Preface

This volume, the tenth in the series *Guides to Sources for British History*, is the first of two volumes that will describe the most extensive and important family and estate collections of the United Kingdom. It breaks new ground in attempting, for each of one hundred and twenty families, to summarise the complete archive. In doing so it reveals the richness of this part of the nation's heritage, and prints for the first time much information not previously available to scholars.

The Commission is most grateful to all the owners of manuscripts who have not only generously assisted it with its enquiries, but have also given permission for the resulting information to appear in print. It is also grateful to all those custodians, both in public repositories and elsewhere, who have responded so helpfully to requests for information or access. In many cases owners or custodians have also kindly commented on draft entries, although the responsibility for their contents must of course rest with the Commission.

As is inevitable with major projects extending over several years and carried out by a small and changing staff, the guide is the work of several hands. It began under the direction of Dr Eileen Scarff, with assistance from a number of colleagues including Dr Anita Travers, Dr JG Parker and Mr DL Prior. The volume has been brought to a conclusion by a team comprising Dr Anthony Smith, Dr Rosemary Hayes and Mr GH Mandelbrote, led by Dr RJ Olney. The text was typed by Mrs Anne Breheny.

The foreword has been contributed by Sir John Habakkuk, a former Commissioner.

CJ KITCHING
Secretary

Quality House, Quality Court
Chancery Lane, London WC2A 1HP

July 1995

The Royal Com

012830300

Guides to Sources for British History
based on the National Register of Archives

10

PRINCIPAL
MILY AND ESTATE
COLLECTIONS
Family Names A–K

Fo

London   HMSO

ISBN 0 11 440265 5

Published by HMSO and available from:

HMSO Publications Centre
(Mail, fax and telephone orders only)
PO Box 276, London SW8 5DT
Telephone orders 0171 873 9090
General enquiries 0171 873 0011
(queuing system in operation for both numbers)
Fax orders 0171 873 8200

HMSO Bookshops
49 High Holborn, London WC1V 6HB
(counter service only)
0171 873 0011 Fax 0171 831 1326
68–69 Bull Street, Birmingham B4 6AD
0121 236 9696 Fax 0121 236 9699
33 Wine Street, Bristol BS1 2BQ
0117 9264306 Fax 0117 9294515
9–21 Princess Street, Manchester M60 8AS
0161 834 7201 Fax 0161 833 0634
16 Arthur Street, Belfast BT1 4GD
01232 238451 Fax 01232 235401
71 Lothian Road, Edinburgh EH3 9AZ
0131 228 4181 Fax 0131 229 2734
The HMSO Oriel Bookshop
The Friary, Cardiff CF1 4AA
01222 395548 Fax 01222 384347

HMSO's Accredited Agents
(see Yellow Pages)

and through good booksellers

Foreword

The estate and family records of the great British landowners are probably, of their kind, unequalled in range and continuity. They form an extraordinarily rich source for the study of what used to be called the Ruling Families, as may be seen from the recent works on the Townshends of Raynham and the Grenvilles of Stowe.[1] But these families occupied until recently so central a role in national life that the records also illuminate the activities of most other groups in society, from the suitors in manorial courts and the tenants of farms to the lessees who in the nineteenth century developed industrial and urban property. There is scarcely an aspect of social and economic history for which these family collections do not provide useful material.

Before the last war few such collections were accessible and fewer still were listed and catalogued. Since then, as a result of the generosity of owners and the interest many of them have taken in their records, and as a consequence of the work of a generation of archivists, this rich vein of material has become very much easier to mine. The records relating to any particular family or property have, however, by the accidents of history, been widely dispersed among different locations, many of them remote and unexpected; and students have found that tracking down the component parts in public and private repositories can be a frustrating and often unsuccessful enterprise. The present guide which, when it is completed by a second volume, will comprehensively cover the contents of 120 collections, makes it possible to exploit these rich resources more fully than ever before; and Dr RJ Olney and his team who are responsible for its preparation deserve the gratitude of all historians.

JOHN HABAKKUK
Oxford, February 1995

---

1. JM Rosenheim, *The Townshends of Raynham*, Middletown, Connecticut 1989; JV Beckett, *The rise and fall of the Grenvilles, Dukes of Buckingham and Chandos, 1710-1921*, Manchester 1994.

Contents

Introduction

Over the last seven or eight centuries, and particularly since the Reformation, successive owners and administrators of some of the country's largest landed estates have built up remarkably full, rich and varied archives. These collections show how estates were acquired and retained, how they were administered, and how they supported a powerful social and political élite. But, as noted in the Foreword to this volume, their importance is not restricted to the history of one social class or one source of wealth. Of value to the social, economic, political, administrative and cultural historian alike, they form a prominent part of the nation's archival heritage.

As with previous volumes in the series *Guides to Sources for British History*, the aim of this guide is to disseminate in edited form some of the extensive information stored in the Commission's National Register of Archives. The Commission is in fact singularly well placed to describe the major British family and estate collections. Not only are they well documented in the National Register of Archives, but the Commission's knowledge of them goes back in many cases long before the foundation of the Register in 1945. Many of the Commission's earliest reports, from 1870 onwards, were the result of investigatory visits to country house libraries and muniment rooms; and since then its knowledge of these collections has been continually supplemented through the generosity of owners and by the efforts of archivists, librarians, historians and members of its own staff. Estate and family collections also meet another criterion of the series: they continue to be in demand as historical sources, and indeed have been the subject of a number of major studies and monographs in the last fifteen years.[1]

It was decided in 1982 to begin the preparation for this publication with a systematic survey, in order to identify gaps in our knowledge and to select a number of major collections for more detailed treatment. The survey took an initial sample of 630 families owning more than ten thousand acres in Great Britain and Northern Ireland in 1883, the date of the fourth edition of John Bateman's *Great Landowners of Great Britain and Ireland*. Whilst many of these families had left important collections, for which considerable information was available in the National Register of Archives, it soon became clear that a process of selection based on acreage alone would produce an uneven volume. In 1883 some very large estates were of low rental value and had never generated many documents, whereas some estates of under ten

---

1. Eg JV Beckett, *The Aristocracy in England 1660-1914*, Oxford 1986; David Cannadine, *Lords and Landlords: the aristocracy and the towns 1774-1967*, Leicester 1980; Heather A Clemenson, *English country houses and landed estates*, 1982; John Habakkuk, *Marriage, debt and the estates system: English landownership 1650-1950*, Oxford 1994; DR Hainsworth, *Stewards, lords and people*, Cambridge 1992; JR Wordie, *Estate management in eighteenth-century England*, 1982; and several important local and family studies.

thousand acres had been reduced to that level by sales but had retained rich and widely-ranging archives. It was decided therefore to evaluate the collections themselves, supplementing the checklist of larger estates with the Commission's own knowledge of the country's most important family archives. Eventually, by a process of investigation and elimination, a smaller total of 120 or so principal collections was chosen for inclusion in the guide, of which the first 58, arranged alphabetically by family name, appear in this volume. These collections satisfy two main criteria: they contain substantial numbers of deeds and other muniments of title, including in most cases two hundred or more medieval charters; and they contain solid and extensive series of estate records, often from the sixteenth century or earlier. These great collections additionally, though not so consistently, include significant quantities of manorial records, records relating to national and local government, and personal and political correspondence and papers. Characteristically, though again not exclusively, they have been accumulated by the country's leading noble (as opposed to gentry) families; they reflect the patterns of marriage and inheritance among those families; and they usually relate to more than one county, if not to more than one part of the United Kingdom.

During the preparation of the guide it was found that the Commission's knowledge was less complete than had initially been thought. In some cases, for instance, it had a good working knowledge of the family papers but fewer details of the estate papers, which had been of less concern to earlier investigators. In other cases the available information turned out to be mainly for the older parts of a collection, with much less known about the nineteenth- and twentieth-century papers. In some instances the Commission could simply request a copy of a catalogue not previously filed in the National Register of Archives, but numerous visits were also necessary to inspect collections in repositories or in private hands. As a result this guide contains a considerable quantity of previously unpublished information. Even where the visit did not result in an entry in the guide, the information obtained has, with the consent of the owners of the records, been added to the Register. An important by-product, therefore, of the guide has been the consolidation of the Commission's knowledge of a number of collections that, whilst not selected for publication in these volumes, are nevertheless of nearly equal size and importance.

For the purposes of this guide a family and estate collection is defined as the whole archive created by a family and its employees. It includes, therefore, not only papers accumulated by successive heads of the family and their wives or husbands but also material created by stewards, land agents, solicitors, architects, housekeepers, private secretaries, librarians and others. It follows that papers may originally have been kept in a number of different places—personal correspondence in the study or business room of a great house, collected manuscripts in the library, household accounts in the housekeeper's room, deeds in the muniment room or solicitor's office and estate records, naturally enough, in the estate office. Some of these archives remain in private custody, although the location of groups within the archive may have changed. A group of deeds for the Yorkshire estates of the Dukes of Devonshire, for instance, was originally kept in Yorkshire, but was moved to Devonshire House, London, and then to Hardwick Hall, Derbyshire, before coming to rest, with muniments from several other family estates, at Chatsworth. In other cases, especially where the principal seat has been sold or given up, the archive is now in the care of one or more public repositories. In fact it is exceptional for principal family and estate collections to be found in fewer than four or five different locations: even if the bulk of the archive remains intact there are usually at least one or two strays elsewhere, and in extreme cases the guide has located twenty or more separate groups. It is part of the purpose of the guide to bring these groups together on paper within their respective entries, to indicate where possible to which of the family's estates specific groups of papers refer, and to show where a single group has been split, by sale or deposit, between two or more locations. Surviving papers of whatever date, even the most recent, are included in the description of the archive if known to the Commission and if the publication of the information has been agreed by their owner. Access to the papers themselves may, however, be restricted. Moreover, the Commission's knowledge of recent estate records varies with the extent to which they have been handed over for permanent preservation in a muniment room or record office.

The surviving archive thus broadly defined is not, of course, limited to the papers remaining in family *ownership* at the present time. Records kept by an agent, for instance, may have passed to *his* family, and hence out of the ownership of the family for whom they were originally created. The family itself may have sold manuscripts or records, either at auction or by private treaty. The guide attempts to record the whereabouts of groups of papers that have left custody in these ways, although it has not been possible to be comprehensive, especially in the case of single items whose provenance is not easy to establish. Where families have purchased items or collections of manuscripts, and have at a later date re-sold them, the resultant dispersal can be only very summarily noted in this guide, although further details of some may be found in the Commission's *Guide to the Location of Collections described in the Reports and Calendars series 1870-1980,* 1982.

Despite the attempt of each entry to be comprehensive in archival terms, it cannot of course contain all the material necessary for the study of a particular estate or family. Thus historians working on the estates of the Earls of Shrewsbury before 1600 could not hope to rely entirely on the papers of the Chetwynd-Talbot family, Earls of Shrewsbury, as defined in this guide. They would also need to examine, for instance, papers now in the archive of the Duke of Norfolk, to whose ancestor many of the old Shrewsbury estates passed in the early seventeenth century. In this case, where the estates, and with them a substantial group of papers, passed by inheritance, the collection of the Dukes of Norfolk is recorded as a *related collection* at the end of the Shrewsbury entry. Where, however, an estate passed from one family to another by sale and purchase, the guide has not normally attempted to trace the subsequent fate of archival material passing with the property. To do so would have been beyond the scope of the publication. (In the exceptional case, however, of the Coke family, Earls of Leicester (no 23), groups of early records were detached from the archive on the sale of outlying portions of the estate in 1910-12 and handed to the purchasers, and these have been included in the entry.)

This leads to the question of how to define the *family* as distinct from the collection. It is necessary to take a date or period as a point of reference, since a group of documents that could be counted, for instance, as part of the Shrewsbury archive in 1550 had become part of the Norfolk archive by 1650. The simplest solution, to adopt a present-day point of reference, was found to have considerable drawbacks. Since 1900 a number of the great landed families have sold or divided their estates. Information relating to the current ownership of estates is not normally in the public domain, and there is no modern official survey comparable to the 1873 *Return of Owners of Land* on which Bateman based his compilation. The period around 1900, on the other hand, was one of comparative stability for the landed interest: few of the great estates had yet been sold, and few of the great country house collections broken up. It was therefore decided to use this period to define the family and hence the name that provides the heading for each entry. Thus the Panshanger archive appears under Cowper, Earls Cowper, since that family was the owner in 1900, although in 1904 the last Earl Cowper died and his estates were divided, Panshanger passing to his daughter Lady Desborough. Another part of the Cowper estates passed to the Marquess of Lothian's family, but this part of the archive, too, has been described in the Cowper rather than the Lothian entry.

The stages by which a great estate was built up, and the marriage alliances through which landed property passed into or out of the family, are described in a brief paragraph or paragraphs at the start of each entry. Where necessary reference is also made to instances where archives descended separately from the estates or families to which they relate, and to major sales or dispersals of manuscripts. This introductory section concludes with a summary, taken from Bateman, of the family's estates in 1883. The brief summary description of the archive begins with the largest or main group of surviving papers, followed, in the case of divided collections, by the smaller or subsidiary groups. Broadly speaking, groups of legal or estate papers are followed by groups of personal or family papers, with collected or miscellaneous papers, and occasionally a secondary archive acquired very late in the family's history, bringing up the rear. Within this pattern, however, groups sharing the same location have for convenience been described consecutively, as have groups derived from the same auction sale.

The brief summary of each group follows a similar order—deeds and legal papers, manorial records, estate and local papers, family papers and miscellaneous or collected papers. Within the section devoted to estate papers, the records of the main estate are usually described first, followed by the records of secondary or outlying estates. With such bulky collections it is possible to give only the barest outline, with the emphasis on groups of papers rather than items, and on whole estates rather than individual parishes within those estates. Where entries go into slightly greater detail it is in order to indicate, for instance, where papers relating to the same subject occur in more than one location. In general the emphasis of the guide is on legal and estate papers: further details of personal and political papers may often be obtained from the Commission's other publications, or by consulting the Personal Index of the National Register of Archives. In general the comparative length of an entry should be a good indication of the comparative importance and size of the collection that it describes. Within an archive, however, it is often the bulkiest sections, the deeds and more recent estate papers, that can be most concisely summarised. It should be added that, where the Commission is working from catalogues compiled by others and not from the results of its own investigations, the summaries may inevitably embody some inconsistencies of scale or methods of description.

The reader should not, therefore, assume that a particular document has not survived merely because it fails to gain a mention in the guide. In many cases further details of a collection or group of papers are available in printed or typescript catalogues or calendars. Each summary is followed by a reference to a published source, or to information available in the National Register of Archives. Registered lists or reports are cited in the form 'NRA 11070', for example, or 'NRA 5950 (partial list)'.

It may be noted that the 1873 *Return*, and in consequence Bateman's figures for 1883, omit the metropolitan area of London. This gives a markedly incomplete picture of the rental income of a family such as the Grosvenors, Dukes of Westminster, much of whose wealth came from London property. In the summary descriptions estates (though not town houses) described as in 'London' should be taken as being in the City of London, not the county of Middlesex, unless otherwise indicated.

The location of papers in this guide is that known to the Commission on 31 December 1994. These collections, however, are subject to frequent change as new material comes to light and as previously recorded material is affected by new custodial arrangements. The student will therefore find it worthwhile to consult the Commission before planning a visit to see papers, and this will be the case particularly with collections in private hands. For its part the Commission is always glad to receive information from custodians and scholars in order to keep its knowledge up to date.

Access to privately owned papers

Privately owned collections of papers deposited on loan in libraries, record offices and other public institutions are normally available for research without restriction. Special conditions, however, may sometimes apply, particularly if a collection is as yet uncatalogued, and advice on access and related matters should be sought from the institutions concerned.

Permission to study papers that remain with a private owner should be sought from the owner in writing, either direct or, where indicated, through an intermediary. The inclusion of such material in this guide does not imply that it is available for research. Where papers can be made available, applicants are reminded that it is often at considerable inconvenience to their owners, and that access for the purpose of research is a privilege and not a right. The conditions of access cited in the guide are those that prevailed in December 1994. Details of the present location of collections whose ownership or whereabouts is not specified in the guide may, where appropriate, be obtained from the Commission.[1]

Those wishing to study papers in private hands are also advised to consult catalogues or other finding aids available in the Commission's search room or elsewhere before approaching owners or custodians.

---

1. Enquiries to the Commission should be addressed to the Secretary, The Royal Commission on Historical Manuscripts, Quality House, Quality Court, Chancery Lane, London WC2A 1HP. Where indicated, enquiries about Scottish collections should be addressed to the Secretary, National Register of Archives (Scotland), West Register House, Charlotte Square, Edinburgh EH2 4DF. For addresses of repositories generally, see the Commission's *Record Repositories in Great Britain, a geographical directory*, HMSO, ninth edition, revised 1994.

Table of
family names and
peerage titles

The following table provides a list of the collections described in this volume as arranged under family names (A–K), with cross-references from the peerage titles of those families as they appear in the entry headings. Other family names and titles connected with the contents of this volume may be traced through the Select Index.

Part II of the Guide, containing entries from a further 60 or so families arranged under family names L–Y, will carry a similar table, but covering both volumes.

Principal family and estate collections
Family names A–K

[1] ANDERSON-PELHAM, Earls of Yarborough

The Anderson and Pelham families were both settled in north Lincolnshire in the late sixteenth century. Charles Anderson of Broughton (1749-1823) inherited the extensive Brocklesby estates on the death in 1763 of his great-uncle Charles Pelham, and was created Baron Yarborough in 1794. His son Charles Anderson-Pelham (1781-1846, created Earl of Yarborough 1837) married in 1806 Henrietta Bridgeman Simpson, who had succeeded to the Appuldurcombe (Isle of Wight) estate on the death of her uncle Sir Richard Worsley, seventh Bt, in 1805. The Isle of Wight estate was sold mainly in the 1850s. In 1886 the fourth Earl married Marcia Lane-Fox, later Baroness Fauconberge and Conyers, co-heir to estates in the North and West Ridings of Yorkshire (including the manor of Wakefield), formerly part of the possessions of the Osborne family, Dukes of Leeds.

Estates in 1883: Yarborough: Lincs 56,795 acres, Berks 98 acres, total 56,893 acres worth £84,649 a year; Conyers: Yorks NR and WR 3,460 acres worth £8,538 a year.

[a] Deeds 12th-20th cent, mainly Lincs; wills, settlements and related papers 17th-19th cent; draft deeds, mortgages and related papers 18th-20th cent, mainly Lincs but incl leasehold property in London (Middlesex) 1771-1900 and Sunninghill (Berks) estate 1873-94; cartularies, registers and schedules of deeds 13th-19th cent, incl Newhouse Abbey cartulary 13th-14th cent; Lincs estate papers 16th-20th cent, incl leases and tenancy agreements from 17th cent, surveys and valuations 1585 (Pelham estates) and 18th-20th cent, plans 17th-19th cent, rentals and accounts 18th-20th cent and papers 18th-20th cent rel to brickyards, woods, tithes, enclosure, and Grimsby estate and docks; papers rel to Claxby ironstone mine 1861-85 and Cleethorpes oyster beds 1856-1909; Isle of Wight rentals and accounts 1848-57; Conyers (Yorks) estate papers

1861-1913; general and household accounts (Yarborough) mid-18th-early 20th cent; household, etc accounts of the 1st Duke of Leeds 1694-1719.

Papers rel to Ancholme drainage 17th-19th cent, Brocklesby Hunt from late 18th cent and Brocklesby Park Hospital 1914-19; appointments and commissions 16th-20th cent; account of Sir William Pelham as Lieutenant of the Ordnance 1578-81 (1 vol); misc Anderson-Pelham family corresp and papers from late 18th cent, with pedigrees and genealogical papers; Worsley family papers 1521-1805 (55 vols), incl Wardrobe account of James Worsley 1521-5, diplomatic papers of Henry Worsley early 18th cent and antiquarian papers of Sir Richard Worsley, 7th Bt; Osborne and Lane-Fox papers 1690-late 19th cent; misc papers, incl Privy Purse accounts of Queen Catherine of Braganza 1663-81 (Worsley MSS) and MS and printed music early 19th cent (Anderson-Pelham and Osborne).

Lincolnshire Archives (YARB, WORSLEY). Deposited by the 7th Earl of Yarborough 1957-87. *Archivists' Report* 9 (1957-8), p46; 15 (1963-4), pp15-21; 17 (1965-6), pp36-8; 20 (1968-9), p45; 27 (1977-82), pp104-9. NRA 5950 (partial list).

[b] Trust and legal papers 18th-20th cent, incl abstracts and schedules, Anderson-Pelham and Worsley settlements 18th-19th cent, wills 18th-early 20th cent, papers rel to sales of Isle of Wight estates 1809-57 and Lincs outliers early 20th cent, and legal corresp 1850s-1950s.

Lincolnshire Archives (2 TALLENTS). Deposited by Hodgkinson & Tallents, solicitors, Newark 1970.

[c] Corresp and papers rel to the development of Immingham docks *c*1903-12.

Lincolnshire Archives (James Martin & Co 4/17). Deposited by James Martin & Co, land agents, Lincoln 1968. NRA 14274.

1

[d] Misc deeds and legal papers mainly 19th-20th cent; Brocklesby estate records 18th-20th cent, mainly 20th cent but incl leases and tenancy agreements from *c*1840, maps from late 18th cent, surveys from mid-19th cent and accounts from *c*1880; Appuldurcombe estate maps ?early 19th cent (3 items); Conyers (Yorks) estate accounts 1898-1935 and coal lease book early 19th cent; drawings and papers rel to Brocklesby Hall, grounds and park 1772-20th cent; catalogues, inventories and valuations, Brocklesby, London house, Appuldurcombe, etc 1802-1981; household accounts 19th-20th cent; Great Limber mausoleum papers, incl building account 1788-96 and register of burials; Brocklesby Hunt papers 1748-1970s; personal and family papers mainly late 19th-20th cent, incl appointments, commissions, and papers of the 4th Earl.

In private possession. Not normally available for research. Enquiries to the Agent, The Estate Office, Brocklesby Park, Habrough, Lincolnshire.

[e] Deeds 13th-18th cent, mainly Isle of Wight but incl Merrick estate in Gloucs and Somerset 1682-1763; wills, settlements and legal papers 16th-19th cent, incl papers rel to the sale of the Appuldurcombe estate 1809-61; Isle of Wight manorial records 14th-19th cent; leases 15th-18th cent; estate surveys, rentals, accounts and other papers 1604-1851, mainly Isle of Wight; inventory of Appuldurcombe House 1565; official papers (shrievalty of Hants, etc) 1559-1831; misc Worsley and Anderson-Pelham papers mainly 18th-19th cent, incl papers of Sir Richard Worsley, 7th Bt, rel to his *History of the Isle of Wight*, etc.

Isle of Wight County Record Office (JER/WA/1-41, GDL/PR/15-16). Transferred from Hampshire Record Office, Carisbrooke Castle Museum, Godshill Parish Council and the Borough of Newport, where the papers had been deposited by CF Worsley, Mr Worsley having obtained them from Clarke & Sewell (later Gummer, Wilson & Jerome), solicitors, Newport. NRA 26748.

[f] Court books for various Isle of Wight manors 1603-30 (2 vols).

Isle of Wight County Record Office (NBC/45/55a-b). Deposited by Medina Borough Council. NRA 26748.

[g] Misc deeds and family papers *c*1300-1805, incl deeds of Appuldurcombe Priory 1399-1443 (4 items), papers of Richard Worsley, Captain of the Isle of Wight 1540-64, papers of Henry Worsley 1701-22, and papers of Sir Richard Worsley rel to his *History*, etc.

British Library, Manuscript Collections (Add Ch 74455-66, Add MSS 46501-4). Presented by CF Worsley 1948.

[h] Wakefield manorial records 1274-1926; Wakefield surveys, plans, accounts and enclosure papers 18th-19th cent, with other papers 1285-1947.

West Yorkshire Archive Service, Yorkshire Archaeological Society (MD 225). Deposited by the 5th Earl of Yarborough 1943 and by Stewart, Chalker & Mosley, solicitors, Wakefield 1956-7. S Thomas, *Guide to the archive collections of the Yorkshire Archaeological Society 1931-83*, 1985, p43.

[i] Conisborough (Yorks) manorial records 13th-20th cent.

Messrs Dawson & Burgess, solicitors, Doncaster. Withdrawn from Doncaster Archives Department 1991.

Related collection: Dukes of Leeds (Yorkshire Archaeological Society DD5, etc, NRA 12923), including Wakefield and Conisborough manorial and estate records.

[2] ARUNDELL, Barons Arundell of Wardour

The Arundells of Lanherne were prominent in Cornish affairs from the thirteenth century, and had property in both Cornwall and Devon. In 1451 Sir John Arundell married Catherine, daughter and co-heir of Sir John Chidiock, who brought estates in Dorset (Chideock, etc), Somerset and Gloucestershire. In 1473 or 1474 Sir Thomas Arundell, son of Sir John, married Catherine, sister of Lord Dinham and co-heir of estates in Devon and other counties. Sir John Arundell (1623-1701) left his estates to his daughter Frances, who in 1671 had married Sir Richard Bellings. Their granddaughter Mary Bellings-Arundell married in 1739 Henry Arundell, later seventh Baron Arundell of Wardour, and on her death in 1769 she was succeeded in the Arundell of Lanherne estates (by now comprising only the Cornish lands and Chideock) by her son the eighth Baron. The Cornish estates were nearly all sold by 1808.

Thomas Arundell, younger son of Sir John Arundell of Lanherne (d1545), received property in Dorset, Somerset and Devon from his father and purchased Wardour Castle (Wiltshire) from Sir Fulke Greville in 1547. This branch of the family acquired further estates in Wiltshire, Dorset, Somerset and Devon. Sir Thomas Arundell (d1639) was created Baron Arundell of Wardour in 1605. The eighth Baron, who built a new Wardour Castle from 1770, married in 1764 Maria Conquest of Irnham (Lincolnshire). On his death in 1808 Irnham passed to a younger daughter, who married the sixth Baron Clifford of Chudleigh, but the Arundell estates (excluding those of the Lanherne line already sold, and other properties alienated by 1808) passed to his elder daughter, wife of her cousin James Everard Arundell, who succeeded as ninth Baron. In 1751 his father, James Everard Arundell senior, had married Anne, daughter and heir of John Wyndham of Salisbury and Norrington (Wiltshire), through whom property in Hampshire, Dorset and Somerset descended to the Arundells. In the late seventeenth century other Hampshire property had been inherited by the Arundells of Wardour from the

Philpott family. By the late nineteenth century, however, the Arundell estates were almost entirely confined to Wiltshire.

Estates in 1883: Wilts 6,037 acres, Cornwall 182 acres, total 6,219 acres worth £9,174 a year.

[a] Deeds c14th-20th cent, Wilts, Dorset, Hants, Somerset, etc; wills, settlements, trust and executorship papers (Arundell, Wyndham, etc) 16th-20th cent; abstracts of title, mortgages, case papers and other legal papers 16th-20th cent; papers rel to forfeitures and recusancy 16th-18th cent; manorial records (court rolls and books, ministers' accounts, etc), Wilts and Dorset (Tisbury, Donhead, etc) 14th-20th cent, Somerset (South Petherton, etc) 16th-17th cent and Hants (Christchurch, Ringwood, etc) 15th-18th cent; Wilts and Dorset estate records 15th-20th cent, incl leases and lease books from 17th cent, maps 17th-19th cent, surveys, rentals, accounts (estate, woods, farms, etc) and misc papers; papers (mainly surveys, rentals and accounts) for Somerset (Kingsdon, etc) estates 17th cent, Hants (Ringwood, Yateley, etc) estates 17th-early 19th cent, Wyndham estates 1614 and Lincs (Irnham) estate 1764-1800.

Papers rel to Wardour Castle and park 17th-20th cent, incl drawings for the new Castle and related papers late 18th cent; drawings for Hatch House, Kent (Wyndham family) by Robert Adam 1761; household accounts, inventories and related papers 16th-20th cent, mainly Wardour Castle but incl London and Breamore (Hants); Wilts yeomanry muster roll 1822; patents and commissions from 16th cent; family corresp and papers c17th-20th cent, Arundell and Wyndham, incl corresp rel to Roman Catholic affairs (especially the movement for Catholic Emancipation 1780-97), notes of the 3rd Baron rel to the Popish Plot 1678, personal accounts 18th cent, corresp of the 8th Baron late 18th cent and printed papers of the 12th Baron; papers rel to Sir Richard Burton (1821-90); misc genealogical and other papers 18th-20th cent; Wilton Abbey accounts 13th-14th cent (2 items).

Wiltshire Record Office (WRO 2667). Purchased 1991. NRA 22502 (partial list).

[b] Accounts of John Benett as steward for the Arundell estates in Wilts, Dorset, Somerset and Devon 1661-77.

Wiltshire Record Office (WRO 413/507). Among the Benett of Pythouse papers deposited by Sir Anthony Rumbold. NRA 7085. For a similar account book 1663-71 see Wiltshire Record Office, WRO 750 (NRA 11070).

[c] Deeds 12th-19th cent, mainly Cornwall (incl Tywardreath Priory) but also Devon (Dinham estates), Dorset (Chideock, etc) and other counties; legal papers c15th-early 19th cent; wills, settlements, trust and executorship papers 15th-18th cent; manorial records (court rolls and books, ministers' accounts, etc), Cornwall and Devon 14th-19th cent, Dorset (Chideock)

14th-16th cent, and Somerset and Gloucs (Pitney, Frampton-on-Severn, etc) 15th-16th cent; Greystoke (Cumberland) barony rolls 9-10 Eliz; Cornish estate records 14th-19th cent, incl leases and lease books 17th-early 19th cent, surveys, rentals, accounts, and papers rel to wrecks 18th cent and to tin mining; estate records for Devon 14th-17th cent, Dorset (Chideock, etc) 15th-18th cent, Somerset and Gloucs 15th-16th cent, and Oxon, Bucks, etc (Dinham properties) 16th cent; Lanherne House building account 1706, plan 1777; household accounts and inventories (Arundell and Dinham families) 14th-18th cent; papal bulls and letters of confraternity 15th-16th cent; recusancy papers 16th-18th cent; family corresp and papers, Arundell, Dinham, etc 14th-18th cent, incl Dinham accounts 14th-15th cent, account book of John Arundell of Lanherne 1506, corresp and papers of Sir Richard Bellings late 17th cent, and corresp of Richard Bellings Arundell (d1724); Tywardreath Priory papers early 16th cent.

Cornwall Record Office (AR). Purchased 1991. HMC *Second Report, App*, 1871, pp33-6. NRA 22502 (partial list).

[d] Survey of Cornish estates 1659.

Royal Institution of Cornwall. Given to CG Henderson by Sir J Langdon Bonython 1919. NRA 1166.

Related collections: Barons Clifford of Chudleigh (Devon Record Office, NRA 20060); Glyn papers (Dorset Record Office D 54, NRA 5760), including Arundell surveys 1541-1601; Mohun MSS (Royal Institution of Cornwall HK, NRA 1166), including Lanherne household account 1466 and other Arundell papers 16th-17th cent.

[3] ASHBURNHAM, Earls of Ashburnham

The Ashburnham family was settled in Sussex from the twelfth century. John Ashburnham, Groom of the Chamber to Charles I, was granted property in Bedfordshire (Ampthill, etc, sold in the early eighteenth century) and Pembrokeshire (Angle, sold 1661). John Ashburnham (1656-1710) married Bridget Vaughan, heiress of estates in Breconshire (Porthamel, etc), Carmarthenshire (Pembrey, etc) and Glamorganshire, and was created Baron Ashburnham in 1689. The second Baron married Katherine, daughter and eventual heiress of Thomas Taylor of Clapham (Bedfordshire). The third Baron (1687-1737) was created Earl of Ashburnham in 1730. The second Earl married in 1756 Elizabeth Crowley, heiress of estates in Suffolk (Barking, etc) and Kent (Blackheath) and ironworks in County Durham. The non-Sussex estates were alienated or reduced in size in the nineteenth and early twentieth centuries. On the death of the sixth Earl in 1924 the remaining estates passed to Lady Mary Ashburnham, his sister, and on her death in 1953 to the Revd JD Bickersteth, a descendant of the fourth Earl.

Estates in 1883: Sussex 14,051 acres, Suffolk 3,372 acres, Carmarthenshire 5,685 acres,

Breconshire 1,381 acres, total 24,489 acres worth £24,136 a year.

[a] Deeds 12th-19th cent, mainly Sussex; wills, settlements, etc 17th-19th cent; schedules of deeds and other documents 17th-20th cent, Sussex and other counties; legal papers 17th-20th cent, incl papers rel to purchases and sales; manorial records, Sussex 15th-20th cent, incl compoti for Burghurst, etc 1418-1526; Sussex estate records 17th-20th cent, incl tenancy agreements 18th-19th cent, surveys, valuations, maps, rentals and accounts, corresp 18th-20th cent, and papers rel to game, timber, churches, tithes and advowsons 18th-19th cent; farm and labour accounts 19th-20th cent; iron, lime and brick accounts 18th-19th cent; venison books 1822-1914; Welsh and Beds estate accounts early 19th cent; papers and drawings rel to Ashburnham Place 18th-20th cent, incl drawings by Lancelot Brown 1767, nd and accounts and papers of George Dance jun early 19th cent; household inventories, London c1675-94 (1 vol) and Sussex and London 19th-20th cent; household accounts, Ashburnham Place, London, etc 19th-20th cent.

Sussex yeomanry papers 1798-1821; papers rel to Sussex roads and railways 18th-early 20th cent; appointments, commissions, etc 17th-20th cent; family corresp and papers 17th-20th cent, incl Civil War narrative of John Ashburnham, letter books of the 1st Baron 1696-1708, Wardrobe accounts 1770-1, papers of the 5th Earl rel to the Spanish Carlists, and pedigrees; papers rel to the Ashburnham library and MSS 19th-20th cent, with misc literary and other papers; Italian documents 1048-1572 (52 items); additional records 19th-20th cent (deposited 1981).

East Sussex Record Office (ASH). Deposited by the Revd JD Bickersteth 1954-91, with additional legal records from Peake & Co, solicitors, London. *The Ashburnham Archives, a Catalogue*, ed FW Steer, 1958. NRA 1000. For out-county material forwarded to other repositories see below and (for the smaller groups, not noticed here) *The Ashburnham Archives*, pp xxii-xxiii. For the Stowe, Libri, Barrois and additional MSS, sold between 1883 and 1901, see HMC *Eighth Report, App III*, 1881, and *Guide to the Location of Collections*, 1982, p3.

[b] Legal and Sussex estate papers 18th-20th cent (mainly 1880-1933), incl case papers, misc manorial papers 18th-early 20th cent, tenancy and shooting agreements, maps, estate corresp 1880-1933 and Warbleton tithe papers 1764-1840.

East Sussex Record Office (RAF). Deposited by Raper & Fovargue, solicitors, Battle 1959.

[c] Accounts and corresp of John Collier as agent for the Ashburnham estate 1736-58.

East Sussex Record Office (Sayer MSS, I/591-615). Deposited by RC Sayer 1965. NRA 28259.

[d] Legal papers 1813-69. incl papers rel to the Sussex estate, Ashburnham House (London) and the Stowe MSS.

Sussex Archaeological Society (SAS/FA 229-265). Deposited by Frere, Cholmeley & Co through the British Record Society 1931. Access through East Sussex Record Office. NRA 10702.

[e] Deeds for Breconshire, Carmarthenshire and Glamorganshire 14th-20th cent (mainly 17th-20th cent), with one for Pembrokeshire 1661; legal papers from c1700, incl papers rel to sales 19th-20th cent; deeds for Montgomeryshire and Salop 18th-20th cent (estate of SR Heap, mortgaged to Ashburnham trustees 1923); misc manorial records, Pembrey 1417, 17th-20th cent and Breconshire 17th-20th cent; Welsh estate records 17th-20th cent, incl leases, surveys and valuations, maps and plans from c1770, rentals and accounts, and corresp from early 19th cent; papers rel to Pembrey tithes, colliery, port and harbour, foreshore and wrecks mainly 18th-early 20th cent, and to Kidwelly (Carmarthenshire) enclosure mid-19th cent.

National Library of Wales (Ashburnham Groups I and II). Transferred from East Sussex Record Office 1954, 1964, 1981. NRA 26986.

[f] Breconshire and Pembrey deeds and papers; Breconshire court rolls 1644-1839.

National Library of Wales. Deposited by Frere, Cholmeley & Co through the British Records Association 1933. National Library of Wales *Annual Report 1933-4*, p37.

[g] Pembrey estate sale papers 1922-3.

Dyfed Archives Service, Carmarthenshire Area Record Office (Bishop collection, box 141). Deposited by the executors of Major JW Bishop 1963. NRA 21543.

[h] Pembrey estate map 1832.

Dyfed Archives Service, Carmarthenshire Area Record Office (CDX/445). Purchased 1992. NRA 29913.

[i] Suffolk deeds 14th-19th cent; misc deeds and legal papers, Sussex and other counties 14th-19th cent; wills, settlements and related papers mainly 18th-19th cent, incl John Crowley (d1728) decd and the Crowley-Ashburnham marriage 1756; misc legal and financial papers 16th-early 20th cent, incl schedules and abstracts of title; Suffolk manorial records 14th-18th cent; Suffolk estate records 16th-early 20th cent (mainly late 18th cent onwards), incl leases, surveys, maps, rentals, accounts and corresp; Beds rentals 1813, 1816; papers rel to contents of and repairs to Barking Hall mainly early 19th cent; account of county bridges 1651; shrievalty papers of Francis Theobald 1664-8; estate corresp of the 4th Earl 1833-50.

Suffolk Record Office, Ipswich (HA1). Transferred from East Sussex Record Office and Ipswich Borough Library 1954. NRA 9718.

[j] Beds deeds and leases 16th-19th cent, with papers rel to sales 1812-62; Clapham enclosure agreement 1667 and court roll 1737; Beds estate records 1710-1862.

Bedfordshire Record Office (S/AM). Transferred from East Sussex Record Office 1954. NRA 30111.

[k] Deeds for Crowley property in Danbury, etc 1566, 1701-28 (11 items).

Essex Record Office (D/DU 279). Transferred from East Sussex Record Office 1954.

[l] Blackheath and Greenwich deeds and leases 1700-1830, with estate records 1801-82.

Centre for Kentish Studies (U 444). Transferred from East Sussex Record Office 1954. NRA 5209.

[m] Deeds, etc rel to Bretherton (Lancs) (settled on the marriage of the 1st Earl to a daughter of the 9th Earl of Derby) 1714-66; survey and valuation of Beds estate nd (18th cent).

Lancashire Record Office (DDX/251). Transferred from East Sussex Record Office 1954. NRA 18537.

[n] Lincs deeds (Vyner trust, etc) 1666-1823 (10 items).

Lincolnshire Archives (MISC DEP 63). Transferred from East Sussex Record Office 1954. NRA 4918.

[o] Middlesex deeds 17th-19th cent, incl Ashburnham House (Westminster Abbey Precincts) and Ashburnham House (Dover Street); inventories and valuations, Ashburnham House (Dover Street) 19th cent; extracts rel to Hyde Park (for the 2nd Earl as Ranger) 1759 (1 vol).

Greater London Record Office (Middlesex Record Office Acc 524). Transferred from East Sussex Record Office 1954. NRA 4816.

[p] Deeds, maps and papers rel to the Chelsea estate 1781-1883.

Kensington and Chelsea Libraries and Arts Service (MSS 43721-96). Deposited 1992.

[q] Deeds for Salisbury Close, Chute Forest and Durnford (Wilts) (Vaughan and Ashburnham families) 1641-1707 (14 items).

Wiltshire Record Office (Acc 261). Transferred from East Sussex Record Office 1954.

[4] ASHLEY-COOPER, Earls of Shaftesbury

The Cooper family had estates in Hampshire, Sussex and Somerset in the sixteenth century. John Cooper of Rockbourne (Hampshire) married Anne, daughter and heiress of Sir Anthony Ashley of Wimborne St Giles (Dorset) and was created a baronet in 1626. Their son, Sir Anthony Ashley Cooper, was created Earl of Shaftesbury in 1672. The Somerset estate passed on the death of the fifth Earl in 1811 to his daughter Barbara, Baroness De Mauley, but the Dorset, Hampshire and Wiltshire estates passed to his brother, who succeeded him as sixth Earl. Estates in northern Ireland were inherited in 1883 through the marriage of Anthony Ashley-Cooper, later eighth Earl, to Harriet, only daughter of the third Marquess of Donegall, but by that date much of the valuable Belfast property had been sold.

Estates in 1883: Shaftesbury: Dorset 17,317 acres, Hants 3,250 acres, Wilts 1,218 acres, total 21,785 acres worth £16,083 a year; Donegall: Co Antrim 14,617 acres, Co Donegal 8,155 acres, Co Londonderry 193 acres, Co Down 31 acres, total 22,996 acres worth £41,649 a year.

[a] Deeds, Dorset, Hants, Wilts, etc 12th-20th cent; schedules of deeds and other legal papers 17th-20th cent; wills, settlements and trust papers 15th-20th cent; manorial records 14th-20th cent, Dorset (incl Knowlton hundred and Shaftesbury borough), Hants, Wilts, Somerset, etc; leases 16th-20th cent, incl Somerset and Wilts; Dorset, etc estate records 14th-20th cent, incl rentals, surveys and maps from 17th cent, accounts and financial papers from 14th cent, vouchers from 17th cent, papers rel to advowsons, tithes, enclosure, etc from 16th cent and papers rel to schools, charities, etc; legal, manorial and estate papers rel to the Cropley family (Yorks and Co Durham) mainly 16th-18th cent; Irish estate corresp 20th cent; papers rel to St Giles House and church 16th-20th cent, incl inventories; household accounts and vouchers mainly 17th-20th cent; Shaftesbury, Dorchester and Dorset election corresp and papers 18th-19th cent; personal and family corresp and papers 15th-20th cent, incl papers of Sir Anthony Ashley 16th-early 17th cent, the 1st, 4th, 7th and 9th Earls of Shaftesbury 17th-20th cent and the 2nd Marquess of Donegall (letter books 1798-1841, 2 vols); photographs and printed items.

In private possession. Access restricted. Enquiries to the Rt Hon the Earl of Shaftesbury, The Estate Office, Wimborne St Giles, Dorset.

[b] Dorchester deeds 17th-19th cent; Dorset and Hants surveys, maps and rentals 1788-1851.

Dorset Record Office. Deposited 1962, and by the Sun Alliance and London Insurance Group 1969 (D 321). HMC *Accessions to Repositories 1962.* NRA 16912.

[c] Irish deeds (copies), legal papers, leases and estate papers 1604-1930 (c1,500 items).

Public Record Office of Northern Ireland (D 811). Presented by Shaftesbury Estates Co, Belfast 1957, 1960. NRA 28831.

[d] Irish deeds and estate papers 17th-20th cent, incl estate maps 1767-70 (3 vols), rentals 1775-1933, accounts, and papers rel to Co Antrim tithes, Belfast Castle, Belfast markets, etc 19th-20th cent.

Public Record Office of Northern Ireland (D 652, 835, 971/5, 1326, 1769, 2083, 2338). Deposited by L'Estrange & Brett, solicitors, Belfast at various dates.

[e] Legal papers 1608-1857 (57 items); leases 17th-20th cent.

Public Record Office of Northern Ireland (D 389, 509). Deposited by the 9th Earl of Shaftesbury through J Bristow, solicitor, Belfast 1935, and by J Bristow 1943.

[f] Legal papers 1830-45.

Public Record Office of Northern Ireland (D 1255, 2223). Deposited by Martin & Henderson, solicitors, Downpatrick 1959, c1966-72.

[g] Co Antrim deeds, leases, testamentary papers and legal papers 1799-1905.

Public Record Office of Northern Ireland (D 3402). Deposited by Pennington, Lewis & Lewis, solicitors, London through the British Records Association 1979.

[h] Belfast estate agency papers 1810-60.

Public Record Office of Northern Ireland (Verner papers, D 1798). *Deputy Keeper's Report 1960-5*, p194. For other stray documents or copies of documents relating to the Donegall estates see also Public Record Office of Northern Ireland D 1787, 2649 (maps c1805 and 1850, etc), D 2249, T 2767 (rentals 1719, 1864) and T 1893 (sub-agent's letter book 1771-4).

[i] Belfast estate accounts 1706-15; papers rel to sales 1800-4.

Public Record Office (C 107/16, 153). For copies see Public Record Office of Northern Ireland (T 455).

[j] Staffs (Donegall estate) deeds 16th-19th cent; legal papers 18th-19th cent, mainly rel to Staffs but incl corresp and papers rel to the Irish affairs of the 1st Marquess of Donegall.

William Salt Library, Stafford (M 520-1, 760). NRA 7279.

[k] Licences, commissions and legal papers mainly 16th-17th cent; Ashley, Cooper and Ashley-Cooper family papers 16th-19th cent, incl personal and official papers of the 1st, 2nd, 3rd and 4th Earls of Shaftesbury and of John Locke.

Public Record Office (PRO 30/24). Given by the 7th Earl of Shaftesbury 1871-81. HMC *Third Report, App*, 1872, pp216-17. NRA 23640.

Related collection: Broadlands papers (Southampton University Library, NRA 25761, and see HMC *Papers of British Politicians 1782-1900*, 1989, p5), including further papers of the 7th Earl of Shaftesbury.

[5] BAGOT, Barons Bagot

The Bagot family was established at Bagot's Bromley (Staffordshire) by c1166, and acquired Blithfield (Staffordshire) by marriage in the mid-fourteenth century. Sir Walter Bagot, third Bt, married in 1670 Jane, daughter and heir of Charles Salesbury of Bachymbyd and Pool Park (Denbighshire), whose family were extensive landowners in both Denbighshire and Merionethshire (Rhug, etc). (Rhug, however, had descended not

to Charles Salesbury but to his brother William, from whom it later passed to the Vaughan family of Nannau and the Wynn family, Barons Newborough.) Pool Park was sold in 1928 and most of the Blithfield estate following the death of the sixth Baron Bagot in 1961, although his widow acquired Blithfield Hall from her late husband's trustees.

Estates in 1883: Staffs 10,841 acres, Denbighshire 18,044 acres, Merionethshire 1,658 acres, total 30,543 acres worth £22,212 a year.

[a] Deeds, mainly Staffs 12th-19th cent but incl some medieval deeds for Bucks and Warwicks; wills and settlements from 16th cent; legal papers 17th-20th cent, incl schedules of deeds; Staffs manorial records 13th-18th cent, incl Blithfield 14th-18th cent and Ferrers manor of Chartley 13th-15th cent; Staffs estate papers 15th-20th cent (mainly 17th cent onwards), incl surveys, maps, rentals, accounts, corresp and papers; home farm accounts late 18th cent; misc Welsh estate accounts 1798-1934; building plans and papers, Blithfield Hall 17th-19th cent and London house 1776-7; catalogues and inventories 18th-19th cent; household accounts, London and Blithfield c1725-1877; papers rel to Staffs administration and elections and to Needwood Forest 17th-18th cent; pardons, grants, patents, commissions, etc 15th-18th cent; family papers 16th-20th cent, incl memorandum book of Walter Bagot 16th cent, papers of Sir Hervey Bagot, 1st Bt 17th cent and papers of the 1st Baron Bagot 18th cent; genealogical and heraldic papers 1586-19th cent; legal, manorial, estate, household and personal records of the Stafford family, Earls of Stafford and Dukes of Buckingham 16th-17th cent, with copies of documents from 13th cent (13 vols, mostly acquired by the 2nd Baron Bagot); misc papers 16th-19th cent, incl household inventories, Earl of Essex decd 1576 and Earl of Kildare decd 1707, papers rel to the Earl of Shrewsbury decd 1615-18 and a Norfolk *Nomina Villarum* c1316 (16th cent copy).

Staffordshire Record Office (D 986, 1404, 1721, (W) 1810, 3108, 3259-60, 3943, 4038, 4173, 4381, 4752). Deposited at various dates since 1946 and partly purchased by the Record Office in 1980. Some papers were transferred from the National Library of Wales in 1983-4. HMC *Fourth Report, App*, 1874, pp325-44. NRA 5471.

[b] Settlements and business papers 1806-99 (c26 items).

Staffordshire Record Office (D 3136/15-22, D 3221/8). Deposited by Eland, Hore & Paterson, solicitors, London through the British Records Association c1977-8.

[c] Legal papers 1634-57, mainly rel to delinquency of and composition by Sir Hervey Bagot, incl survey and rental 1647-8.

In private possession. (Copies in Staffordshire Record Office.) Purchased 1946 (Sotheby's, 25 Feb, lot 248A). NRA 10591. For other family papers sold principally in 1946 by the Bagot

Trustees see (d), (e) and (f) below and HMC *Guide to the Location of Collections*, 1982, p3. Some other papers, including inventories and accounts (Sotheby's, 25-27 Feb 1946, lots 254, 259) have not been traced.

[d] Bagot family papers 16th-19th cent, incl notebook of Richard Bagot late 16th cent, corresp of Sir Hervey Bagot, 1st Bt, *c*1640-59 and corresp of the 1st Baron Bagot with the Revd T Townson *c*1749-92; misc legal, financial and other papers 17th-20th cent.

Staffordshire Record Office (D 5121). Deposited 1992 through the British Records Association by the National Trust, to which the collection had been bequeathed by NES Norris of Brighton. NRA 5471.

[e] Further family corresp *c*1693-1706, incl corresp with the Wagstaffe family.

William Salt Library, Stafford (WSL 141/1-10/60). Purchased 1959.

[f] Family letters and papers 16th-17th cent, incl many rel to Staffs affairs; misc papers, incl accounts for Lord Paget's ironworks 1583-5 and list of Cannock freeholders and commoners *c*1590.

Folger Library, Washington (L.a.1-1076). Acquired mostly at the André de Coppet sale, Sotheby's, 4 July 1955, lots 774 *et seq.* Microfilm in Staffordshire Record Office. NRA 20980.

[g] Welsh deeds 13th-early 19th cent, mainly Denbighshire (Bachymbyd, etc) and Merionethshire (Rhug, etc); Salesbury wills and related papers, incl inquisitions 1551 and 1612; legal papers from 16th cent, incl schedule *c*1600, sequestration papers 1640s, case papers rel to the Salesbury inheritance 1674-7 and papers rel to the barony of Dinmael 1660-1751; bailiff's account, commote of Collion (Denbighshire) 1546-7; Welsh estate records, incl leases 15th-18th cent, surveys and plans 18th-20th cent and rentals and accounts 17th-19th cent; family corresp and papers 16th-19th cent, incl papers of William Salesbury as governor of Denbigh Castle 1643-6; Ferrers and Devereux receiver-generals' and ministers' accounts 1404-9, 1525-51.

National Library of Wales. Deposited from Pool Park 1928 and by Nancy, Lady Bagot 1974-5. Purchased 1978-9, 1986-7. National Library of Wales *Annual Report 1942-3*, p29, *1943-4*, p29, *1974-5*, p63. NRA 29973 (partial list).

[h] Tachbrook (Warwicks) and Bachymbyd rentals 1699-1711.

Public Record Office (C 109/89, Bagot *v* Oughton).

Related collection: Barons Newborough (Caernarfon Area Record Office XD 2, NRA 16601).

[6] BAILLIE-HAMILTON, Earls of Haddington

Sir Thomas Hamilton (1563-1637), Secretary of State and Lord Privy Seal of Scotland, was created Earl of Haddington in 1627. He acquired a compact landed estate in East Lothian (Haddingtonshire), where he bought Tynninghame in 1628, and in Roxburghshire, mainly by purchase of former monastic lands such as those of Melrose Abbey. In 1674 his great-grandson the fifth Earl married the daughter and heiress of John, Duke of Rothes (d1681), but the earldom of Rothes was inherited by his eldest son and that of Haddington by his second son Thomas, who became sixth Earl.

Lord Binning, son of the sixth Earl, married in 1717 Rachel, daughter and in her issue heiress of George Baillie of Jerviswood (Lanarkshire) and Mellerstain (Berwickshire). In 1759 their second son George (d1797) inherited the estates of his maternal grandfather and took the surname Baillie. George Baillie's grandson George (1802-70) succeeded his cousin as tenth Earl in 1858, adopting the surname Baillie-Hamilton and uniting the estates of the two families.

In 1854 George Baillie, later eleventh Earl of Haddington, married Helen Catherine, only daughter of Sir John Warrender, fifth Bt, by his second wife Frances, daughter of Richard Pepper Arden, first Baron Alvanley. On the death of the third Baron Alvanley in 1857 he inherited the Arderne (Cheshire) estate of the Arden family through his wife.

Estates in 1883: Berwickshire 14,279 acres, E Lothian 8,302 acres, Roxburghshire 4,708 acres, Lanarkshire 501 acres, Cheshire 6,256 acres, total 34,046 acres worth £46,616 a year.

[a] Writs 14th-19th cent, mainly E Lothian and Roxburghshire; registers of title 16th-17th cent, incl cartulary of the 1st Earl of Haddington 1620-1; settlements 1608-1802; trust, legal and case papers 16th-19th cent, incl minutes and accounts of the 6th Earl's guardians 1685-99 and papers rel to quarrying early 19th cent; tacks 17th-19th cent, mainly E Lothian and Roxburghshire; Tynninghame (E Lothian and Roxburghshire) estate surveys, maps, valuations and rentals 16th-20th cent, accounts 19th-20th cent and corresp and papers 16th-20th cent, incl papers rel to teinds 16th-19th cent, timber accounts 1743-55 and papers rel to wood sales late 19th cent; Mellerstain (Berwickshire and Lanarkshire) estate rentals and accounts 1870-20th cent and letter books 20th cent; Dumfriesshire estate rentals 1883-1952 and accounts late 19th-20th cent; inventories of plate, furniture, etc (Hamilton family) 17th cent.

Papers rel to E Lothian lieutenancy 1797 and militia in Scotland 1783-1820; patents and commissions 17th-19th cent; personal and political papers 16th-19th cent, incl legal and other papers of the 1st Earl, official and political papers of the 9th Earl and military diaries of Lord Binning 1882, 1884-5; misc family accounts and papers 16th-19th cent; literary, genealogical and other papers 14th-19th cent, incl MS catalogue of English royal household and nobility 16th cent, and naval orders of Sir Thomas Hardy 1707-9.

In private possession. Enquiries to the National Register of Archives (Scotland) (NRA(S) 104). HMC *Papers of British Cabinet Ministers 1782-1900*, 1982, p28. NRA 10114.

[b] Writs 1484-1815, mainly Berwickshire and Lanarkshire; inventories of title; executors' accounts and papers of George Baillie 1841-4; legal and case papers 16th-19th cent, incl some rel to Robert Baillie the Patriot 1679-90; tacks *c*1765-1887 (mainly Berwickshire and Lanarkshire); Mellerstain and Jerviswood estate maps 18th cent, particulars and rentals 1659-1884, accounts and vouchers 1630-1884, corresp 1711-19th cent, factor's notes 1777-1883 and estate papers 16th-20th cent, incl peat accounts 1659-84 and Mellerstain accounts of teinds 1692-4, timber accounts *c*1752-1885 and drainage papers *c*1824-47; estate rental of Sir John Dun of Garthock (Ayrshire) 1714.

Mellerstain plans 18th cent, incl some of Robert and William Adam; Mellerstain household accounts 1699-1872, incl cellar books 1739-43 and carriage accounts 1765-6, and household papers 18th-19th cent, incl bills of fare 18th cent, inventories 1844-8 and library catalogues and accounts 1719-96; misc household accounts 1711-52, incl London 1719-40 and Barnet 1722-9; inventories, George Baillie of Jerviswood 1693 and Jerviswood 1694; corresp rel to alterations at Arderne Hall (Cheshire) *c*1862-72.

Election papers (Berwickshire, Dumfriesshire and Lanarkshire) 1701-1812; Mellerstain school accounts and papers *c*1755-8; Baillie family and political corresp, accounts and papers 17th-19th cent, incl official, political and diplomatic papers of George Baillie (1664-1738), letters of James 'Secretary' Johnston (1665-1737) and Alexander Hume-Campbell (1674-1740), papers of the 2nd Earl of Marchmont, misc papers of Robert Baillie the Patriot (d1684) and hunting diaries *c*1796-1819; genealogical, literary and misc papers mainly 16th-19th cent, incl Tynninghame charter of King Duncan 1094, Sir John Skene's 'Tabill of the Cheker Rollis' 1595, log of the *Defyance* 1707-8 and MS treatises on tree planting by the Earl of Haddington *c*1733 (2).

In private possession. Enquiries to the National Register of Archives (Scotland) (NRA(S) 104). NRA 10114. Seventeenth- and eighteenth-century pamphlets were sold, with other library volumes from this collection, by the 12th Earl of Haddington in 1956 (Sotheby's, 23 Oct, lots 217-376).

[c] Official and other corresp and papers of the 9th Earl of Haddington 1834-46, mainly as First Lord of the Admiralty 1841-6; misc corresp and papers 1501-1936, incl the Tynninghame letter-book of James V 1529-42, corresp of James VI and I, letters of George Canning to Lord Binning 1809-27 and 7 letters of Sir Walter Scott *c*1828-9.

Scottish Record Office (GD 249). Deposited by the 12th Earl of Haddington 1968, 1982. HMC

Papers of British Cabinet Ministers 1782-1900, 1982, p28. NRA 10114.

[d] Corresp and papers of the Hall family as agents for Lady Grizel Baillie 1712-50.

Scottish Record Office (Hall of Dunglass papers, GD 206/2/262-7.)

[e] Legal and antiquarian papers of the 1st Earl of Haddington, incl copies of minutes of Parliament 1400-1622.

National Library of Scotland. Summary Catalogue of the Advocates' Manuscripts, 1971, nos 712, 914, 919, 1481.

[f] Estate accounts of the 7th Earl 1744-68.

National Library of Scotland (MSS 14833-4). Purchased 1977 (Phillips, Edinburgh, 18 May, lot 163).

[g] Cheshire deeds and papers (Done, Crewe, Arden and Baillie-Hamilton families) 13th-20th cent, incl deeds from 13th cent, legal papers, settlements and manorial court records (Bredbury, etc) 16th-19th cent, estate surveys, valuations, rentals, accounts and vouchers 17th-20th cent, household accounts and papers (Harden, Utkinton, etc) mainly 18th cent, Delamere Forest records 14th-19th cent, and misc family, genealogical and literary papers 16th-20th cent.

Cheshire Record Office (DAR). Deposited 1958, 1962 by Lady Helen O'Brien, granddaughter of the 11th Earl of Haddington. NRA 16207.

[h] Cheshire deeds and papers 17th-20th cent, mainly deeds, abstracts of title and leases 17th-19th cent but incl wills and settlements (Arden and Done families) 17th-19th cent, surveys, particulars and maps 18th-19th cent, and misc legal papers from 17th cent.

John Rylands University Library of Manchester. Deposited 1955, 1987 by Sale, Lingards & Co on behalf of Lady Helen O'Brien. NRA 14301.

[7] BERKELEY, Earls of Berkeley

The Fitzhardinges, later Berkeleys, were lords of Berkeley (Gloucestershire) from the twelfth century. The tenth Lord Berkeley (d1417) married Margaret, daughter and heiress of Warin De Lisle, Lord Lisle. William, Marquess of Berkeley (d1492) succeeded to part of the estates of the Mowbray Dukes of Norfolk in Leicestershire, Lincolnshire, Sussex and elsewhere (see also no 37). He settled much of his property with remainder to the King, but his brother Maurice (who married Isabel Mead, heiress of Thornbury (Gloucestershire) and property in Somerset) and Maurice's great-grandson the seventh Baron Berkeley recovered some of the alienated possessions.

Thomas Berkeley (dvp1611), son of the seventh Baron, married Elizabeth Carey, daughter and co-heir of the second Baron Hunsdon: she purchased

Cranford (Middlesex) in 1618. Their son the eighth Baron married in 1614 Elizabeth Stanhope, heiress of other property in Middlesex (including East Bedfont, sold to the Duke of Northumberland in 1656). The ninth Baron was created Earl of Berkeley in 1679. In 1773 the fifth Earl of Berkeley inherited valuable London (Middlesex) property and the Portisham (Dorset) estate from a distant cousin, Lord Berkeley of Stratton.

In the early nineteenth century the Berkeley Castle estates passed to a natural son, created Baron Fitzhardinge in 1841. In the twentieth century they descended to the eighth Earl of Berkeley (a descendant of the eldest legitimate son of the fifth Earl) and on his death to the Berkeleys of Spetchley (Worcestershire). The London property was sold in 1919 and Cranford mainly in 1932. The Bosham (Sussex) estate was held by the Hon CPT Berkeley, second son of the first Baron Fitzhardinge, in 1883.

Estates in 1883: Fitzhardinge: Gloucs 18,264 acres, Dorset 1,471 acres, Middlesex 539 acres, total 20,274 acres worth £33,717 a year; Robert Berkeley (of Spetchley): Worcs 4,811 acres.

[a] Deeds 12th-19th cent (over 400 pre-1250), mostly Gloucs but incl Berks (Lisle properties), Leics (Seagrave family, etc from 12th cent), Middlesex, Norfolk, Somerset, Sussex, Yorks, etc; wills, settlements, inquisitions *post mortem* and related papers 13th-19th cent; Berkeley cartulary 15th cent; abstracts and copies of charters, with particulars of properties 15th cent (37 rolls); legal and case papers from 15th cent, incl papers rel to the Norfolk estates early 16th cent, the Berkeley peerage, precedence, etc; manorial records 13th-19th cent, mostly Gloucs (hundred of Berkeley, etc) but incl Leics (Melton Mowbray, etc) 16th-17th cent, Somerset 14th-17th cent, Yorks 15th-16th cent and Berks (Abingdon Abbey manors) 15th-16th cent.

Gloucs estate records 13th-19th cent (mainly 16th cent onwards), incl leases, surveys, maps 18th cent, rentals and accounts, timber accounts and papers, Severn fishery papers, and duck decoy records 1840-87; estate records for other counties 15th-19th cent, incl Mowbray estates 14th-early 16th cent, Cornwall and Devon (Berkeley of Stratton estates) 16th-18th cent, Dorset (Portisham estate), Kent, etc (Hunsdon estates) late 16th-early 17th cent, Hunts late 16th cent, Leics 16th-17th cent, Middlesex 16th-19th cent, Somerset (Portbury, etc) mainly 16th cent, Sussex (Bosham) 16th-early 19th cent, and Berkeley Square (Middlesex) estate 18th-19th cent; misc accounts for building work at Berkeley Castle 18th-19th cent; household and general accounts 14th-19th cent (Berkeley, Yate, London houses, etc); inventories and other papers 16th-19th cent.

Papers rel to Gloucs affairs 15th-19th cent, incl a military survey of Gloucs 1522, subsidy rolls 16th cent, muster rolls and papers 16th-early 17th cent and election papers 18th-19th cent; commissions, patents, etc 15th-19th cent; personal accounts from 14th cent (Berkeley and

Mowbray); family corresp and papers 16th-19th cent, incl diplomatic and Irish papers of the 2nd Earl 1689-1701, naval papers of the 1st Baron Fitzhardinge and Sir MFF Berkeley 19th cent, scientific papers of the 8th Earl 20th cent, papers of the 2nd Baron Hunsdon (1547-1603), account book 1604 and inventory 1622 of Sir Michael Stanhope, and antiquarian and other papers of John Smyth of Nibley early 17th cent (incl his 'Lives of the Berkeleys'); genealogical, literary and other papers from late 14th cent; cartularies, registers, etc of St Augustine's Abbey Bristol, St Andrew's chantry Berkeley and Croxton Abbey (Leics) 13th-14th cent; Berkeley parish registers and transcripts 1562-1650; Alkington (Gloucs) overseers' book 1700-12; Star Chamber papers nd (1 bundle).

In private possession. Access restricted (enquiries to the Hon Archivist to the Trustees of the Berkeley Castle muniments, c/o the Gloucestershire Record Office). HMC *Fourth Report, App*, 1874, pp364-7; IH Jeayes, *Descriptive catalogue of the charters and muniments . . . at Berkeley Castle*, 1892. NRA 21647.

[b] Gloucs estate plans 1739-*c*1850.

Gloucestershire Record Office (D 650). Deposited by the Berkeley Estates Company 1951-93. NRA 9859.

[c] Misc Gloucs, Middlesex and Sussex deeds 17th-19th cent; wills, settlements and trust papers 18th-20th cent; legal papers 19th-20th cent, incl Severn fishery papers 1907-9; Cam and Coaley (Gloucs) enclosure award 1876; Berkeley Square lease book 1896-1920; Cranford inventory 1917.

Gloucestershire Record Office (D 4462; BRA 2351). Deposited by Boodle, Hatfield & Co, solicitors, London through the British Records Association 1982-91. NRA 4632, 21647.

[d] Legal, manorial and estate papers *c*1840-70, incl draft deeds and leases, papers rel to Severn salmon fisheries *c*1860-70, Berkeley hundred court book 1863-5 and enclosure papers 1863-70.

Gloucestershire Record Office (D 177). Deposited by Haines & Sumner, solicitors, Gloucester. Gloucestershire Record Office *Handlist*, 1988, p181.

[e] Naval papers of Capt H Berkeley 1843-98, incl some corresp of his father FHF Berkeley.

Gloucestershire Record Office (D 3752). Deposited by Major RG Berkeley 1978. NRA 22750.

[f] Papers of John Smyth of Nibley as steward of the Berkeley estates mostly early 17th cent, incl particular of Seagrave (Leics) estate, household regulations 1594, Berkeley Castle constable's account 1612-13, taxation papers, genealogical papers, etc, with other papers rel to the Smyth family and their properties.

Gloucester Public Library. NRA 16645. Part of the Smyth papers that descended to the Cholmondeley family of Condover and were dispersed by sale in 1877 (HMC *Fifth Report, App*, 1876, pp333-60; *Guide to the Location of Collections*, 1982, p13). Other ex-Berkeley material may now be found in Bristol University Library (Kingswood Abbey deeds 13th-15th cent), Gloucestershire Record Office (muster books 1608; legal and estate papers *c*1580-1732, with a Berkeley Castle inventory 1663, in the Denison-Jones papers of Leonard Stanley papers (D 225, NRA 6128)), and in private hands (stewardship and other papers of John Smyth (photocopies in Gloucestershire and House of Lords Record Offices, NRA 16645, 20336)).

[g] Middlesex deeds 16th-19th cent (Cranford, Harlington and London (Spring Gardens)); Cranford and Harlington manorial records 15th-20th cent, with Northaw (Herts) court roll 1572-4; misc Middlesex estate records 17th-20th cent, incl leases 17th-19th cent, maps 19th-20th cent, Harlington enclosure papers 1819-24 and Cranford rental 1917-23; particulars of Dorset and Sussex estates ?late 19th cent; household account book, Lady Berkeley 1629-35; pedigree late 19th cent.

Greater London Record Office (Accs 530, 867, 2599, etc). Deposited *c*1955-88. NRA 3512 (for Acc 867), 4632.

[h] Letter book of the 7th Baron Berkeley rel to his keepership of Kingswood and Michaelwood forests 1571-1610.

Norfolk Record Office (MS 21509/42).

Related collection: Fitzalan-Howard, Dukes of Norfolk (no 37).

[8] BOWES-LYON, Earls of Strathmore and Kinghorne

John Lyon (d1382), Chancellor of Scotland in 1377, married Johanna, daughter of Robert II, and acquired estates in Aberdeenshire, Fife, Forfarshire and Perthshire. In the seventeenth century some of the older estates were sold, but the Forfarshire and Perthshire estates were consolidated, with Glamis Castle (Forfarshire) and Castle Lyon (Perthshire) rebuilt as the principal seats. Patrick Lyon, ninth Baron Glamis, was created Earl of Kinghorne in 1606, and his grandson obtained a new patent as Earl of Strathmore and Kinghorne in 1677.

In 1767 John Lyon, ninth Earl of Strathmore and Kinghorne, married Mary Eleanor, daughter and heir of George Bowes, of Streatlam and Gibside (County Durham) and Wemmergill (Yorkshire, North Riding), by Mary, daughter and heir of Edward Gilbert, of St Paul's Walden (Hertfordshire). On the death of the tenth Earl in 1820 the Bowes estates in the north of England passed to a natural son, John Bowes, but on the latter's death in 1885 they reverted to his cousin the thirteenth Earl. Smaller English estates were acquired through the marriages of the eighth Earl to Jean Nicholson, of Hetton and West Rainton

(County Durham) in 1753, and of the eleventh Earl to Mary Carpenter, of Redbourn (Hertfordshire) in 1800. The Shadwell (London) estate appears to have been acquired through the marriage of Lord Glamis, son of the eleventh Earl, to Charlotte Grinstead in 1820.

In 1923 some fifty-seven bound volumes of Bowes papers were accidentally sold with the library from Streatlam Castle. Many were recovered by the family but some are now in other custody (see (g)-(l) below and BLH Horn and FJ Shaw, 'Bowes bound correspondence and papers', *Archives*, XIV, no 63, 1980, pp134-40).

Estates in 1883: Strathmore: Forfarshire 22,600 acres, Perthshire 270 acres, Herts 1,800 acres, Sussex 16 acres, total 24,686 acres worth £28,502 a year; Bowes: Yorks NR 34,887 acres, Co Durham 8,313 acres, total 43,200 acres worth £21,071 a year.

[a] Writs for Forfarshire (Restennet Priory, etc), Perthshire, Fife and Aberdeenshire from 12th cent; deeds for other counties 17th-20th cent, incl Herts, London, Co Durham, Northumberland, Yorks NR and Sussex; wills, settlements and trust papers, incl papers rel to the Earls of Erroll mid 17th cent, sederunt book for the Earl of Strathmore 1776-95 and trust accounts and papers 19th cent; legal papers *c*16th-20th cent, Bowes and Lyon, incl case papers and inventories of writs; barony court books, mainly Glamis, 1622-1754.

Forfarshire estate records mainly 16th-20th cent, incl tacks, maps, rentals, accounts, corresp and other papers, particularly full for the 17th cent; Fife, Perthshire and Aberdeenshire estate records mainly 17th-18th cent; Co Durham and Yorks NR (Bowes) estate records 1598-*c*1920, mainly late 18th-early 19th and late 19th-early 20th cent, incl papers rel to Co Durham collieries and mineral rights; records for the Nicholson estate (Co Durham, etc) 18th cent, Herts estates (Redbourn and St Paul's Walden) *c*1765-1934, Bognor (Sussex) estate 1864-71, London (Shadwell) estate late 18th-late 19th cent and Biarritz property 1880s; trust, legal and misc estate papers rel to the Ridley Hall (Northumberland) estate 18th-20th cent; Scottish household accounts, inventories, building plans and papers, etc (Glamis and Castle Lyon) from early 17th cent, incl papers rel to the rebuilding of Glamis Castle late 17th cent and account of honey from the gardens 1743-5; Streatlam and Gibside household papers 18th-20th cent, incl Gibside inventory 1761 and Streatlam inventories *c*1826, 1887; papers rel to chapels at Gibside and Barnard Castle 19th-20th cent.

Papers rel to Scottish county, burgh and parish affairs 17th-20th cent, incl Forfarshire elections 18th cent; commissions, patents, etc *c*16th-20th cent; family corresp and papers, Lyon and Bowes 16th-20th cent, incl papers of Sir George Bowes late 16th cent, letter books of Robert Bowes 1582-3, 1590, Co Durham election papers 1675-81, book of record of Patrick, Earl of

Strathmore 1684-9, game books 19th-20th cent and diaries of the 13th Earl 19th cent; genealogical and other papers, incl papers of Sir Cuthbert Sharp.

In private possession. Enquiries to the National Register of Archives (Scotland) (NRA(S) 198, 885). HMC *Second Report, App*, 1871, pp185-6; *Fourteenth Report, App III*, 1895, pp174-90. NRA 381.

[b] Deeds 12th-19th cent, mainly Co Durham and Yorks but incl Northumberland, Middlesex and other counties; wills, settlements and related papers 16th-20th cent; legal and case papers 14th-20th cent, mainly from 17th cent, incl cases rel to the descent of the Bowes estate and boundary disputes with the Barnard (Raby) estates; manorial records for Mickleton (Yorks NR) 15th-19th cent, Streatlam (Co Durham) 1721-1802, etc; Streatlam and general estate records 16th-20th cent, mainly from early 18th cent, incl surveys and maps, rentals and accounts, corresp, and papers rel to tithes, farms, woods, drainage, brick and tile manufacture, enclosure, etc; papers rel to the Wemmergill and Kirklevington estates (Yorks NR) 17th-20th cent, the Gibside estate (Co Durham and Northumberland) 18th-20th cent (incl papers rel to paper milling 18th cent), the Winlaton and Hylton (Co Durham) estates 18th-20th cent and the Herts and London estates mainly 18th cent.

Building plans and papers 18th-20th cent, Streatlam Castle, Gibside, Hylton Castle (19th cent) and Holwick Hall (Yorks NR) (20th cent); household accounts and inventories 18th-20th cent, mainly Streatlam Castle and Gibside; papers rel to Co Durham and Yorks affairs 16th-20th cent, incl Teesdale Forest and the Sunderland Navigation; Bowes and Bowes-Lyon family corresp and papers 16th-20th cent, incl papers of Sir George Bowes rel to the Northern Rebellion 1569-78, business and political corresp of George Bowes *c*1715-60, and corresp and papers of John Bowes rel to South Durham elections 1832-41, the Bowes Museum, etc; genealogical and misc papers 18th-20th cent; agency papers rel to the Co Durham estate of the Crichton-Stuart family 19th-20th cent and the Lartington (Co Durham) estate 20th cent.

Durham County Record Office (D/St). Deposited by the 16th and 17th Earls of Strathmore 1964-73, 1986, 1990 (except for a volume of Gibside accounts 1765-7, purchased 1962). NRA 32740.

[c] Papers rel to the Bowes estates (Co Durham and Yorks) mainly 17th-20th cent, incl deeds, legal and case papers, wills and settlements, manorial records (Cotherstone, Mickleton, Lune, etc) and estate papers (mainly Co Durham and Lunedale (Yorks NR) but also a few for Kirklevington late 18th cent).

Durham County Record Office (D/HH). Deposited by ER Hanby Holmes (former steward and solicitor to the estate) 1975-86. NRA 18998.

[d] Winlaton manorial and partnership estate records 16th-20th cent.

Durham County Record Office (D/CG). Deposited by Sir WW Gibson and Messrs Wilkinson, Marshall, Clayton & Gibson, solicitors, Newcastle-upon-Tyne 1963-76. NRA 26390.

[e] Misc Bowes legal and estate papers 1476-1901, mainly Co Durham, incl surveys, plans, etc for the Streatlam estate *c*1804-55 (papers of Thomas Bell as surveyor); papers rel to the Bowes Museum, Barnard Castle 1862-1942, incl letters and papers of its founder John Bowes.

Durham County Record Office (D/BO/A-G). Transferred from the Bowes Museum 1963, 1970. NRA 23425.

[f] Streatlam rentals, accounts, etc 1852.

Public Record Office (C 114/172, Bowes *v* Strathmore).

[g] Cumberland, Co Durham, Yorks NR, etc deeds 12th cent-1635, with misc papers 12th cent-1615; letters to Sir George Bowes from his brother Robert 1578, etc (1 vol).

British Library, Manuscript Collections (Add Ch 66317-66488; Add MSS 34208, 40746-8). Purchased 1892 and 1923 (Sotheby's, 28 Mar, lot 691).

[h] Papers rel mainly to Bowes estates and local affairs *c*1567-1664 (1 vol), incl lordship of Sutton and Teesdale Forest, boundaries of honour of Richmond and royal parks at Barnard Castle.

In private possession. Sotheby's, 28 Mar 1923, lot 674.

[i] Corresp and papers of Sir George Bowes rel to the 1569 rebellion (1 vol); misc papers 1653-1744 (1 vol), mainly rel to Bowes family coal mines.

Bowes Museum, Barnard Castle. Sotheby's, 28 Mar 1923, lots 655, 672.

[j] Bowes family corresp and papers 1568-1629 (1 vol), incl lists of rebels 1569.

Durham University Library (MS 534). Sotheby's, 28 Mar 1923, lot 684.

[k] Misc Bowes family corresp 1662-1760 (1 vol).

Durham County Record Office, Darlington Library (U 415e BOW 5546). Sotheby's, 28 Mar 1923, lot 686.

[l] Misc Bowes family corresp and papers 1696-1728 (1 vol), incl papers rel to coal mining, Berwick election 1723, etc.

Chicago University Library. Sotheby's, 28 Mar 1923, lot 650.

[m] Trustees' corresp and papers rel to the St Paul's Walden estate and parish affairs 1830-55 and nd (50 items).

Hertfordshire Record Office (D/EX 253). Deposited by Rachel, Lady Bowes-Lyon 1970. NRA 18330.

[9] BOYLE, Earls of Glasgow

The Boyle family was in possession of Kelburne (Ayrshire) by the thirteenth century, and acquired land in Buteshire (Cumbrae, etc) during the sixteenth century. The first Earl of Glasgow (1666-1733) acquired further Ayrshire property by marriage from the Mure family of Rowallan, but this later passed to the Campbell family, Earls of Loudon. Hawkhead (Renfrewshire) was acquired through the marriage of the third Earl to Elizabeth, sister and eventual heir of the thirteenth Lord Ross, in 1755. A Northumberland estate, Etal, came from the Carr family through the first wife of the fourth Earl. The Crawford Priory (Fife) and Kilbirnie (Ayrshire) estates were inherited from a distant kinswoman, Lady Mary Lindsay-Crawford (d1832).

On the death of the fifth Earl in 1869 he was succeeded by his brother in the Scottish estates but by his sister, Lady Augusta FitzClarence, in the Etal estate. Hawkhead was sold c1884, and the manuscripts reported on by the Commission transferred to Crawford Priory. On the death of the sixth Earl in 1890 the earldom and the Ayrshire estates passed to a cousin, David Boyle of Shewalton, grandson of David Boyle, Lord Justice General, but Crawford Priory passed to the sixth Earl's daughter Gertrude. She was the wife of the Hon Thomas Cochrane, later Baron Cochrane of Cults, third son of the eleventh Earl of Dundonald.

Some of the Lindsay muniments at Crawford Priory were transferred to the collection of the Earl of Crawford and Balcarres.

Estates in 1883: Earl of Glasgow: Ayrshire 25,613 acres, Fife, 5,625 acres, Renfrewshire 4,579 acres, Buteshire 1,833 acres, Dunbartonshire 175 acres, total 37,825 acres worth £34,588 a year; David Boyle of Shewalton: Ayrshire 2,358 acres worth £2,708 a year.

[a] Writs 1392-19th cent, predominantly Ayrshire and Buteshire but a few for Renfrewshire; heritable bonds and other legal papers 1576-19th cent; Ayrshire estate papers 16th-20th cent, mainly Kelburne and Shewalton, incl tacks, rentals and accounts, factors' accounts, stock and timber accounts, Shewalton colliery records 1676-1866 and papers rel to Shewalton mills; household and building records c1631-20th cent, mainly Fairlie (Ayrshire), Kelburne and Shewalton, incl accounts, plans and inventories; family corresp and papers 16th-19th cent, incl papers of the 1st, 4th and 7th Earls of Glasgow, and extensive papers of David, Lord Boyle and his son Patrick Boyle of Shewalton.

In private possession. Enquiries to the National Register of Archives (Scotland) (NRA(S) 94). NRA 10152.

[b] Writs and related legal papers c1210-19th cent (mainly 16th-18th cent), Lindsay estates in Ayrshire and Fife, Ross lands in Renfrewshire, Midlothian and West Lothian, etc; extensive estate papers 17th-19th cent, mainly Ayrshire (Lindsay estates), Fife and Renfrewshire, incl tacks, rentals and accounts, factors' accounts and papers, corresp and colliery records; household accounts and inventories 17th-20th cent, Hawkhead, Crawford Priory, etc, with other household and garden papers; family corresp and papers 16th-20th cent, mainly Boyle and Cochrane, incl papers of the 4th Earl of Glasgow (Renfrewshire lieutenancy, politics, etc), papers of the 6th Earl as representative peer and Lord Clerk Register, and papers of the Countess of Dundonald 1886-1914 and the 1st Baron Cochrane of Cults.

Scottish Record Office (GD 20). Deposited 1953 (from Crawford Priory) and 1974. HMC *Third Report, App,* 1872, pp405-6; *Eighth Report, App I,* 1881, pp304-8. NRA 29330.

[c] Legal, financial and estate papers 1620-1867, Boyle, Campbell of Lawers (Perthshire), etc, incl accounts for Lawers House 1732, Rowallan estate accounts 1743-5, and Hawkhead and Neilston rental 1752; papers rel to Renfrewshire affairs 1762-1844, incl commission of the 5th Earl as lord lieutenant 1844.

Scottish Record Office (GD 237/97-9, 149, 156-7, 181-2, 192). Deposited by Tods, Murray & Jamieson, WS, Edinburgh. NRA 32483.

[d] Corresp of the Hon Patrick Boyle of Shewalton 1740-96 (42 items).

Scottish Record Office (GD 1/481). Presented by John S Allison 1967. *Annual Report 1967,* p10.

[e] Letters from the 7th Earl to his solicitor CG Shaw 1892-5; misc legal papers 1893-1918.

Strathclyde Regional Archives, Ayrshire Subregional Archives (ATD 8/4-5). Deposited by David W Shaw & Co. NRA 23182.

[f] Cartularies (with plans), Boyle estates 1762-20th cent (10 vols).

In private possession. Enquiries to the National Register of Archives (Scotland) (NRA(S) 596). NRA 14949.

[g] Hawkhead library catalogues 1819-46 (2 vols).

National Library of Scotland (MSS 14242-3). Purchased 1970.

[h] Justiciary notebooks of David, Lord Boyle 1811-48 (26 vols).

National Library of Scotland (Adv MSS 36.3.1-36.4.10).

[i] Religious corresp of the 6th Earl of Glasgow.

Dundee University Library (Brechin Diocesan Library MSS (Br MS 1/5-8); College of Cumbrae MSS). NRA 22376, 33180.

Related collections: Crichton-Stuart, Marquesses of Bute (NRA 15459), including Mure of Rowallan papers 17th cent; Crawford and Balcarres papers (National Library of Scotland, NRA 11004); Kilbirnie writs 1491-1846 (Scottish Record Office GD 1/113); misc Crawford of Kilbirnie and Jordanhill papers 14th-19th cent (National Library of Scotland Acc 6518); Etal and Howtel deeds and papers 18th-20th cent (Northumberland Record Office Acc 2802).

[10] BRIDGEMAN, Earls of Bradford

John Bridgeman (1577-1652), Bishop of Chester, acquired estates at Great Lever and elsewhere in Lancashire. His son Sir Orlando Bridgeman, first Bt (1609-74), Keeper of the Great Seal, married in 1628 Judith Kynaston, through whom the Morton (Shropshire) estate was inherited. He purchased further lands in Shropshire (Knockin, Ness, etc), and Warwickshire (Castle Bromwich). His son Sir John Bridgeman, second Bt (1631-1710), married in 1663 Mary Cradock of Caverswall (Staffordshire), who brought property in Stafford; and Sir John Bridgeman, third Bt (1667-1747), married Ursula, daughter and heir of Roger Matthews of Blodwell (Shropshire).

Sir Henry Bridgeman, fifth Bt (1725-1800), married in 1755 Elizabeth Simpson of Stoke Hall (Derbyshire), and in 1762 succeeded to the Weston (Staffordshire) estate on the death without issue of his maternal uncle the fourth (Newport) Earl of Bradford. He was created Baron Bradford in 1794. (Other estates of the Newport family, Earls of Bradford, in Shropshire and elsewhere were acquired by the Pulteney family, and later descended to the Vane family, Earls of Darlington and Dukes of Cleveland.)

The second Baron Bradford (1762-1825) married in 1788 Lucy Byng, co-heir of the fourth Viscount Torrington, and was created Earl of Bradford in 1815. He succeeded in 1802 to property in Norfolk (Weeting) on the death of his cousin Charles Coote, seventh Earl of Mountrath, but the Weeting estate was sold to John Julius Angerstein (1735-1823). The second Earl bought the St Catherine's estate, Applethwaite (Westmorland) from Miss Ann Agnes Parker in 1830-1.

Estates in 1883: Salop 10,883 acres, Staffs 6,843 acres, Lancs 1,958 acres, Warwicks 1,906 acres, Westmorland 62 acres, Worcs 13 acres, Leics 6 acres, Denbighshire 24 acres, Montgomeryshire 15 acres, total 21,710 acres worth £41,982 a year.

[a] Deeds for Staffs (incl Walsall) 14th-19th cent, Salop 15th-19th cent, Warwicks (Castle Bromwich, etc) 12th-19th cent, Worcs 13th-17th cent, Lancs 18th-20th cent, Cheshire (Newport estates) 17th-18th cent, Denbighshire, etc 16th-18th cent and other counties (incl London) 13th-18th cent; settlements, wills and trust papers 15th-20th cent, Bridgeman, Byng, Coote, Cradock, Matthews, Newport and Simpson families; legal and case papers 15th-20th cent, incl abstracts of title and solicitors' corresp; manorial records 14th-19th cent, incl Knockin and Ness (Salop), Castle Bromwich and Walsall.

Staffs (incl Walsall) estate records 16th-20th cent, incl leases, surveys, maps and plans, rentals and accounts, agents' corresp, etc; records for Salop estates 17th-20th cent, Warwicks estates 15th-20th cent, Newport family estates in Cheshire, Staffs and Salop 1739-54 and Irish estates (Coote family) 18th-early 19th cent; misc papers for Lancs estates (incl Bolton) 18th-20th cent; papers for other estates 17th-18th cent, incl Devereux (Warwicks and Worcs) estate rentals 1626-48, Wilbraham (Cheshire) estate rental and accounts 1693, Byng (Kent) estate survey 1793, Simpson (Notts) estate rentals and surveys 1744-87 and Newport family (Co Tipperary) rental 1752; papers rel to houses late 16th-20th cent, incl inventories for Weston Park, Castle Bromwich and London houses, corresp rel to William Winde's alterations at Castle Bromwich 1688-1702 and Weston Park building plans 19th cent; household accounts 17th-19th cent; agreements rel to Weston with Lancelot Brown 1766-7; Weston garden and plantation accounts 19th cent.

Papers rel to county and local affairs 16th-19th cent, incl subsidy rolls 1564-1698 (mainly Staffs), recusant rolls 1629-32, Salop election corresp 17th-19th cent and papers rel to churches at Tong (Salop), Castle Bromwich, etc 19th cent; Preston (Salop) Hospital Charity deeds and papers 17th-20th cent; papers rel to tithes, advowsons, schools and charities 16th-20th cent; commissions and patents 16th-20th cent; Bridgeman family papers 17th-20th cent, incl papers of Bishop Bridgeman and Sir Orlando Bridgeman 17th cent, and letters from Disraeli to Lady Bradford and Lady Chesterfield 1871-81; papers of Mathew Cradock, mayor of Stafford early 17th cent; Byng family corresp and papers *c*1768-1817, incl papers of the 4th Viscount Torrington as ambassador to Brussels 1781-91; genealogical and misc papers.

Staffordshire Record Office (D 1287). Deposited by the 6th Earl of Bradford in 1972 and subsequently. NRA 430 (partial list).

[b] Walsall estate lease book (with plans) 1827-76; Walsall estate terriers 1860-76; rentals and accounts 19th-20th cent, mainly Walsall but incl Salop, Warwicks and Worcs 1825-63 and Warwicks (Castle Bromwich) 20th cent.

Staffordshire Record Office (D 1287 ADD). Deposited by the Walsall Borough Librarian from the papers of the Potter family, solicitors and agents to the Bradford estate. NRA 9943.

[c] Papers rel to family affairs 1777-1919, incl wills and settlements.

Staffordshire Record Office (D 1287 ADD). Deposited by Baileys, Shaw & Gillett, solicitors, London, through the British Records Association 1992 (BRA 1690).

[d] Deeds early 13th cent-1715, mainly Staffs; Staffs manorial records (especially Biddulph and Bucknall) 1389-1711; Staffs rentals (Biddulph, etc) 16th-17th cent (3).

William Salt Library, Stafford. Presented 1896. NRA 7953.

[e] Walsall leases and related legal papers 19th-20th cent; business accounts, letter books and diaries of the Potter family, Walsall agents 1830-1914.

Walsall Archives Service (Acc 35/20-22, 59). Transferred from Walsall Borough Library. NRA 9943, 21950, 23874.

[f] Drafts and copies of trust deeds, abstracts of title, etc 1718-1836; corresp and papers 1715-1820, mainly rel to Salop militia 1803-20.

Shropshire Record Office (SRO 190, 922). Deposited by the 5th and 6th Earls of Bradford 1948-58. NRA 11197, 11563.

[g] Lancs deeds 14th-19th cent; Lancs surveys and rentals 17th-19th cent, plans 18th cent and colliery accounts 17th-19th cent; papers rel to Wigan rectory late 16th-early 19th cent.

Lancashire Record Office (DDBm). Deposited by the 6th Earl of Bradford and from the Bolton estate office 1967. *Guide to the Lancashire Record Office*, 1985, p 200.

[h] Bishop Bridgeman's register 17th cent, incl copies of Lancs, Cheshire and Denbighshire deeds from 13th cent and Lancs leases 16th-17th cent, surveys 1628, etc, and lists of tenants 1662; Lancs estate records 17th-20th cent, incl agreements and legal papers 18th-19th cent, surveys and valuations 19th cent, maps and plans 1770-1890 and nd, rentals and accounts 17th-20th cent, colliery accounts and papers 17th-19th cent, and corresp 1742-1885; financial papers of Bishop Bridgeman 1624-39; rental 1812 and account 1784-5 for the Duke of Devonshire's Cumberland estates.

Bolton Archive Service (ZBR). Deposited from the Bolton estate office 1967. NRA 18677.

[i] Bishop Bridgeman's ledger rel to Wigan rectory and manor 1615-42 (18th cent transcript).

Wigan Archives Service (D/DZ A13/1). NRA 13277.

[j] Bishop Bridgeman's register, incl transcripts of records collected by him 1619-43.

Cheshire Record Office (EDA 3). *Guide to the Cheshire Record Office*, 1991, p70.

[k] Deeds and papers rel to the St Catherine's estate, Applethwaite 1712-1899.

Cumbria Record Office, Kendal (WD/NT/77). Deposited by the National Trust 1990.

[l] Deeds, manorial records and estate records rel to the Weeting (Norfolk) estate 16th-early 19th cent; inventory 1803 and plan of wine cellar 1806; Weeting parish settlement papers 1748-70; bank account of the 7th Earl of Mountrath 1764-7.

Norfolk Record Office. Formerly Norwich Central Library MSS 13428a-13809. Deposited by the Earl of Bradford through Norwich Record Society. NRA 4652.

[m] Papers of the 1st and 2nd Earls of Bradford as trustees for Henrietta Anderson-Pelham (née Simpson, d1813), incl papers rel to the Anderson-Pelham family (later Earls of Yarborough), and to Sir Richard Worsley, 7th Bt decd (d1805) and his Appuldurcombe (Isle of Wight) estate.

Lincolnshire Archives (BRAD). Deposited by the 6th Earl of Bradford 1961. NRA 9551.

[n] Trust papers 1673-1735 rel to the Teddington (Middlesex) estate settled by Sir Orlando Bridgeman, 1st Bt, on his son Francis.

Greater London Record Office (Acc 1225). *List of Accessions*, Dec 1973-May 1974.

[o] Corresp and papers of the 4th Viscount Torrington as ambassador to Brussels 1782-92.

In private possession. Access through Staffordshire Record Office. HMC *Second Report, App*, 1871, p30.

Related collections: Barons Barnard (in private possession, not open for research); Earls of Mountrath, Irish estate maps 1730-70 (Trinity College Library, Dublin, NRA 24842).

[11] BRUDENELL, Earls of Cardigan

By the fifteenth century the Brudenell family owned property in several midland counties, including Buckinghamshire (Stoke Mandeville). The Deene (Northamptonshire) branch was established by the lawyer Sir Robert Brudenell (d1531), who in the early sixteenth century bought Deene, Glapthorne and Stanion (Northamptonshire), Slawston and Cranhoe (Leicestershire), Ayston and Wardley (Rutland) and much land elsewhere. He also acquired Stonton Wyville (Leicestershire) by marriage. The estates were consolidated by purchase, and Deene Hall was completed in 1570. Thomas Brudenell of Doddington (Huntingdonshire) (d1663) succeeded his uncle at Deene in 1606, sold outlying property in Buckinghamshire and Warwickshire in 1606-8, and was created Earl of Cardigan 1661. His descendant the fourth Earl married in 1730 Mary, co-heir of John Montagu, second Duke of Montagu, and was himself created Duke of Montagu in 1766. The dukedom became extinct on his death in 1790, when the Montagu estates passed to the family of his daughter Elizabeth, Duchess of Buccleuch, but the Brudenell estates devolved on his brother as fifth Earl of Cardigan.

Hougham and Marston (Lincolnshire) entered the family on the marriage in 1539 of Sir Thomas Brudenell to Agnes, heiress of John Bussey, and were sold by the fifth Earl to Sir John Thorold, ninth Bt, in 1791. The Howley Hall (Yorkshire, West Riding) estate, including property in Wakefield, Headingley, Bramley, and East and West Ardsley, was acquired through the marriage of Francis, Lord Brudenell, father of the third Earl of Cardigan, to Lady Frances Savile, sister of the second Earl of Sussex (d1671). The Rutland properties devolved upon Caroline Brudenell (d1803), wife of Sir Samuel Fludyer, first Bt, and at her death on her younger son George Fludyer of Ayston (d1837).

When the seventh Earl of Cardigan died in 1868 he was succeeded in the earldom by the second Marquess of Ailesbury (see no 12), but his estates passed to his widow with remainder to Robert Thomas Brudenell-Bruce (1845-1912), fourth son of the third Marquess of Ailesbury, and then to his son George (who assumed the name of Brudenell only) in 1917.

Estates in 1883: Northants 7,210 acres, Yorks WR 5,583 acres, Leics 2,931 acres, total 15,724 acres worth £35,357 a year.

[a] Deeds, mainly Leics and Northants 13th-19th cent, Lincs and Rutland 13th-18th cent and Yorks 14th-19th cent but with some for Beds, Bucks, Cambs, Hunts, Lancs, etc 13th-18th cent; inventories of deeds and abstracts of title 16th-19th cent; wills and settlements 15th-19th cent; inquisitions *post mortem* 13th-16th cent; legal and trust papers 14th-19th cent, incl Civil War sequestration papers and executorship accounts and papers for Sir Henry Shirley, 2nd Bt (d1633); manorial records 14th-18th cent, Northants, Leics, Lincs, Rutland, etc; hundred court rolls for Corby (Northants) 1571-89, 1742, Gartree (Leics) 1557, 1578 and Loveden (Lincs) 1687, 1694.

Leases, terriers, maps, surveys, valuations, rentals and accounts, mainly Northants and Leics 15th-20th cent and Lincs and Rutland 14th-18th cent, incl survey of the estates of Sir John de Reynes late 14th cent, Stoke Mandeville accounts 1473-7, Oakley Reynes (Beds) survey 1614, and survey book for the whole Brudenell estate c1633-7; misc estate corresp and papers 17th-20th cent, incl Lincs enclosure papers early 17th cent, survey of Northants and Leics woods 1796, Northants wood accounts 1705-17, 1741-3, and Deene labour accounts 1869-1921 and dairy accounts 1844-1916; Yorks WR estate records 17th-19th cent, incl leases late 18th-19th cent, particulars of leases 1658-1744, valuation 1798, maps and terriers 1711 and 1735, rentals, accounts and corresp 18th-19th cent, and wood and colliery accounts 1789-91; papers 16th-18th cent rel to the Hornby (Lancs) estate of the Parker family, Barons Morley, incl misc surveys 1576-1709 and rentals 1711; Clitheroe (Lancs) estate accounts of the Dowager Duchess of Montagu 1709-43; plan of Deene house and park 1601; Glapthorne building accounts 1599 and inventories 1617, 1636; Twickenham Park House inventory 1685; misc household papers 16th-20th cent, incl accounts of Glapthorne household 1636 and Deene household 1706-7.

Papers rel to Rockingham Forest (Northants) 16th-19th cent and to the Forest of Dean c1617-18; shrievalty and taxation papers 16th cent; patents and commissions 16th-20th cent; family papers 16th-19th cent, incl recusancy and political papers 17th cent and acquittances, bonds and personal accounts 17th-19th cent; misc papers of the Duke of Montagu as Constable of Windsor Castle 1752-90; acquittance

roll of the 5th Earl of Cardigan as Master of the Robes 1790-1; corresp and papers of the 7th Earl (1797-1868); genealogical and misc papers 16th-19th cent, incl survey of Owston Abbey (Leics) 1536, justice of the peace's precedent book 16th cent, genealogical papers of the 1st Earl (d1663) and papers rel to the debts of the Tresham family of Lyveden (Northants) 17th cent; rent ledger 1734-53 and personal accounts of Sir Nathaniel Dance-Holland (1735-1811), painter.

Northamptonshire Record Office (BRU). Deposited by GLT Brudenell 1936-59. NRA 34693.

[b] Executorship papers of the 5th Earl 1761-1823; accounts for the sale of Hougham and Marston 1792; Windsor Castle governorship bills 1762 and misc appointments of deputy governors, etc 1714-52.

Northamptonshire Record Office (Acc 1956/46b, YZ 1481-1521). Deposited by Nichol, Manisty & Co, solicitors, London through the British Records Association 1956. NRA 4039.

[c] Great and Little Oakley (Northants) deeds 13th-16th cent (7).

Northamptonshire Record Office (Acc 1956/64, BRU.Z.110-116). Deposited by GT Brudenell 1956. NRA 4039.

[d] Leics and Northants conveyances and related papers 20th cent, returned by the family's London solicitors; misc deeds 13th-16th cent, with volume of copies of medieval charters for the Bucks estate, abstracts of Bucks leases c1558-62 and Sir Robert Brudenell's book of purchases early 16th cent; will of Sir Thomas Brudenell 1587 and probate of the 3rd Earl 1703; misc Northants maps and plans 17th-19th cent, mainly for Deene, incl plan of Deene manor by John Hawstead 1612; valuation of Lord Brudenell's estates 1628, Leics estate surveys 1637, note book 1638, steward's accounts 1657-80, 1713-24 and estate accounts (Leics and Northants) 1727-32; papers rel to the household at Deene 18th-19th cent, incl plastering account 1726, inventory of plate and linen 1706-30, servants' wages book 1709-32, household accounts 1757-65, 1793-1801 and garden accounts 1722-30; catalogue of the library at Howley Park 1716; household accounts of Sir Nathaniel Dance-Holland 1757-65.

Lincs poll book c1721 and Northants canvass book ?1832; misc pardons, etc 15th-16th cent; misc family papers 17th-20th cent, incl antiquarian papers of the 1st Earl (d1663), misc corresp of the Rous family of Courtyrala (Glamorgan) 1775-1848, military note book of 7th Earl 1856 and Deene game book 1905-10; misc papers, incl MS account of Francis Tresham's death in the Tower 1605.

In private possession. Enquires to Northamptonshire Record Office. NRA 34693. The 1297 inspeximus of Magna Carta from the collection was sold in 1984 to a collector in the

USA. The whereabouts of three agreements for Sir Humphrey Gilbert's expedition 1582, sold at Sotheby's in 1964 (2 Nov, lots 278-80), and of a seventeenth-century commonplace book and other family papers, sold at Sotheby's in 1967 (20 Feb, lots 228-49), have not been traced. Corby manor records 1799-1934 and court rolls for Glapthorne 1793-1914, Headingley with Burley 1735-1832 and Bramley 1735-1816 are known to have been in the custody of WW Mills, steward of the Brudenell manors, in 1934, but were subsequently lost, most probably destroyed in the Second World War.

[e] Abstract of title to an estate at Bramley 1749-96; misc Yorks WR manorial records 1704-1832; Yorks WR tenancy papers 1779-1851, maps and plans late 18th cent, *c*1827-49, valuations 1813, 1848-9, surveys *c*1823-38 and rentals and accounts 1759-1852; corresp of George Hayward, agent for the Yorks estate 1830-52; Yorks WR tithe papers 16th-19th cent and enclosure papers 1789-1839, mainly for East and West Ardsley and Headingley; misc papers rel to sales 1839-53 and to timber, collieries and quarries on the Yorks estate 1708-1853; papers rel to turnpikes near Leeds 1830-53; misc papers 18th-19th cent.

Leeds District Archives (DB/220). Deposited by Dibb Lupton, solicitors, Leeds 1966. NRA 34058.

[f] Yorks deeds, mineral leases, particulars, plans and papers 18th-19th cent, incl estate rental 1756, legal accounts *c*1850-70 and papers rel to New Park colliery 1794-1869.

Wakefield Libraries, Department of Local Studies (Goodchild Loan MSS: Cardigan MSS). NRA 23595.

Related collections: Dukes of Buccleuch (Northamptonshire Record Office 1965/212, etc, NRA 4039, 23059, and in private possession), including papers of the Montagu family, Dukes of Montagu; Dukes of Marlborough (British Library, Manuscript Collections Add MSS 61101-61710, etc), including papers of the 1st Earl of Cardigan that passed to the Spencer family (Add MSS 61481-2).

[12] BRUDENELL-BRUCE, Marquesses of Ailesbury

Edward Bruce of Blairhall (Clackmannanshire) (1548-1611) received the Whorlton and Jervaulx Abbey (Yorkshire) estates from the Crown and was created Baron Bruce of Kinloss (Fife) in 1608. His son Thomas (1599-1663) married a daughter of the second Earl of Exeter (see no 19), and was created Earl of Elgin in 1633. His grandson the second Earl was created Earl of Ailesbury in 1664.

The second Earl of Ailesbury inherited the Seymour estates of Tottenham and Savernake Forest (Wiltshire), which included Shalbourne (Berkshire), through his marriage in 1676 to Elizabeth Seymour, to whom they had passed on the death in 1671 of her brother the third Duke of Somerset. With these came the hereditary wardenship of Savernake Forest, originally granted to the Seymours' ancestor Richard Esturmy by William I. (Other Seymour estates passed to her uncle the fourth Duke of Somerset and later to the co-heirs of the seventh Duke on his death in 1750.)

On the death of the third Earl of Ailesbury in 1747 the earldom of Elgin passed by special remainder to his cousin Charles Bruce, ninth Earl of Kincardine, but the Kinloss title passed to his elder daughter Mary, Duchess of Chandos (see no 44) and the English estates to his nephew Thomas Brudenell-Bruce (1729-1813), youngest son of the third Earl of Cardigan (see no 11). Thomas Brudenell-Bruce was created Earl of Ailesbury in 1776, and his son Charles Marquess of Ailesbury in 1821. The second Marquess succeeded a cousin as eighth Earl of Cardigan in 1868, but did not inherit the Deene (Northamptonshire) estate.

The Brudenell-Bruces added to their Wiltshire property by purchase, most notably buying in 1779 the Marlborough estate (a former Seymour property) from the heirs of the Marquess of Granby, but by 1892, when a projected sale to Lord Iveagh for £750,000 failed, it was heavily mortgaged. Much of the Wiltshire estate was sold in 1929, and in 1938 Savernake Forest was conveyed to the Forestry Commission. The Yorkshire estates were alienated in the years from 1886, Jervaulx Abbey being sold to Samuel Cunliffe-Lister, Baron Masham of Swinton.

The Houghton Park (Bedfordshire) estate was granted to the first Earl of Elgin by James I. The neighbouring Maulden estate was added by purchase in 1635. The leasehold of Ampthill Great Park was brought from the Earl of Ashburnham in 1666 but sold back again in 1690. The remaining Bedfordshire possessions were sold to the Duke of Bedford in 1738.

Estates in 1883: Wilts 37,993 acres, Yorks NR 15,369 acres and WR 133 acres, Berks 1,556 acres, total 55,051 acres worth £59,716 a year.

[a] Deeds 13th-20th cent, mainly Hants and Wilts, with some for Beds, London and Surrey 17th-18th cent, Lincs 14th-18th cent, etc; abstracts of title 14th-18th cent; wills and settlements 15th-20th cent; inquisitions *post mortem*, William Sturmy 1427 and the Earl of Hertford 1626; trust, legal and case papers 16th-19th cent, incl some rel to disputes with the Duke of Marlborough and Lord Verney in Marlborough and Great Bedwyn *c*1760 and proposed sale of Wilts estate to Lord Iveagh 1890-4; Wilts manorial court records 14th-19th cent and hundred court records (Selkley and Kinwardstone) 1696-1861; leases and agreements 14th-19th cent, mainly Wilts but incl some for Beds and Yorks 17th cent, etc; Wilts surveys, maps, particulars, valuations and rentals 15th-20th cent, vouchers and accounts 17th-20th cent, tithe papers 17th-18th cent, and other corresp and papers 16th-20th cent; misc rentals, accounts and papers rel to Beds, Yorks and other estates

late 17th-early 19th cent; valuation of estates of Edward, Earl of Hertford 1621 and rental of Hougham and Marston (Lincs) (Cardigan estate) 1741.

Papers rel to Tottenham House and chapel mid-18th-early 19th cent, incl work by Lancelot Brown; household and library accounts and papers 17th-19th cent, mainly Houghton House and Tottenham House but also Ampthill and St John's, Clerkenwell (Middlesex) 1675-90; stable accounts 1796-1820; inventories 17th-20th cent, mainly from late 19th cent, incl valuation of portraits 1945; deer park accounts 1814-24 and tree nursery book 1785-7; Savernake Forest records 13th-20th cent, incl warden's roll 1332 and forest court books 1541-57, 1577-1613; Wilts, Marlborough and Great Bedwyn election accounts and papers 18th-early 19th cent; Wilts militia and Royal Wiltshire Yeomanry records 1758-1820; Wiltshire Emigration Association minutes and register 1849-51.

Patents and commissions 15th-20th cent; family and political corresp and papers (Seymour, Bruce and Brudenell-Bruce families) 16th-20th cent, incl papers of Diana, Countess of Ailesbury 1672-90, the 4th Earl of Ailesbury, and the 1st, 5th and 6th Marquesses; misc Sturmy family papers 14th-15th cent, incl funeral expenses of Henry Sturmy 1381 and other accounts 1381-3; genealogical, literary and other papers 14th-20th cent, incl legal treatises and year books 14th-early 15th cent, two parliamentary diaries 1621, 1624 and 1654, 1659, and inventory of Sir Peter Lely's collection of paintings 1682.

Wiltshire Record Office (WRO 9, 111, 1300). Deposited by the 7th and 8th Marquesses of Ailesbury 1946, 1975, and by Merriman & Co, solicitors, Marlborough 1950. HMC *Fifteenth Report, App VII*, 1898, pp152-306. NRA 30725. A pedigree and miscellaneous charters and plans remain in family possession but are closed to research. Copies of some of these are available at Wiltshire Record Office, to which further enquiries should be addressed.

[b] Wilts manorial court records (mainly Seymour family) 14th cent-1700, incl hundreds of Alderbury 1560-3, 1576 and Selkley 1544-1700; misc Wilts surveys, rentals and accounts 14th-18th cent, incl Savernake rentals 1738-58; account of the lands of John de Vere, Earl of Oxford 1548; Monkton Farleigh Priory (Wilts) charter roll 15th-16th cent and rental 1417; Savernake forest plea rolls 1371-81; Wilts sheriff's tourns 1511-12 and county court amercements roll 1450.

Wiltshire Record Office (WRO 192). Deposited 1933 with Bradford City Corporation by Mary, Countess of Swinton and transferred 1952. NRA 30725.

[c] Manorial court records 1319-17th cent and accounts 1338-1597, mainly Tanfield, Thornbrough, Wath, etc (Yorks NR), but also Beds, Lincs, Rutland, Somerset, Wilts, etc, incl some

for the estates of Muchelney Abbey and Glastonbury Abbey (Somerset) and court rolls for Cecil (Exeter) manors in Lincs and Rutland 15th-early 17th cent; Beauchamp of Hatch (Somerset) cartulary early 15th cent; Yorks leases, mainly 18th cent; surveys, valuations, particulars and terriers 1613-1907; maps and plans 17th-19th cent, incl 19 by William Senior 1627-8; rentals, accounts and vouchers c1790-1889; estate corresp and papers 18th-19th cent, incl misc enclosure papers 1763-1803, Tanfield tithe papers 1756-62 and drainage papers 1844-77; Tanfield Hall inventories 1747-97.

Accounts 1573-4 and surveys 1608 of the former Lincs estates of Charles Brandon, Duke of Suffolk and his daughter Frances, Duchess of Suffolk; auditors' account for the Earl of Exeter's estates 1618-19; Monks Kirby (Warwicks) survey 1619; Yorks election papers 1733-42; Yorks (NR) militia accounts 1715; East Witton Without (Yorks NR) overseers' accounts 1770-1850 and poor rate assessments 1867-77; muster rolls of the hundreds of Isleworth, Elthorne and Spelthorne (Middlesex) 1573, 1578; Sussex estate accounts of Syon Abbey (Middlesex) 1454-5; Bury St Edmunds Abbey chamberlain's accounts 1515-16.

North Yorkshire County Record Office (ZJX). Deposited with Bradford City Corporation by the Countess of Swinton 1933 and subsequently acquired by Bradford District Archives. Further Yorkshire material was sent to Bradford from Wiltshire Record Office in 1952 and 1976. In 1977 the papers were transferred to North Yorkshire County Record Office. *Guide no 1, 1985 and supplements 1986, 1987, 1989*. NRA 33897 (partial list).

[d] West Tanfield manor court books 1576-97, 1625-35.

North Yorkshire County Record Office (ZAX). Purchased 1951.

[e] Misc Somerset manorial records (Seymour family) 15th-17th cent, incl Muchelney court rolls and rentals 1411-75; abstract of accounts for the Duke of Somerset's estates in Somerset 1671.

Somerset Archive and Record Service (DD/AB). Given by the 7th Marquess of Ailesbury 1946. NRA 1399.

[f] Somerset deeds 1254-1719, admissions and enfranchisements 1633-1712 and leases 1556-1715 (Seymour family); Pilton survey 1719 and Puriton particulars 18th cent.

Somerset Archive and Record Service (DD/AB). Deposited in Wiltshire Record Office by the 7th Marquess of Ailesbury 1946 and transferred by the 8th Marquess 1976. NRA 1399.

[g] Muchelney Abbey charter 995.

Somerset Archive and Record Service (DD/SAS, PR 502). Deposited by the 7th Marquess of Ailesbury 1946.

[h] Cartulary of Muchelney Abbey c1300.

British Library, Manuscript Collections (Add MS 56488). Sold by the 7th Marquess at Christie's 1970.

[i] Terrier of Somerset estates of Glastonbury Abbey 1514-17.

British Library, Manuscript Collections (Egerton MS 3034). Acquired 1923. (In the possession of the 2nd Marquess of Ailesbury in 1877.)

[j] Northants forests assart roll 1362-4.

Northamptonshire Record Office (Acc 1947/14, ZA 438). Presented by the 7th Marquess of Ailesbury 1947.

[k] Houghton House (Beds) household account book of the 1st Earl of Ailesbury 1676-82.

Bedfordshire Record Office (X 289). Deposited by the 7th Marquess of Ailesbury 1952. NRA 15702.

[l] Account of the trial of the Earl of Strafford 1641.

British Library, Manuscripts Collections (Add MS 41688). Presented by the 6th Marquess of Ailesbury 1929.

Related collections: Bourne-Arton of Tanfield Lodge (North Yorkshire County Record Office ZBS, NRA 33698); Earls of Elgin (in private possession, NRA 26223); Marquesses of Bath (in private possession).

[13] CAMPBELL, Dukes of Argyll

The medieval estates of the Campbells were much increased by Colin Campbell of Lochow (Argyllshire) (d1493), who was created Earl of Argyll in 1457. Through marriage to a daughter and co-heir of John Stewart, Lord Lorne, he acquired the lordship of Lorne (Argyllshire). In 1489 he was granted the Rosneath (Dunbartonshire) estate by the Crown and in 1493 he acquired the lordship of Castle Campbell (Clackmannanshire). These estates were added to in the sixteenth century by royal grants of Abernethy and Muckart (Perthshire), both subsequently alienated, and the acquisition through marriage of Barbreck (Argyllshire), sold in the 1750s. They were further expanded by James VI and I's grant to the seventh Earl of the whole lordship of Kintyre in 1617. There were subsequent additions to the Argyllshire estates, including Lismore in the nineteenth century, but the Clackmannanshire estate was apparently disposed of in the late eighteenth or early nineteenth century.

Duddingston (Midlothian) passed to the Campbells from Elizabeth, Duchess of Lauderdale (d1698), whose daughter married the first Duke of Argyll (so created in 1701). It was sold in 1745 to the eighth Earl of Abercorn. The mansion known as The Whim (Peeblesshire) was built by the third Duke, but sold at his death in 1761 to James Montgomery, Chief Baron of the Exchequer. The Chirton (Northumberland) estate acquired by the first Duke was apparently sold soon after his death. The English acqusitions of the second and third Dukes did not remain in family possession, the former (Sudbrooke, Surrey, and Adderbury, Oxfordshire) being inherited by the second Duke's daughter Caroline, Countess of Dalkeith, and the latter, including Whitton (Middlesex), being bequeathed by the third Duke to his mistress Ann Williams.

Papers of the Callander family presumably entered family possession through the marriage in 1869 of Archibald, second son of the eighth Duke, to his father's ward Janey Sevilla, daughter of James Henry Callander (d1851) of Craigforth (Stirlingshire) and Ardkinglas (Argyllshire).

Estates in 1883: Argyllshire 168,315 acres, Dunbartonshire 6,799 acres, total 175,114 acres worth £50,842 a year.

[a] Writs, Argyllshire and Inverness-shire 13th-20th cent, and Dunbartonshire, Midlothian and Stirlingshire 16th-19th cent; bonds of manrent 16th-17th cent; inventories of writs 16th-18th cent; wills, settlements and executry, legal and trust papers 16th-20th cent; bonds, discharges and other financial papers 16th-20th cent, incl some rel to the debts of Archibald, Bishop of the Isles c1683-96; tacks, maps, plans, surveys, valuations, rentals, accounts, vouchers, corresp and other records of the Argyllshire and Ivnerness-shire estates (Inveraray, Kintyre, Mull and Tiree) 16th-20th cent (mainly from mid-18th cent), incl accounts of the earldom of Argyll 1624, Kintyre survey c1630 and rental c1653, Morvern rental 1662, rental of the Earl of Argyll's estates 1669-72, Kintyre coal and salt book 1673 and coal accounts 1694, and valuations of Inveraray burgh 1712, 1810 and Campbeltown burgh 1714; other Argyllshire estate papers 18th-19th cent, incl some rel to the Campbeltown Coal Company, the Achaleck Woollen Company, the Craignure and Coilevraid copper and nickel mines, the Glenure manufactory and the Argyllshire woodlands; estate papers rel to Lismore c1860-20th cent, Rosneath c1792-1831, Duddingston 18th cent and the lordship of Campbell (Clackmannanshire) late 17th cent-1801.

Accounts and papers rel to building work at Inveraray Castle 1720-2, c1745-65, 1861-80, and to the rebuilding of Rosneath Castle early 19th cent, incl plans by Joseph Bonomi (1739-1808); accounts of work at Holyrood House 1719; misc inventories 17th-20th cent, incl Dumbarton Castle 1639, the Chirton household 1703 and plate of James, Duke of Queensberry 1703; Inveraray Castle household records 17th-19th cent, incl wine accounts 1692-3 and cellar inventories 1749-53; other household records, incl some rel to Whitton 18th-20th cent and accounts of the household at Holyrood House 1782; papers rel to Argyllshire affairs 17th-19th cent, incl the risings of 1715 and 1745 and Argyllshire lieutenancy, militia, fencibles and volunteers; minutes, reports, accounts, corresp and other records of the Synod of Argyll 1689-1845; Kintyre parish heritors' papers 1747-1866; Inveraray church building accounts 1796; vice-admiralty papers of the 6th Duke of Argyll *c*1803-16.

Patents, commissions and family, personal and political papers 16th-20th cent, incl accounts of the Marquess of Argyll's expenditure on the army for Ireland, etc 1642-4, misc papers of the 1st, 2nd, 3rd and 5th Dukes; letters of Lord John Campbell about the Walcheren expedition 1799, corresp of Elizabeth, Duchess of Argyll (1733-90), and papers of the 8th and 9th Dukes; letters of the 1st Earl of Breadalbane 1678-81 and the 7th Earl of Carlisle 1829-58; papers of John Campbell, advocate, of Stonefield 1730-59 and accounts of Archibald Campbell of Succoth, WS 1767-70; misc accounts of the Earl of Argyll's Regiment of Foot 1691-3; genealogical papers 18th-20th cent, transcripts of the Argyll records by the 10th and 11th Dukes and Sir William Fraser, and Gaelic manuscripts of Highland folklore and history (the Dewar collection); misc papers 17th-20th cent, incl Scottish parliament roll 1700.

Legal, financial, estate and family papers of the Callander family of Craigforth 17th-20th cent, incl Craigforth rentals 1685-6, 1767, 1790, corresp and papers of George Callander (d1824) and James Henry Callander MP (1803-51), and letters of General William Dyott (1761-1847); papers rel to James Campbell of Ardkinglas 18th-19th cent, incl misc estate papers and Edinburgh house building accounts 1765-7; legal, financial and other papers of the Maclaine family of Lochbuie (Mull) 17th-early 18th cent, incl Duart estate rental 1671-3 and diary of military actions against the family by the Earl of Argyll 1679; misc papers of the Menzies family, baronets, of Castle Menzies 1504-1713, incl Enzie estate account 1648 and Castle Menzies inventory 1713.

In private possession. Access restricted. Enquiries to the National Register of Archives (Scotland) (NRA(S) 1209, partial list). HMC *Fourth Report, App,* 1874, pp470-92, and *Sixth Report, App,* 1877, pp606-34; *Papers of British Cabinet Ministers 1782-1900,* 1982, p8; *Papers of British Colonial Governors 1782-1900,* 1986, p9. NRA 9955.

[b] Papers of the 5th Duke rel to the British Fisheries Society 1773-1802.

Scottish Record Office (GD 9/1-4). Presented by the 11th Duke of Argyll 1949-50. NRA 28867.

[c] Political and military corresp 1653-1715, mainly of the 1st Duke.

Scottish Record Office (GD 1/1158). Purchased at Phillips 1992.

[d] Letter books 1722-38 and papers *c*1740-72 of John and Archibald Campbell of Stonefield as agents to the Dukes of Argyll, incl corresp rel to the rising of 1745; other misc papers 17th-19th cent.

Scottish Record Office (GD 14). Deposited by Colonel GCP Campbell of Stonefield 1948. NRA 28972.

[e] Papers of Andrew Fletcher, Lord Milton (d1766), agent to the 3rd Duke of Argyll, incl executry and legal papers of the 2nd and 3rd Dukes 1682-1762, general, household and personal accounts *c*1724-61, Argyllshire estate papers 1629-1761 (mainly leases, rentals and accounts 1706-61 but incl Argyllshire chamberlain's accounts 1690 and estate papers for Kintyre from 1629 and Barbreck 1678-1757), accounts and papers rel to The Whim *c*1729-64, to Rosneath 1743-63 and to Duddingston 1703-58, teinds papers 1738-60, Inveraray building papers 1740-63, incl drawings by John Adam, Rosneath drawings by William Adam and Roger Morris *c*1744-7, accounts of Archibald Campbell of Succoth 1744-60, and patents, commissions and other papers 1549-1756.

National Library of Scotland (MSS 17610-94, 17878-9, Ch 14911-41). Deposited with other Fletcher of Saltoun papers by JTT Fletcher 1959.

[f] Executry papers of the 1st Duke and related papers 1682-1720, incl some concerning his Chirton estate; legal and financial corresp of Elizabeth, Duchess of Argyll 1691-1729, mainly rel to her affairs after the death of the 1st Duke.

National Library of Scotland (Advocates' MSS 29.3.5, 29.5.4).

[g] Business and family corresp 1589-1690 and household and family accounts 1642-96 of the Earls of Argyll, incl accounts rel to masons' work at Inveraray and Rosneath.

National Library of Scotland (MS 975). Presented by AO Curle 1933.

[h] Family corresp 1604-90 and financial papers, mainly discharges, 1637-77 of the Earls of Argyll.

National Library of Scotland (MS 3138, Ch 2448-74). Bequeathed by Thomas Yule, WS 1941.

[i] Corresp and papers of the 4th Duke rel to the rising of 1745-6.

National Library of Scotland (MSS 3733-6). Purchased 1947 (Christie's, 15 Dec).

[j] Family and business corresp of the Dukes of Argyll *c*1800-1940, mainly of the 7th and 8th Dukes but incl letters of Charles Howard, MP, to the Duchess of Argyll 1839-69.

National Library of Scotland (Acc 8508). Purchased 1983. NRA 29218.

[k] Letters of the 8th Duke to the 9th Duke and Princess Louise, Duchess of Argyll 1862-85; misc papers 1892-1930.

National Library of Scotland (Acc 9209). Presented by IFC Anstruther 1986. NRA 29218.

[l] Letter book of the 2nd Duke as Commander-in-Chief of British forces in Spain 1711-12.

Cambridge University Library (Add MS 6570). Purchased 1924. *Summary Guide*, p27.

[m] Further military letter books of the 2nd Duke 1711-12 (4).

Bedfordshire Record Office (DDWY 897-901). Deposited with papers of the Stuart family of Tempsford by Mrs K Wynne 1948. NRA 19616.

[n] Letters on Indian affairs from the Earl of Mayo to the 8th Duke of Argyll (5 vols).

British Library, Oriental and India Office Collections (MS Eur.B 380). Purchased from Francis Edwards, bookseller, 1983.

[o] Letters to the 9th Duke from Sir JA Macdonald rel to Canadian affairs 1878-84.

Public Archives of Canada (MG27 IB4). Presented by Lady Doughty 1938. HMC *Papers of British Colonial Governors 1782-1900,* 1986, p9.

[p] Campbeltown local history collection, incl Kintyre estate corresp 1890-8 and misc papers of the Dukes of Argyll 17th-20th cent.

Argyll and Bute District Archives (DR 4). Deposited by the trustees of Duncan Colville 1981. NRA 27756.

Related collections: Dukes of Buccleuch (Scottish Record Office GD 224 and in private possession, NRA 6184; Northamptonshire Record Office Acc 1977/23, NRA 23059, and in private possession), including records of the Adderbury estate; correspondence of the Earls of Argyll 17th cent among the Menzies of Castle Menzies papers (HMC *Sixth Report, App,* 1877, pp688-709, nos 56-69, 72-81, dispersed by sale 1914 and partly untraced: for nos 75-77 see Scottish Record Office GD 50/128, and for nos 72 and 74 see West Highland Museum, Fort William, MSS A 3, 4).

[14] CAMPBELL, Earls of Breadalbane

Duncan Campbell, grandfather of the first Earl of Argyll, gave Glenorchy (Argyllshire) to his younger son Sir Colin Campbell in 1432. Sir Colin was granted Lawers (Perthshire) by James III in 1473, while his son Sir Duncan Campbell (d1513) acquired lands near Loch Tay (Perthshire), including the baronies of Glenlyon and Finlarig, and was in 1498 appointed bailiary of Disher and Toyer, the territory situated around Loch Tay. The Perthshire and Argyllshire estates grew through purchase and royal grant during the sixteenth and seventeenth centuries. In 1617 James I granted the hereditary forestership of Mamlorne (Perthshire) to Sir Duncan Campbell, 1st Bt (1625).

John Campbell (d1716), created Earl of Breadalbane in 1681, obtained the Caithness-shire estates of the sixth Earl of Caithness, but they were all sold by c1730. In 1693 he also acquired the estates of Lord Neil Campbell of Armaddy

(Argyllshire), younger son of the Marquess of Argyll, in settlement of extensive debts. John Campbell of Carwhin (Perthshire) succeeded his cousin as fourth Earl in 1782 and was created Marquess of Breadalbane in 1831. By his marriage to the daughter and co-heir of David Gavin in 1793 he acquired Langton (Berwickshire), which passed to his sister Elizabeth, wife of Sir John Pringle, Bt, of Stichill (Berwickshire). When the second Marquess died in 1862 the marquessate became extinct, but the earldom and estates devolved on his cousin John Campbell (1824-71), who had inherited Glenfalloch (Perthshire) in 1850.

Preston (Kirkcudbrightshire), acquired through the marriage in 1761 of Lord Glenorchy, son of the third Earl, to Willielma, co-heir of William Maxwell, does not appear to have remained in the family's possession after Glenorchy's death in 1771. Sugnall (Staffordshire) entered the family through the third Earl's marriage in 1730 to Arabella, daughter and co-heir of John Pershall, but was sold in 1772.

Estates in 1883: Perthshire 234,166 acres, Argyllshire 204,192 acres, total 438,358 acres worth about £55,700 a year.

[a] Deeds, writs and registers of title, Argyllshire and Perthshire 14th-19th cent, Caithness 16th-early 18th cent and Sugnall (Staffs) 15th-18th cent; bonds of manrent and fosterage 16th-17th cent; inventories of deeds, wills, settlements and executry and trust papers 16th-20th cent, incl curatory papers of the Maxwell family of Preston (Kirkcudbrightshire) 1740-62 and 3rd Earl of Aberdeen 1801-10; legal papers 16th-20th cent, incl accounts from 17th cent; bonds, receipts and other financial papers 15th-20th cent; records of the baillie court of Disher and Toyer 1573-1748; minutes of Kenmore (Perthshire) justice court 1580 and of courts at Lawers 1634 and Killin 1721 (Perthshire); Thurso (Caithness) baillie court minutes 1687.

Argyllshire and Perthshire tacks, plans, valuations, surveys, rentals, accounts, vouchers, corresp and papers 16th-20th cent, incl rentals of Lord Neil Campbell's Argyllshire estates 1692-4; tenants' petitions 18th-mid 19th cent; papers rel to drainage and improvements 1728-1918; papers rel to teinds, mainly Perthshire, 16th-19th cent; records of Argyllshire and Perthshire woodlands late 17th-20th cent, incl survey 1792; papers rel to Black Mount (Argyllshire) deer forest 1839-1912 and to shooting 19th cent; Loch Etive and west coast fishery papers 1610-1920; papers rel to minerals and mining 17th-20th cent, incl records of Barrs (Argyllshire) granite quarry 1839-53, Easdale (Argyllshire) slate quarries 1742-1912 and Tyndrum (Perthshire) lead mines 18th cent-1862; papers rel to Argyllshire farms 1815-63; Caithness tacks, valuations, rentals, accounts, vouchers, corresp and other estate papers 16th-early 18th cent; Langton (Berwickshire) estate papers 18th-19th cent, incl rentals 1832-55 and accounts and vouchers 1795-1871; Preston (Kirkcudbrightshire) rental

1761 and accounts 1754-65; misc Sugnall (Staffs) estate papers 17th-18th cent; rentals of the Duke of Lauderdale's E Lothian estate 1685 and lands acquired by the Duke of Argyll 1716.

Building records, Finlarig, Kenmore and Taymouth Castle (Perthshire) 17th-19th cent, Armaddy Castle (Argyllshire) 18th-19th cent and Castle Kilchurn (Argyllshire) late 17th-early 18th cent; papers rel to work at Holyrood House 1692-3 and London houses late 18th-early 20th cent; Dumbarton Castle glasswork accounts 1690-1; household inventories 16th-20th cent, incl Finlarig c1632-1828, Carwhin 1686, Holyrood House 1716-95, Sugnall Hall 1768 and Frisky Hall (Dunbartonshire) 1846; inventory and valuation of Langton House 1863 and the Duke of Buckingham's residence at Auchlyne House (Perthshire) 1847; Taymouth Castle and other Scottish household records 16th-20th cent, incl diet books 1582-1713 and cellar accounts from 1749; papers rel to parks and gardens 18th-19th cent, incl Taymouth nursery book 1796-1803 and Achmore (Perthshire) garden accounts 1827-8; Bath household accounts 1693; London household papers 18th-20th cent.

Mamlorne forest court records 1744-64; papers rel to Argyllshire and Perthshire schools, churches and ecclesiastical matters 16th-20th cent, and to roads, bridges, canals, navigation and railways 18th-20th cent; papers rel to local and political affairs 17th-19th cent, incl election expenses for Coupar Angus 1788-90, Perth Burghs 1790-1 and Perthshire 1831-3, papers rel to Perth and Oban prisons 1839-61, and Oban harbour papers mid-19th cent; military records 18th-20th cent, incl muster roll of the companies of Breadalbane 1706, records of the Breadalbane Fencibles 1783-1804 and Volunteers 1799-1811, Argyllshire militia, volunteers and lieutenancy papers c1808-1901, and muster rolls (copies) of the Cambrian Regiment of Fencibles 1793-1802.

Patents and commissions 1488-1914; family inventories and accounts 16th-20th cent; family and political corresp and papers 15th-20th cent, incl papers rel to feuds with the MacGregors, the Massacre of Glencoe 1692 and to peerage elections 18th-19th cent, papers of the 3rd Earl as minister to Denmark 1720-31, and corresp and papers of the 2nd Marquess as Lord Chamberlain of the Household; accounts and papers of Colin Campbell of Carwhin, WS (d1715); misc financial papers of the 6th Earl of Caithness (d1676); business corresp of the Pershall family 1719-35; genealogical papers 16th-19th cent, incl the Black Book of Taymouth 1432-1648; literary and misc papers 15th-20th cent, incl MS narrative of the reign of Edward II late 15th cent, protocol book of Gavin Hamilton, notary 1569-1604, and MS of Sir James Balfour's *Practicks* c1603.

Papers of the Mercer family of Aldie (Perthshire) 1757-1805, incl Pitkeathly (Perthshire) rentals and accounts 1766-73, accounts of work at Pitkeathly House 1768-73 and family corresp 1757-1805; legal, family and estate papers of the

Menzies family of Weem (Perthshire) 16th-19th cent.

Scottish Record Office (GD 112). Mainly deposited on loan by the ninth Earl 1926 and presented by the Countess of Breadalbane 1973. Other deeds were presented 1971. Family correspondence was presented by Dundas & Wilson, Davidson & Syme, Edinburgh 1976. The Black Book of Taymouth was purchased 1977. HMC *Fourth Report, App,* 1874, pp511-14; *Papers of British Politicians 1782-1900,* 1989, p18. NRA 31601.

[b] Inventory of writs 17th cent; rentals 1682, 1688, 1731, 1761, 1784; misc family corresp and papers 17th-18th cent.

Scottish Record Office (GD 50). Bequeathed by John MacGregor 1937. NRA 30103.

[c] Cartulary of the Caithness estate 1470-1708.

Scottish Record Office (GD 1/1072). Presented 1988.

[d] Misc Kenmore estate papers 1818-1944.

Scottish Record Office (GD 1/641). Deposited by Miss JK Macdonald 1972-3.

[e] Papers of the Campbell family of Barcaldine as chamberlains 17th-early 18th cent.

Scottish Record Office (GD 170). NRA 33900.

[f] Executry and trust papers 1821-94; marriage contract of Mary, daughter of the 1st Earl 1719; corresp and papers 17th-19th cent, mainly of the 1st Marquess, but incl letters of Elizabeth Campbell of Carwhin 1803-7, papers rel to works of art 17th-19th cent, warrants and commissions, etc 18th-19th cent and papers rel to the Dumbartonshire Fencibles 1755-97; business papers of David Gavin c1747-74, with Langton estate papers c1765-1845 and other papers of the Gavin family 18th-19th cent; misc papers rel to the Dukes of Buckingham 17th-19th cent, incl rentals of the Bucks, Northants, Oxon and Somerset estates 1831 (2), financial and other corresp and papers 1831-49, and Bucks election accounts 1830-5.

In private possession. Enquiries to the National Register of Archives (Scotland) (NRA(S) 2238). NRA 25302.

[g] Misc Campbell of Glenorchy family papers 15th-17th cent, incl royal letters and warrants 1565-1626.

In private possession. Enquiries to the National Register of Archives (Scotland) (NRA(S) 1522). NRA 20973.

[h] Rentals of the Breadalbane estates 1727-57 (4 vols).

In private possession. Enquiries to the National Register of Archives (Scotland) (NRA(S) 27). NRA 10121.

[i] Household book of the 1st Earl 1659-71.

Glasgow University Library, Special Collections Department (MS Gen 1473). Bought from JF Kellas Johnstone 1926.

[j] Corresp of the Campbell family of Achalader as factors 18th cent.

In private possession. Enquiries to the National Register of Archives (Scotland) (NRA(S) 657). NRA 16065.

[k] Staffs estate survey book 1731.

William Salt Library, Stafford (D 1798/318). Deposited by Hand, Morgan & Owen, solicitors, Stafford 1958. NRA 5900.

Related collection: Pershall of Sugnall estate and family papers 17th-18th cent (William Salt Library, Stafford WSL 48/2/23).

[15] CAMPBELL, Earls Cawdor

On the death in 1498 of John, eighth thane of Cawdor (or Calder), Cawdor Castle and estates in Nairnshire and Inverness-shire passed by marriage to a younger branch of the Campbell family, Earls of Argyll. Estates in Argyllshire, including the island of Islay, were acquired in the lifetime of Sir John Campbell (d1642) but sold in the 1720s.

The Stackpole Court (Pembrokeshire) estate was acquired through the marriage of Sir Alexander Campbell of Cawdor to Elizabeth Lort in 1689. Their son John Campbell married in 1726 Mary, daughter and co-heir of Lewis Pryse of Gogerddan (Cardiganshire). The Golden Grove (Carmarthenshire) estate was bequeathed to the first Baron Cawdor by John Vaughan in 1805. Further South Wales property was purchased by the first Earl, and the family's principal seat remained Stackpole Court until the early twentieth century, when it reverted to Cawdor Castle.

Estates in 1883: Nairnshire 46,176 acres, Inverness-shire 3,943 acres, Carmarthenshire 33,782 acres, Pembrokeshire 17,735 acres, Cardiganshire 21 acres, total 101,657 acres worth £44,662 a year.

[a] Scottish writs 1236-19th cent, mainly Inverness-shire, Nairnshire and Morayshire but incl Argyllshire (Islay and Muckairn) 1511-1717; legal papers 15th-19th cent, mainly 18th-19th cent but incl papers rel to the thanes of Cawdor 15th cent and bonds of manrent, Campbell family 16th-17th cent; Nairnshire and Inverness-shire estate papers 15th-20th cent, especially full from the early 18th cent, incl tacks, maps and sketches of boundaries 18th-19th cent, factors' and general estate accounts, and related financial papers 17th-20th cent; Argyllshire estate tacks, rentals, accounts and sale papers c1625-1722; papers rel to Cawdor Castle 1578-19th cent, incl building plans and papers from 1639, inventories and household accounts; garden accounts 17th-18th cent; papers rel to Nairnshire and Inverness-shire affairs 16th-19th cent, incl Nairnshire politics and elections 18th-19th cent, commission of supply, hereditary jurisdictions, parish affairs, etc; family corresp and papers 15th-20th cent, incl corresp of the Lords Cawdor with factors and solicitors 18th-20th cent;

accounts of the thanes of Cawdor as chamberlains for royal lands beyond Spey 1456-8.

In private possession. Enquiries to the National Register of Archives (Scotland) (NRA(S) 1400). Cosmo Innes, ed, *The Book of the Thanes of Cawdor: a series of papers selected from the charter room at Cawdor Castle 1236-1742*, 1849; HMC *Second Report, App*, 1871, p193. NRA 8147.

[b] Cawdor writs, bonds and legal papers 1623-1942.

Scottish Record Office (GD 236/29-41). Deposited by Dundas & Wilson, CS, Edinburgh. NRA 32486.

[c] Factors' accounts 1911-13 (3 vols), incl Nairnshire and Inverness-shire rentals.

Scottish Record Office (CS 96/2480-2).

[d] Welsh deeds (mainly Carmarthenshire and Pembrokeshire) c13th-20th cent; wills, settlements and related trust and legal papers 16th-20th cent, Vaughan, Lort and Campbell families; manorial records, Carmarthenshire (Kidwelly, Newcastle Emlyn, etc) from 1630 and Pembrokeshire (Castlemartin, Stackpole) from 1375; Carmarthenshire and Pembrokeshire estate records 16th-20th cent, incl leases, surveys and maps, rentals and accounts (mainly Carmarthenshire, from 1656), and papers rel to coal and lead mining (18th-20th cent) and to enclosure and transport (Llanelly, Kidwelly, etc mainly 19th cent); Carmarthenshire and Pembrokeshire home farm accounts mainly 19th cent; misc Cardiganshire, Merionethshire and Montgomeryshire estate papers ?late 18th cent; estate and other papers of the Brigstocke, Gwynn and Phillips families, Wales and Surrey 1626-1780; rentals, accounts, etc for Cawdor Scottish estates c1804-20th cent; household and building papers 16th-20th cent, incl inventories of Golden Grove, Stackpole Court and London houses (Hanover Square, etc) and building plans and papers for Golden Grove 1827-34.

Papers rel to Welsh affairs 17th-early 20th cent, incl Carmarthenshire tax assessments, Carmarthenshire and Pembrokeshire politics c1754-1880, Carmarthenshire and Pembrokeshire militia and volunteers 1781-1902, and Carmarthen castle and gaol early 19th cent; Vaughan, Lort and Campbell family papers 17th-20th cent, incl papers of the 1st Baron Cawdor rel to the French landing in Pembrokeshire 1797, etc, papers of the 1st Earl as 1st Lord of the Admiralty 1905, journals, diaries, accounts and corresp; genealogical papers, incl a Vaughan pedigree roll 1641 and the Golden Grove Book of Welsh genealogies 18th cent.

Dyfed Archives Service, Carmarthenshire Area Record Office. Mostly deposited by the 5th and 6th Earls Cawdor and by Cooke & Arkwright, estate agents, Bridgend 1962-90. The Golden Grove Book was transferred from the Public Record Office and the 1641 pedigree from the

College of Arms in 1978. HMC *Second Report, App*, 1871, p31; Dyfed Archives *Quarterly Newsletter*, spring 1990, p5. NRA 21492, 21493.

[e] Misc legal papers *c*1919-40.

Dyfed Archives Service, Carmarthenshire Area Record Office. Deposited by the executors of Major JW Bishop 1963. NRA 21543.

[f] Cenarth (Carmarthenshire) rental and account 1720-75.

National Library of Wales (MSS 21798-9A). Given by DLP Evans. *Annual Report 1981-2*, p49.

[g] Copies of naval papers, 3rd Earl as 1st Lord of the Admiralty 1905 (1 vol).

Ministry of Defence, Naval Historical Library.

[16] CAPELL, Earls of Essex

Sir William Capell (d1515), a London merchant, acquired estates in west Essex and east Hertfordshire, Norfolk, Suffolk and Somerset. Further Somerset estates were acquired through the marriage of his son, Sir Giles Capell (d1555/6). Arthur Capell (d1649), created Baron Capell 1641, married in 1627 Elizabeth Morrison of Cassiobury (Hertfordshire), which became the principal seat. She also brought, through her mother Elizabeth, younger daughter of the first Viscount Campden, former Hicks properties in Warwickshire (Ilmington) and Gloucestershire (Tewkesbury and Cheltenham). (Other Hicks estates descended, however, to the Noel family, Earls of Gainsborough.) The second Baron Capell was created Earl of Essex in 1661. Many Capell and Hicks family lands were sold in the later seventeenth and eighteenth centuries. Through the marriage of the fourth Earl of Essex in 1754, however, the Capells inherited estates in Warwickshire (Shuttington), Herefordshire (Hampton Court, sold in 1808) and Ireland (Roscommon, Trim, etc) from the Coningsby family.

Estates in 1883: Herts 5,545 acres, Essex 3,090 acres, Warwicks 690 acres, Co Roscommon 2,906 acres, Co Meath 1,303 acres, Co Wicklow 678 acres, Co Dublin 658 acres, total 14,870 acres worth £18,936 a year.

[a] Deeds *c*1200-19th cent, mainly Herts and Essex but incl a few for Beds and Norfolk 16th cent; wills, settlements and related papers 16th-19th cent, mainly Morrison and Capell, incl trust papers rel to the Hampton Court estate 18th-early 19th cent; legal papers 16th-19th cent; manorial records 14th-19th cent, Herts (Cashio, Watford, Walkern, etc), Essex (Stebbing, etc), Norfolk (Great and Little Fransham) and other counties, incl St Albans Abbey manors (Cashio, Watford, etc 14th-early 16th cent); Herts estate records 16th-19th cent, incl leases, surveys, rentals, accounts, tithe papers mainly 17th cent and farm bailiff's account 1758-60;

Essex rentals, accounts, etc, mainly 17th-18th cent; misc Gloucs, Lincs, Norfolk and Suffolk estate accounts, etc 17th-18th cent; rental of Morrison and Hicks estates 1634-9; Ellesmere estate accounts 1609-16 (6 rolls); household accounts 17th-19th cent; Cashio hundred subsidy roll late 16th cent; Morrison and Capell family papers from late 15th cent, incl pardons, commissions, delinquency papers 1644-5, personal account 1644-6, Irish Council minutes 1696 and letters rel to the Prince of Wales 1781.

Hertfordshire Record Office. Transferred from the Hertfordshire County Museum, St Albans 1930 and deposited by Viscount Malden 1955. HMC *Various Collections VII*, 1914, pp297-350 *passim*. NRA 7244.

[b] Deeds for Herts, Essex, Gloucs, Norfolk and Suffolk 15th-20th cent; deeds for other counties (Herefs, Warwicks, etc) and Ireland 17th-19th cent, and Albemarle House (London) 1695-1788; settlements, etc 18th-20th cent; legal papers 17th-20th cent, incl schedules; manorial court rolls 17th-20th cent, Herts and Essex; English estate papers 18th-20th cent, mainly Herts and Essex but incl a Herefs rental 1796 and Warwicks estate papers 19th-20th cent; Irish estate papers 17th-20th cent, incl leases, maps 18th-19th cent, rentals and accounts; agreements rel to letting of Cassiobury House 1887-1921.

Hertfordshire Record Office (D/ECp; Acc 1895, 1988). Deposited by Messrs Lee & Pembertons, solicitors, London 1971, 1981, 1983. NRA 7244 (partial list).

[c] Marriage settlements and related papers 1777-1834; manor of Park (Herts), minute book 1728-54 and presentment book 1733-96; appointment of steward for Irish estates 1806.

Hertfordshire Record Office (Acc 1919, 2067, 2406). Deposited by Boodle, Hatfield & Co, solicitors, London, through the British Records Association 1982-8.

[d] Estate surveys, Essex and Herts 1674, 1798.

Hertfordshire Record Office (Acc 2205). Presented by J Crozier through Hertford Museum 1986.

[e] Cartulary of Sir William Capell *c*1515.

Essex Record Office. Deposited through the British Records Association 1990.

[f] Letters patent, barony of Capell of Hadham 1641; Cassiobury visitors' books 1805-22, 1893-1921; Lord Essex's directions for his funeral 1886; letters rel to the naval career of the Hon RA Capell 1832-57.

Watford Museum.

[g] Deeds 12th-18th cent, Beds, Berks, Bucks, Cambs, Essex, Herts, Middlesex, Norfolk, Notts, Somerset, Suffolk, etc; schedules of deeds, extracts, etc; bonds, acquittances, etc 14th-18th cent; manorial records 13th-18th cent, Essex (Stebbing, etc), Devon, Dorset, Gloucs, Notts, Somerset and other counties; St Albans Abbey, copies of Herts court rolls, etc 1237-1537

(2 vols, 1 roll); misc estate papers 16th-19th cent, incl survey and map of Cheltenham estate c1800 and Hampton Court estate account 1801; Morrison and Capell family and household papers mainly 16th-18th cent, incl letter of Sir Richard Morrison at Augsburg 1552, letters rel to Herts musters 1586-8, sequestration papers 1640s, papers rel to Watford almshouses 1580-1799, papers of and rel to Arthur, Lord Capell 17th cent, papers of Sir Henry Capell as First Commissioner of the Admiralty 1679-80 and letters from the 3rd Earl of Essex as ambassador at Turin 1732-5; misc papers, incl valor of Peterborough Abbey 1539 and inventory of goods of the Earl of Hereford 1322.

British Library, Manuscript Collections (Add Ch 64889-66125, 71032-74; Add MSS 40625-32, 43461-3, 60385-9). Given by Adela, Countess of Essex 1922 and purchased 1937 and 1978. See also HMC *Various Collections VII*, 1914, pp297-350 *passim*. For other Herts deeds, etc 13th-17th cent see Add Ch 18136-94 (acquired 1869).

[h] Accounts of John Elcock as receiver for Sir Henry Capell of Ubley (Somerset) 1550-7.

British Library, Manuscript Collections (Add MS 64064). Purchased 1986.

[i] Manorial records for Norfolk (Great and Little Fransham, etc) and Suffolk (Icklingham) 14th-17th cent, with court book 1609-16 (various manors); Norfolk and Suffolk leases 16th-18th cent.

Norfolk Record Office (MSS 13034A-13416). Presented to Norwich Castle Museum by Adela, Countess of Essex 1922. NRA 30577.

[j] Norfolk (Great and Little Fransham and Gooderstone) deeds, court rolls and estate records mainly late 14th-late 16th cent.

Norfolk Record Office. Deposited in Norwich Central Library 1953. HMC *Various Collections VII*, 1914, pp324-7. NRA 4638.

[k] Bramfield (Suffolk) court roll 1542-3.

Suffolk Record Office, Ipswich branch. Transferred from Hertfordshire Record Office 1960.

[l] Manorial records for Somerset (Ubley, etc), Devon (Chillington), Dorset (Child Okeford) and Gloucs (Aust) 14th-17th cent; misc Somerset deeds and estate papers 13th-18th cent.

Somerset Archive and Record Service (DD/S/HY). Purchased from Messrs B Halliday, booksellers, Leicester 1946. NRA 35090.

[m] Further manorial records, Wrington, Winterhead, etc 15th-17th cent.

Somerset Archive and Record Service (DD/X/PRO). Deposited by the Public Record Office 1957.

[n] Deeds and papers rel to the Hampton Court estate 1724-1802 (31 items); inventory of Ashwood Park 1807.

Hereford Record Office. Transferred from Hertfordshire Record Office to Hereford City Library 1955.

[o] Cheltenham court books 1714-1808, lists of officers and jurors 1740-75, surrenders 1645-1787, survey 1617 and rentals 1698-1713.

Public Record Office (C 116/133-152).

[p] Papers of the 1st Earl of Essex as Lord Lieutenant of Ireland 1672-7.

British Library, Manuscript Collections (Stowe MSS 200-217). Purchased by the Marquess of Buckingham from the Earl of Essex 1808, acquired by the British Museum from the Ashburnham collection in 1883. HMC *Eighth Report, App III*, 1881, pp1, 39.

[17] CAVENDISH, Dukes of Devonshire

The Cavendish family became established in Derbyshire as a result of the marriage of Sir William Cavendish (d1557) to Elizabeth Barlow, heiress of Hardwick and later Countess of Shrewsbury. Chatsworth (purchased in 1549) and other estates were added to the Barlow and Hardwick properties, and these eventually all passed to William Cavendish, created Earl of Devonshire in 1618. He married as his first wife Anne Keighley of Keighley (Yorkshire, West Riding), and at his death in 1626 owned large estates in both Derbyshire and Yorkshire, together with properties in several other counties.

Over the next two hundred years the Yorkshire property was reduced, but the Derbyshire estates were consolidated, and Chatsworth House was rebuilt by the first Duke between 1686 and his death in 1707. The fourth Duke married in 1748 Charlotte, *suo jure* Baroness Clifford and heir of her father Richard Boyle, third Earl of Burlington. Through her came not only the major part of the extensive Irish estates of the Boyle family, Earls of Cork and later of Burlington, but also the Craven (Bolton Abbey) and Londesborough estates in Yorkshire (West and East Ridings), inherited from the Clifford Earls of Cumberland, and property in Derbyshire and elsewhere inherited from the Saville family, Marquesses of Halifax. (Other Clifford and Saville estates, however, descended to the Tufton family, Earls of Thanet and later Barons Hothfield.) The Londesborough estate was sold by the sixth Duke in 1845.

Lord George Augustus Henry Cavendish, second surviving son of the fourth Duke, married in 1782 Lady Elizabeth Compton, daughter and heir of the seventh Earl of Northampton (see no 24), and through her inherited estates in Sussex (including Compton Place near Eastbourne) and Somerset. Some outlying Cavendish properties, including Latimer (Buckinghamshire) and Keighley, were settled on him, and he also inherited the Holker (Lancashire) estate from his uncle Lord George Augustus Cavendish, to whom it had passed from the Lowther family. Lord GAH Cavendish was created Earl of Burlington in 1831 and died in 1834. His grandson the second Earl succeeded his cousin as seventh Duke of Devonshire in 1858, bringing back various properties into the main line of the Cavendish family, but Latimer and other properties were settled on the Hon Charles Compton Cavendish, youngest son of the 1st Earl of Burlington, who in 1858 was created Baron Chesham. The Holker estate later passed to Lord Richard Cavendish, younger brother of the ninth Duke.

Estates in 1883: Derbys 89,462 acres, Yorks WR 19,239 acres, Lancs 12,681 acres, Sussex 11,062 acres, Somerset 3,014 acres, Lincs 1,392 acres, Cumberland 983 acres, Middlesex 524 acres, Notts 125 acres, Cheshire 28 acres, Staffs 26 acres, Co Cork 32,550 acres, Co Waterford 27,483 acres, Co Tipperary 3 acres, total 198,572 acres worth £180,750 a year.

[a] Deeds from 12th cent, mainly Derbys but also Yorks (incl Londesborough and Craven estates from c1200), Sussex (Compton estates from 13th cent), Lincs and other Saville estates, Lancs (incl Holker estate from 1363), Hunts, Kent, Middlesex, etc; schedules of deeds, incl Cavendish estates c1627, Saville estates c1700 and Hardwick muniment room 1821; Cavendish wills, settlements, trust papers and executorship papers 16th-20th cent; Cavendish legal papers 16th-20th cent, incl papers of Messrs Currey and Co (London agents and solicitors); Clifford, Boyle and Compton legal papers 16th-18th cent; manorial records 14th-20th cent, mainly Derbys and Yorks from 16th cent, but incl Cumberland (soke of Carlisle 17th cent) and Sussex (hundred rolls late 13th cent, Eastbourne and other manors 14th-18th cent).

Derbys estate records mainly 16th-20th cent, incl leases, survey by William Senior 1609-28, other maps, plans and misc surveys from late 16th cent, rentals and accounts from 16th cent, auditors' and agents' corresp and papers from late 17th cent, and records for individual estates (Chatsworth, Buxton, High Peak, Shottle and Pentrich, Hardwick, etc) from late 18th cent (extensive); Derbys lead mining records 18th-20th cent, with some Ecton (Staffs) copper mining records; Staveley Coal and Iron Co papers 19th-20th cent; Chatsworth farm accounts 1708-50; papers rel to the development of Buxton, incl accounts for the building of the Crescent 1780-6.

Clifford estate papers 15th-17th cent, mainly Yorks (Londesborough and Craven) but incl some for Cumberland and Westmorland 16th cent; Cumberland estate papers (Carlisle, etc) 17th-20th cent; Yorks (Burlington, later Devonshire) estate records 17th-20th cent, incl rentals, accounts, corresp, maps and plans; Keighley and Wetherby (Yorks WR) estate leases and papers mainly 18th-20th cent; Dore (Yorks WR, formerly Derbys) estate papers 19th-20th cent; Irish estate records 17th-19th cent, incl surveys 1774-5 and letter books 1693-1758; Compton (Sussex) estate papers 15th-20th cent, incl Eastbourne building plans and papers rel to the Devonshire Parks and Bath Co 19th-20th cent; Polegate (Sussex) stud records early 20th

cent; estate papers for other counties, incl Bucks (Latimer, etc) 18th-19th cent, Hunts (Sawtry) 18th-19th cent, Lancs (Holker 17th-19th cent, Brindle and Inskip 18th-19th cent), Lincs (Barrowby) 18th-early 20th cent and Northants (Fotheringhay) 1688-98.

Building accounts for Hardwick 1588-98 and Chatsworth 1686-1706; plans for the north wing of Chatsworth by Sir Jeffry Wyatville 1818, 1820-39, with accounts 1820-48; inventories, Hardwick, Chatsworth and Devonshire House from 17th cent; household accounts, Chatsworth 16th-20th cent and Hardwick and Devonshire House 17th-20th cent; Chatsworth garden papers 17th-20th cent; Skipton (Yorks WR) and Londesborough inventories 16th-17th cent, household accounts 1510-1667 and later; architectural drawings, Chiswick House, etc 18th-19th cent; Chiswick accounts 18th-early 19th cent, library catalogue 1818; papers rel to Derbys politics and county affairs mainly 18th cent; papers rel to the borough of Knaresborough 18th-19th cent, incl burgage tenements; Edensor (Derbys) parish accounts 1637-1793 and school log book 1863-1908.

Cavendish family papers 16th-17th cent, incl patents and commissions, papers of Sir William Cavendish as Treasurer of the Chamber (1546-57), misc personal accounts of Elizabeth, Countess of Shrewsbury, papers of the 1st and 3rd Earls of Devonshire 17th cent, and personal and family corresp of Rachel Russell, wife of the 2nd Duke, 1656-90; political and personal papers of the 3rd and subsequent Dukes 18th-20th cent, incl Irish lord lieutenancy papers of the 3rd and 4th Dukes, political papers of the 4th Duke 1756-62, personal corresp of the 5th Duke and his wife, and political corresp and papers of the 8th Duke.

Clifford family corresp 1551-c1640; Boyle family papers late 16th-mid-18th cent, incl Irish corresp and papers of the 1st Earl of Cork c1594-1643 and of the 3rd Earl of Burlington; Saville family papers mid-17th-early 18th cent, incl papers of the 1st Marquess of Halifax; Compton family papers 18th cent, incl papers of the Earl of Wilmington and the Hon Charles Compton (d1755); philosophical papers of Thomas Hobbes; scientific papers of Henry Cavendish c1771-8; corresp of Sir Joseph Paxton mainly 1826-65; misc political, literary and other papers 15th-20th cent, incl Earl of Shrewsbury's ministers' accounts 19-20 Edward IV, Irish Vice-Treasurer's accounts 30-32 Henry VIII, trust papers for the 12th Duke of Hamilton decd c1890-1910, Chatsworth weather records 1861-1985 and Cavendish family photographs; Bolton Priory compotus 1287-1325; register of Abingdon Abbey mid-14th cent; cartulary of St Albans Abbey late 14th cent; Fountains Abbey charters from 12th cent; Thwaites cartulary 15th cent.

In private possession. Access restricted. Enquiries to the Librarian and Keeper of the Devonshire

Collections, Chatsworth House, Derbyshire. NRA 20594 (partial lists).

[b] Lead mining accounts 1750-1875 (duplicate series).

Derbyshire Record Office (1288 M). Deposited from Chatsworth 1973. NRA 19305.

[c] Misc estate letters and papers 1729-1928, rel mainly to NE Derbys.

Chesterfield Public Library. NRA 9187.

[d] Ecton and Whiston copper mining and smelting account 1783-92.

In private possession. Microfilm in Staffordshire Record Office (MF 57). NRA 16699.

[e] Derbys estate accounts and papers 1707-1836 (Barker family as stewards), incl Dore rental 1792-1802, Chatsworth estate accounts 1743-4, 1755-6, 1771, and Hardwick Hall accounts 1734-82.

Sheffield Archives (Bagshawe collection 496-500, 505, 509, 595, 627, 632, 697-8). Given by the executors of EG Bagshawe 1956 and purchased. NRA 7871.

[f] Misc corresp and papers of Thomas Clarke of Kirkby (Notts) as agent for the Staveley and other estates 1804-13.

Nottinghamshire Archives (Acc 244/69-73). Presented by P Wood 1955. NRA 5953.

[g] Court books for Wetherby 1608-1846, Keighley 1782-1825 and wapentake of Staincliffe 1810-25; manorial and legal papers, Yorks estates 1721-1856; Wetherby sale particulars 1824.

West Yorkshire Archive Service, Leeds (DB 98, 246). Deposited by Dibb, Lupton & Co, solicitors, Leeds. NRA 34058.

[h] Carlisle and Castle Sowerby estate papers 19th-early 20th cent, incl architects' certificates for Carlisle building estate 1896-1934.

Cumbria Record Office, Carlisle. County Archivist's Report Nov 1972, June 1985.

[i] Sussex manorial records 13th-19th cent (236 items).

Sussex Archaelogical Society (CP 1-236). Deposited by the Chatsworth Estates Co 1931-2. Access through East Sussex Record Office. *Sussex Arch Coll* LXXIII (1932), p lxv; XCI (1956), pp144-57. Sussex estate papers 19th-20th cent remain in the Compton Estate Office, Eastbourne (David Cannadine, *Lords and Landlords: the aristocracy and the towns 1774-1967*, 1980, p436).

[j] Somerset (Compton estate) manorial and estate records 17th-19th cent.

Somerset Archive and Record Service (DD/DEV). Sent to Chatsworth from the office of RMP Parsons, Misterton, 1938, and deposited in the record office by the Chatsworth Trustees 1970. NRA 17716.

[k] Deeds and legal papers, mainly Cos Cork and Waterford 17th-19th cent; copies of charters, etc

rel to Youghal borough and college 14th-17th cent; copies of wills and settlements 17th-18th cent; Irish estate papers *c*1570-1870, incl surveys and valuations, maps and plans, rentals, accounts, agents' corresp, memoranda and reports; Lismore household accounts 1656-7; misc Dungarvan and Youghal election papers 18th cent; personal corresp and papers mainly 17th cent, incl some of the 1st Earl of Cork 1601-43; misc items, incl a list of Munster undertakers 1595, an account of military operations in west Cork 1641 and a geometrical treatise by Robert Boyle nd.

National Library of Ireland (MSS 6136-7220, 13226-56 and unnumbered). Deposited from Lismore Castle 1952. *Analecta Hibernica* 22 (1960), pp272-4. NRA 29337.

[l] Misc deeds and legal papers 1625-1965, incl papers rel to Blackwater fisheries and Irish Land Commission sales 19th-20th cent; surveys and valuations 1717, 1816-79; maps and plans 1776-1965; rentals, accounts and vouchers 19th-20th cent, mainly from 1870; agents' corresp and papers from 1791, incl election corresp 19th cent; wage books, etc rel to farm, woods, fisheries, etc mainly 20th cent; papers rel to Lismore Gas Co 1853-1934 and Waterford, Dungarvan and Lismore Railway 1878-1909; Lismore household and garden accounts 20th cent.

In private possession. Access restricted. Enquiries to the Librarian and Keeper of the Devonshire Collections, Chatsworth House, Derbyshire. NRA 29337.

[m] Papers rel to the administration of the Burlington estates mainly 1724-5 (16 items), with items rel to the Boyle and Fairfax families 17th-18th cent.

Greater London Record Office (Q/CML). In part agency papers of Ferdinando Fairfax. Sold as part of the Christie Miller collection, Sotheby's, 21 Apr 1877, lots 4, 24. NRA 13152.

[n] Indian corresp and papers of the 8th Duke 1880-5 (6 vols, 6 boxes).

British Library, Oriental and India Office Collections (MSS Eur. D 604). Deposited by the 11th Duke of Devonshire 1962.

[o] Misc official papers of the Earl of Wilmington 1714-43.

British Library, Manuscript Collections (Add MSS 38618-19, 45733; Add Ch 71290-7). Presented 1912, 1941.

Related collections: Compton, Marquesses of Northampton (no 24); Barons Hothfield (Centre for Kentish Studies, Maidstone U 455, 991, 1095, 2538, NRA 4391; Cumbria Record Office, Kendal WD/Hoth, NRA 12905; West Yorkshire Archive Service, Yorkshire Archaeological Society DD 121, NRA 12905); deeds and estate papers for Cavendish (Chesham) estates 15th-20th cent (Buckinghamshire, Cambridgeshire (Huntingdon), Hertfordshire, Lancashire, Greater

London and Staffordshire Record Offices and the William Salt Library, Stafford, NRA 570, 571, 28429); deeds and estate papers for the Holker estate 15th-20th cent (Lancashire Record Office DDCa, NRA 5965); Pitchford MSS (National Library of Wales, NRA 9005), incl corresp of Elizabeth, Duchess of Devonshire 1792-1812.

[18] CAVENDISH-BENTINCK, Dukes of Portland

Sir Charles Cavendish, third son of Sir William Cavendish of Chatsworth (see no 17), aquired Welbeck (Nottinghamshire) in 1598 and Bolsover (Derbyshire) in 1608, both from the Talbot family (see no 20). His second wife, Catherine, Baroness Ogle, brought the Bothal (Northumberland) estates. Their son was created Earl (1628), Marquess (1643) and Duke (1665) of Newcastle. Following the death of the second Duke in 1691 these Cavendish estates passed to his daughter Margaret, wife of John Holles, fourth Earl of Clare. Lord Clare was created Duke of Newcastle in 1694. On his death in 1711 the Clare estates and a portion of the Cavendish estates passed to his nephew Thomas Pelham, created Duke of Newcastle in 1715, but the bulk of the Cavendish lands, together with the manor of Marylebone (Middlesex) and Wimpole (Cambridgeshire) passed to his daughter Henrietta, who married Edward Harley, later second Earl of Oxford.

Lord Oxford sold Wimpole, and on his death in 1741 the Harley estates in Herefordshire (Brampton Bryan, etc) passed to a cousin, but his widow continued in possession of the Welbeck estates, which on her death in 1755 passed to her daughter Lady Margaret Cavendish Harley. Lady Margaret married William Bentinck, second Duke of Portland, and her estates were inherited by the third Duke on her death in 1785.

Hans Willem Bentinck (1649-1709), an associate of William III, was created Earl of Portland in 1689 and acquired extensive estates in Buckinghamshire (Bulstrode), Hertfordshire (Theobalds), Cumberland, Middlesex (Soho) and elsewhere, plus, in his son's name, a large estate in Ireland. His son, Viscount Woodstock, later second Earl of Portland, married in 1704 a daughter of the second Earl of Gainsborough, through whom came a moiety of the Titchfield (Hampshire) estates formerly belonging to the Wriothesley Earls of Southampton. The Bentinck estates, however, were largely disposed of by sale in the eighteenth and early nineteenth centuries.

Lord Titchfield, later fourth Duke of Portland, married in 1794 Henrietta Scott, heiress of the Balcomie (Fife) estate, whose trustees also acquired for her the Cessnock, Dean and Kilmarnock estates in Ayrshire. The fourth Duke sold Balcomie but increased the Ayrshire estates by purchase, notably Fullarton in 1803. The Langwell (Caithness) estate was acquired by the fifth Duke between 1857 and 1869. On the death of the fifth Duke in 1879 most of the estates passed to the cousin who succeeded him as sixth Duke, but part of the Ayrshire estates were divided between the fifth Duke's sisters Lady Ossington and Lady Howard de Walden, the latter also inheriting the Marylebone property.

Estates in 1883: Notts 43,036 acres, Northumberland 12,337 acres, Derbys 8,074 acres, Lincs 903 acres, Norfolk 591 acres, Worcs 9 acres, Bucks 5 acres, Caithness 101,000 acres, Ayrshire 17,244 acres, total 183,199 acres worth £88,350 a year.

[a] Deeds 12th-20th cent, mainly Notts and Derbys but incl Cambs (Holles) 14th-18th cent, Dorset and Wilts (Holles) 16th-18th cent, Gloucs and Somerset (Cavendish) 14th-17th cent, Herefs (Harley) 13th-17th cent, London and Middlesex 16th-18th cent, Northumberland 13th-19th cent, Staffs (Cavendish and Holles) 14th-17th cent, Yorks 12th-18th cent and other counties; Holles cartulary c1660; wills, settlements and related papers, Cavendish, Ogle, Holles, Harley, Bentinck, Pierrepont and other families 14th-19th cent; legal and case papers 14th-19th cent, incl papers rel to the recovery of the Cavendish estates after the Civil War, case papers rel to John Holles, Duke of Newcastle 1680-1715, and calendars of deeds, etc 17th-18th cent; manorial records 14th-20th cent, incl Mansfield (Notts) 1315-1876, Bolsover (Derbys) 1485-1876 and Chesterfield and hundred of Scarsdale (Derbys) 16th cent; Sherwood Forest court records and related papers 13th-19th cent; Waltham Forest (Essex) court rolls and related papers 1481-1606.

General rentals and accounts for Cavendish, Holles and Bentinck estates 17th-19th cent; Welbeck (Notts and Derbys) estate records 14th-20th cent, incl leases from late 16th cent, surveys, maps 18th-19th cent, rentals and accounts 17th-20th cent, corresp mainly 17th-19th cent, and papers rel to timber, minerals, forests, game, enclosure, tithes, schools, charities, etc; misc Northumberland estate papers 14th-20th cent, incl leases 14th-17th cent and accounts 17th-19th cent; London (Middlesex) estate papers 16th-19th cent, incl papers rel to markets and to Clare House property 1693; Scottish estate papers 19th cent, incl Ayrshire estate accounts 1819-46, maps, and papers rel to harbours; Herefs (Brampton Bryan, etc) estate papers 17th-early 18th cent, incl leases, surveys, corresp, and papers rel to fairs; papers rel to the Holles (Newcastle) estates 1680-1714 and to the Holles of Ifield (Sussex) estates 1680-1711; misc papers rel to estates in Devon, Yorks, Lincs and elsewhere 14th-19th cent, and to the Earl of Thanet's estates c1684; building accounts, Bolsover Castle, Welbeck Abbey, etc 17th-19th cent; inventories 1795-1893, mainly Welbeck; household accounts and papers 17th-19th cent, mainly Welbeck house, gardens and farms but incl Nottingham Castle 1687-91 and London houses 18th-19th cent.

Papers rel to local administration 17th-19th cent, incl Notts lieutenancy book of the 1st Duke of

Newcastle 1660-77, Herefs Civil War and militia papers 17th-early 18th cent, Scarsdale (Derbys) coronership papers 1669-1750, Stepney and Hackney (Middlesex) court of record bonds 1672, 1680-3, Notts and Cumberland election papers mainly 18th cent, and papers rel to Middlesex Volunteers 1798-1804; appointments, Cavendish, Bentinck and Harley 16th-20th cent; Cavendish and Cavendish-Bentinck family papers 17th-early 20th cent, incl corresp of the 3rd, 4th and 5th Dukes of Portland; accounts of the Duke of Newcastle 1693-1711 and the Earl of Portland 1691-8; Harley papers 16th-18th cent, incl roll of Sir Robert Harley as Master of the Mint 1626-35, Dunkirk accounts of Sir Edward Harley 1660-1 and Barbados papers of Sir Robert Harley 1663-5; accounts of the 4th Earl of Southampton 1660-3; genealogical papers 16th cent-c1900; misc maps, plans and printed material 17th-20th cent; papers of RW Goulding rel to the Welbeck art collections 1890-c1930; documents 12th-19th cent collected by HA Strong; misc MSS, incl account of Duke of Ormonde's Irish estate arrears 1698-1703, Dublin Castle account of the Duke of Dorset 1731, rental of the Earl of Bristol's Suffolk estates 1754-60 and Dronfield (Derbys) guild papers 16th cent.

Nottinghamshire Archives (DD/P). Papers deposited by the 7th Duke of Portland 1950-69 were accepted for the nation in lieu of tax 1986 and allocated to Nottinghamshire Archives 1987. An additional deposit (1985) was catalogued as DD/P6. NRA 5959. Further papers, including a volume of Newcastle estate maps by William Senior c1629-40 and more recent maps and drawings, remain in private possession.

[b] Rent accounts, Mansfield estate 1749 and Notts and Derbys estates 1777-8.

Nottinghamshire Archives (DD 104/1-2). Deposited by EW Mellors 1959. NRA 6885.

[c] Red Books by Humphry Repton 1790-1803(3).

In private possession. Enquiries to the Historical Manuscripts Commission.

[d] Deeds 14th-20th cent (mainly 18th-20th cent), Notts, Derbys and Northumberland (Cavendish estates), Bucks (Bulstrode estate), Herts (Theobalds estate), Middlesex (Soho and Marylebone), Cumberland, Lincs, Norfolk and other counties; settlements, wills, etc 17th-19th cent; legal papers mainly 19th-20th cent, incl cases rel to the Butterley Company c1907-12 and to the claims of the Druce family c1896-1907, and solicitors' corresp 19th-20th cent; Bolsover manorial books and papers 1634-51; misc estate papers 17th-20th cent, Bucks, Cumberland, Herts, Middlesex (Soho), etc, incl rentals, accounts, valuations and corresp; misc family papers 17th-20th cent, incl commonplace book of Lady (Brilliana) Harley c1622, and misc political and personal papers of the 3rd Duke of Portland.

Nottingham University Library, Manuscripts Department (Portland (London) collection). Presented by the 7th Duke of Portland through his London solicitors 1947-8. NRA 28916 (partial list).

[e] Cavendish, Holles and Cavendish-Bentinck family corresp and papers 16th-19th cent (c38,000 items), incl the Cavendish and Holles Dukes of Newcastle, the 1st Earl and 1st-5th Dukes of Portland, Lord William Bentinck (1774-1839) and Lord George Bentinck (1802-48); Harley family papers c1579-1741 (c1,500 items), incl papers of Sir Edward Harley as Governor of Dunkirk 1660-1 and semi-official papers of the 1st Earl of Oxford; literary papers, incl many of Harley provenance; misc collected and other papers, incl Yorks forest pleas mid-16th cent (1 vol), particulars of Welbeck Abbey lands 1587/8 (1 vol), rental of the barony of Hepple (Northumberland) 1652-60 (1 vol), rental of Viscount Woodstock's Irish estates 1699 (2 vols), valuation of Henrietta Scott's estates 1796 (1 vol), and diplomatic papers of William Blathwayt 1676-99.

Nottingham University Library, Manuscripts Department. Deposited by the 7th Duke of Portland 1949, 1968; allocated to the Library 1987. NRA 7628.

[f] Papers of the Sample family as agents for the Bothal estate 1780-1947, incl leases 1807-32, maps and plans from 1780, misc surveys and valuations 1861-1932, rentals and accounts 1827-1942, coal papers 1825-1947, estate company minutes 1907-45 and corresp of William Sample with the 4th and 5th Dukes of Portland 1828-66; inventory of Bothal Castle 1923.

Northumberland Record Office (ZSA 1-24, 51). NRA 24807.

[g] Deeds 13th-18th cent, mainly Hants (Titchfield Abbey, Beaulieu Abbey and other Wriothesley properties); legal and family papers 16th-18th cent, Earls of Southampton and Gainsborough and Dukes of Beaufort and Portland; manorial records 14th-18th cent, incl court book of Titchfield Abbey estates 1521-30; rentals, valuations, accounts and misc estate papers 16th-18th cent; misc financial and official documents, Earls of Southampton 1535-1670.

Hampshire Record Office (3M53). Deposited by the 7th Duke of Portland 1953; allocated to the Record Office 1987. NRA 8800.

[h] Ayrshire deeds and legal papers 1408-1845 (501 items), incl Campbell of Cessnock, Lockhart of Bar and Fullarton of Fullarton.

Scottish Record Office (GD 163). Deposited by the 7th Duke of Portland through Melville and Lindesay, WS 1955, 1956. NRA 10990.

[i] Ayrshire estate papers 1798-early 20th cent, mainly plans (estates, cropping, Troon Harbour, Cessnock Castle, etc) and factor's papers; a few personal papers late 19th-early 20th cent.

Strathclyde Regional Archives, Ayrshire Subregional Archives (ATD 13). Deposited by Welbeck Estates Ltd 1976. NRA 24996.

[j] Abstract of title, Marylebone estate 1710; copy of rental 1710; observations on the Marylebone estate 1759, with summary of rentals 1712-37

Greater London Record Office (O/341). Acquired 1971.

[k] Middlesex estate rentals (7 vols) and letter book 1720-54; misc financial and legal papers, Harley family early 18th cent, incl legal note-books of Robert Harley (d1774).

British Library, Manuscript Collections (Add MSS 18237-66). Purchased 1850.

[l] Harley family corresp and papers c1582-1740, incl extensive papers of the 1st and 2nd Earls of Oxford and papers rel to the Brampton Bryan estate and Herefs affairs; papers of Matthew Prior and Humfrey Wanley; Cavendish, Holles and Vere corresp and papers c1597-1715; cartulary, registers, etc rel to Hants religious houses (6 vols); misc MSS, incl Scottish charters, a Pierrepont cartulary 15th cent and a volume of William Blathwayt's papers.

British Library, Manuscript Collections (Add MSS 70001-70523, Add Ch 76671-76767). Deposited by the 7th Duke of Portland c1947-53; allocated to the Library 1987. HMC *Portland II-X*, 1893-1931. NRA 20953.

[m] Welbeck Abbey cartulary (MS 3640) and charters (*passim*); Notts and Derbys shrievalty account 1558 (MS 5070); misc Cavendish, Holles and Harley family papers, incl Privy Seal papers of John Holles, Duke of Newcastle (MSS 2262-4, 7344-51) and official papers of the 1st Earl of Oxford (MSS 7405-7500, 7639 A, B).

British Library, Manuscript Collections. Among the Harleian MSS, rolls and charters acquired from Henrietta, Countess of Oxford 1753.

[n] Additional Harley family letters and papers 1688-1719 (1 vol), mainly corresp and papers of Thomas Harley as envoy to Hanover 1712, 1714.

British Library, Manuscript Collections (Add MS 40621). Acquired 1922.

[o] Harleian Library catalogues by Humfrey Wanley and others c1708-c1761 (13 vols).

British Library, Manuscript Collections (Add MSS 45699-45711). Acquired 1941.

[p] Welbeck weather records 1802-52 (51 vols).

British Library, Manuscript Collections (Add MSS 16882-7). Presented by the 4th Duke of Portland from 1847.

[q] Welbeck weather records 1827-76 (35 vols).

National Meteorological Library and Archive (Royal Meteorological Society collections).

[r] Architectural drawings 18th cent, mainly rel to Welbeck Abbey, incl designs by William Talman and Sir John Vanbrugh.

British Architectural Library, Drawings Collection. Deposited by the 7th Duke of Portland 1969 and by Lady Anne Bentinck 1977. NRA 5959.

[s] Rental of the 1st Earl of Portland's estates 1714 (1 roll).

Bodleian Library, Oxford (MS Eng. misc.c.12(R)).

[t] Civil War letters and papers c1640-52 (25 vols).

Bodleian Library, Oxford (Dep. c. 152-176). Collected by the Revd John Nalson (d1686) and subsequently acquired by the Dukes of Portland. Deposited by the 7th Duke 1946; allocated to the Library 1987. HMC *Portland I (Thirteenth Report, App I)*, 1891.

Related collections: Dukes of Newcastle (Nottingham University Library, Manuscripts Department Ne, Ne2, NL, NRA 7411); Counts Bentinck 17th-18th cent (British Library, Manuscript Collections Eg MSS 1704-56) and 18th-early 19th cent (Nottingham University Library, Manuscripts Department); Barons Howard de Walden (City of Westminster Archives Centre Acc 449, 458, 503, NRA 31668); Dukes of Beaufort (Gloucestershire Record Office D 2700, NRA 6282), including the Titchfield estate early 18th cent; Kilmarnock estate records 14th-20th cent (Dick Institute, Kilmarnock KIMMG, NRA 29118); Harley of Brampton Bryan (in private possession, NRA 686); Marquesses of Bath (in private possession), including Harley papers.

[19] CECIL, Marquesses of Exeter

The Cecil family was established at Bourne and Stamford (Lincolnshire) by the early sixteenth century. Extensive estates in Lincolnshire, Northamptonshire (including the Soke of Peterborough) and Rutland were acquired by Richard Cecil (d1553), Groom of the Stole to Henry VIII, and his son William Cecil, Baron Burghley (d1598), Secretary of State to Edward VI and Elizabeth and Lord Treasurer 1572-98. On the latter's death almost all these properties passed to his son by his first wife, Thomas Cecil, created Earl of Exeter in 1605: other Cecil estates, however, in Hertfordshire and elsewhere, passed to Robert Cecil, Thomas's half-brother, who was created Earl of Salisbury (see no 41). Thomas Cecil also acquired property in the North Riding of Yorkshire (Snape and Well) and Bedfordshire (the barony of Bedford, etc) through his marriage in 1564 to Dorothy, daughter and co-heir of John Nevill, Lord Latimer (d1577).

On the death of the second Earl of Exeter without male issue in 1640, some Lincolnshire property (Stamford, etc) passed to his youngest daughter Anne, wife of the second Baron Grey of Groby, who was created Earl of Stamford in 1628. But the estates centred on Burghley House were consolidated in the eighteenth and nineteenth centuries and the family interest in Stamford strengthened, notably by the reacquisition of the Earl of Stamford's estate in the mid-eighteenth century. A large estate near Crowland (Lincolnshire) was purchased by the second Marquess of Exeter *c*1829 but sold after his death in 1867. The Yorkshire and Bedfordshire estates were sold in the late eighteenth and early nineteenth centuries, and the London (Middlesex) property (in the Strand) *c*1850.

Estates in 1883: Northants 15,625 acres, Rutland 8,998 acres, Lincs 3,095 acres, Leics 553 acres, total 28,271 acres worth £49,044 a year.

[a] Deeds 11th-20th cent, incl medieval charters and grants rel to Bourne, Peterborough and Revesby (Lincs) abbeys, and medieval and later deeds for Lincs, Northants and Rutland, with smaller groups for Beds, Middlesex and Yorks NR; wills, settlements and related legal and trust papers 14th-20th cent, incl Cecil wills and settlements from 16th cent, Latimer and Nevill settlements, etc 14th-16th cent (incl some items rel to the Beauchamp Earls of Warwick), legal papers of the Earls of Stamford 18th cent and solicitors' papers mainly 19th-20th cent; manorial records 14th-20th cent, mainly Lincs, Northants and Rutland but incl Roos in Holderness (Yorks ER) 1307-1422; Nassaburgh hundred (Northants) records 1384-1730; Bedford barony court papers 16th-18th cent; Wrangdike (Rutland) hundred and soke of Kirton-in-Holland (Lincs), records ?mainly 18th cent.

Lincs, Northants and Rutland estate records mainly 16th-20th cent, incl leases 16th-19th cent, surveys and valuations 16th-19th cent, maps from early 17th cent, rentals and accounts mainly 17th-20th cent, corresp 18th-20th cent, papers for individual parishes 16th-19th cent, and papers rel to chief rents 18th-19th cent, enclosure 18th-19th cent, Stamford market 18th-19th cent, Stamford water supply late 18th-mid-20th cent, Crowland estate *c*1829-68, and ironstone mining early 20th cent; misc estate and legal papers rel to Beds 15th-early 19th cent, Middlesex (London property) 15th-19th cent and Yorks (Snape, Well, Ingmanthorpe, etc) 15th-18th cent; extent of Lord Burghley estates (Herts, etc) 1598; Latimer and Warwick estate accounts 1510-34; Stamford rentals *c*1721-50 (Earl of Stamford's property); valuation 1841 and sale papers rel to Cowdray (Sussex) estate; household accounts 18th-19th cent, mainly Burghley House; papers rel to Burghley House 17th-19th cent, incl inventories 1688-90, 1804 and 1891, vouchers for work by Verrio and others late 17th cent and accounts and plans for alterations 1828-33; papers rel to gardens, park and home farm mainly 18th-19th cent.

Soke of Peterborough records 15th-20th cent, incl grant of jurisdiction 1493, commissions of oyer and terminer, commissions of the peace, and quarter sessions files 1623-89; papers rel to the recordership of Stamford 1682-1754, Stamford, etc charities 15th-18th cent and Stamford Volunteers 1797-1804; election papers (Stamford, Lincs, Northants and Rutland) 18th-19th

cent; papers rel to drainage, railways, charities, etc 19th cent; Stoke Dry (Rutland) parish account book *c*1685-1735; Burghley Park Hospital papers 1914-18; Well Hospital papers *c*17th-18th cent; Cecil family appointments and commissions 16th-19th cent; misc family papers 16th-20th cent, incl de Sitsilt pedigree roll late 16th cent, papers rel to benefactions to St John's College Cambridge 1577-86 and Clare Hall 1613, game books, and collected letters and papers 1499-1678; Peterborough Abbey rental late 14th cent, homage roll 1299-1478 and account rolls (Barnack, etc) early 16th cent.

In private possession. Not available for research while extensive cataloguing is in progress. Enquiries to the Historical Manuscripts Commission. HMC *Sixth Report, App,* 1877, pp234-5. NRA 6666 (partial list). Many of the Revesby charters noticed in the Report were given to the Hon Edward Stanhope of Revesby Abbey in 1881 and are now deposited in Lincolnshire Archives (RA, NRA 6329; and see E Stanhope, ed, *Abstracts of the Deeds and Charters relating to Revesby Abbey 1142-1539,* 1889). Two Peterborough Abbey registers were presented by the 9th Earl of Exeter to the Society of Antiquaries in 1778 (GRC Davis, *Medieval Cartularies,* 1958, nos 754, 759; NRA 27819). The letters and papers 1499-1678 represent a collection *penes* the Revd Francis Hopkinson in 1872 but acquired for the Burghley archive in the early twentieth century (HMC *Third Report, App,* 1872, pp261-7).

[b] Burghley household papers 1934-42; appointments, diaries and related papers of the 5th Marquess 1920-56; corresp and papers of Myra, Marchioness of Exeter (wife of the 5th Marquess) 1861-1965, mainly rel to local affairs.

Northamptonshire Record Office (Acc 1950/75; ZB 441; Acc 1975/95, X 4374-6). NRA 4039, 23653, 26759.

Related collections: Brudenell-Bruce, Marquesses of Ailesbury (no 12), including records descending through Diana, Countess of Elgin; Gascoyne-Cecil, Marquesses of Salisbury (no 41); Milbank of Thorpe Perrow and Halnaby (North Yorkshire County Record Office ZAL, NRA 13275), including Snape and Well records.

[20] CHETWYND-TALBOT, Earls of Shrewsbury

The Talbot family had lands in Herefordshire in the twelfth century. The fifth Baron Talbot married the heiress of the Furnivall estates in Yorkshire, Nottinghamshire, Staffordshire and Derbyshire and was created Earl of Shrewsbury in 1442. On the death of the eighth Earl in 1618 the Sheffield (Yorkshire, West Riding), Worksop (Nottinghamshire) and Glossop (Derbyshire) estates passed to the Howard family (see no 37), but the Alton (Staffordshire) estate passed with the Shrewsbury earldom to a cousin.

George Talbot (1566-1630), who succeeded as ninth Earl in 1618, was grandson and eventual heir of Sir John Talbot of Grafton (Worcestershire), Albrighton (Shropshire) and Burghfield (Berkshire). His descendants also acquired property in Oxfordshire (Bampton and Heythrop) and Cheshire. On the death without issue of the seventeenth Earl in 1856 all or most of the Shrewsbury estates passed to a distant cousin, the third Earl Talbot of Hensol, who succeeded as eighteenth Earl of Shrewsbury. Certainly by 1883 the Staffordshire, Cheshire, Worcestershire and Shropshire estates were all in the possession of his son the nineteenth Earl, the Berkshire and Oxfordshire estates having been sold since 1850. Some Talbot records, however, passed to a younger son of the fourteenth Duke of Norfolk, Lord Edmund Howard (later Viscount Fitzalan of Derwent).

Henry Chetwynd-Talbot, third Earl Talbot of Hensol, who succeeded to the Shrewsbury earldom in 1856, was a representative of the Talbot family formerly of Salwarpe (Worcestershire), descended from Sir John Talbot (d1581), a younger son of Sir John Talbot of Grafton, etc. Charles Talbot, a great-grandson of Sir John Talbot (d1581), married in 1708 Cecil Matthews, granddaughter and heir of David Jenkins of Hensol (Glamorganshire), and was created Baron Talbot of Hensol in 1733. (Hensol Castle was sold c1790 but mineral rights were retained.) His son was created Earl Talbot in 1761 but died without male issue in 1782, when some of the Welsh estates passed to his daughter, *suo jure* Baroness Dinevor. The Talbot barony, however, passed to his nephew John Chetwynd-Talbot, who through his mother inherited the Chetwynd estates centred on Ingestre (Staffordshire), some of which had been held by the Chetwynd family since the thirteenth century. He was created Earl Talbot in 1784.

Estates in 1883: Staffs 18,954 acres, Cheshire 9,500 acres, Worcs 3,608 acres, Salop 2,186 acres, Derbys 1,359 acres, Northants 20 acres, Berks 19 acres, Oxon 2 acres, Glamorganshire 81 acres, total 35,729 acres, worth £62,382 a year exclusive of Welsh minerals.

[a] Staffs deeds 13th-20th cent, with a few for other counties 18th-19th cent; Chetwynd and Talbot settlements 15th-19th cent, with related trust and executorship papers; legal papers 16th-20th cent, incl the Shrewsbury peerage case; schedules of deeds c1793-20th cent; Staffs manorial records 15th-19th cent; Staffs (Alton and Ingestre) estate records 16th-20th cent, incl leases and agreements, surveys and maps, rentals and accounts, corresp, and papers rel to coal mining, brick making, salt making, quarrying, tithes, timber, buildings and repairs, railways, etc; records for Cheshire, Oxon, Salop and Worcs estates, mainly c1870-20th cent but incl some items from 18th cent; particular of Ashton Gifford (Wilts) 1657; Alton and Ingestre farm accounts mainly 19th cent; shooting accounts 20th cent.

Building plans and papers 19th-20th cent, incl rebuilding of Ingestre Hall 1883-4; Ingestre and Alton inventories late 19th cent; household accounts 1622-75 (Ingestre) and 19th-20th cent; Alton and Ingestre garden accounts 19th cent; parochial papers 18th-19th cent, incl Ingestre overseers' accounts 1831-53; family papers 16th-20th cent, incl Staffs lieutenancy, shrievalty and other papers of Walter Chetwynd late 17th cent, diplomatic corresp of John Chetwynd (later 2nd Viscount) early 18th cent, and papers of the 2nd Earl Talbot as Lord Lieutenant of Ireland 1817-22 and of Staffs 1822-42; papers rel to agency for Wolseley estates c1853-71; inventory of Ralph de Grendon (Warwicks) 1332; Chetwyndorum Stemma 1690.

Staffordshire Record Office (D 240, D(W) 1744, D 4597). Part deposited in the record office 1952-87, part deposited in the William Salt Library, Stafford 1949 and subsequently transferred. *Staffordshire Family Collections*, 1984, pp5-7. NRA 8481, 7275.

[b] Deeds and papers 1663-1852, mainly Staffs and Cheshire; legal papers rel to division of estate 1858-62.

Staffordshire Record Office. Deposited by Withers, solicitors, London, through the British Records Association 1994.

[c] Misc Staffs deeds, mortgages and legal papers 1871-1924; estate papers 1802-1938, mainly Staffs, incl Ingestre survey 1802-3.

Staffordshire Record Office (D 3984). Deposited by Williams & James, solicitors, London, through the British Records Association 1983. NRA 8481.

[d] Misc deeds, wills and legal papers 1865-87.

Staffordshire Record Office (D 1091). Deposited by Waterhouse & Co, solicitors, London, through the British Records Association 1970.

[e] Legal and trust papers 1863-86, incl Shrewsbury *v* Talbot and settlement on marriage of Lady Adelaide Talbot to Earl Brownlow 1868; misc Staffs estate papers 1866-87, incl rentals, accounts and Brereton colliery leases.

Staffordshire Record Office (D 1434). Presented by Peter Eaton, bookseller, through the Bodleian Library 1974. NRA 8481.

[f] Papers of Richard Bill as agent for the Earl of Shrewsbury's Staffs estates 1686-1751, incl rental 1729 and accounts 1693-1751, with misc papers rel to the Shrewsbury estate late 18th-mid-19th cent.

Staffordshire Record Office (Bill of Farley papers, D 554). Deposited by Mrs P Clifford (née Bill). NRA 6841.

[g] Chetwynd deeds, Staffs 13th-19th cent and Warwicks 14th-15th cent (c100 medieval); misc deeds for Herefs, Wales, Ireland, etc 13th-18th cent; Chetwynd settlements, wills and related papers 15th-18th cent; legal papers and bonds 16th-18th cent, with schedule of deeds 1833; Staffs manorial records (Ingestre, etc) 15th-17th

cent; Staffs and Warwicks leases 14th-18th cent; misc Staffs surveys, rentals, accounts, etc 15th-18th cent; Glamorganshire estate survey *c*1750; Staffs militia, shrievalty and other papers 16th-17th cent; Stafford borough papers 17th-18th cent, incl poll books; agreement for equipment of archers *temp* Henry VI.

William Salt Library, Stafford (HM Chetwynd; HM 27/9). Deposited by Hand, Morgan & Co, solicitors, Stafford. NRA 7274.

[h] Chetwynd legal and family papers 1594-1666, incl Staffs and Warwicks lieutenancy corresp 1661-6.

William Salt Library, Stafford (William Salt's original collection no 565). NRA 8254.

[i] Glamorganshire deeds 15th-18th cent, with related Jenkins and Talbot wills, settlements and legal papers; leases 16th-18th cent; fragment of estate accounts 1751-6.

National Library of Wales (Talbot of Hensol deeds and documents). Deposited by HR Thomas for SAH Burne of Stafford 1939-40. NRA 28334.

[j] Glamorganshire deeds, leases and related legal papers 18th-20th cent; Glamorganshire estate records 19th cent, incl rentals 1838-47.

Glamorgan Record Office (D/D Hen). Deposited by the 21st Earl of Shrewsbury 1978. NRA 26425.

[k] Deeds 12th-18th cent (mainly medieval) for Talbot estates, principally Cheshire, Salop, Staffs, Worcs and Yorks but also Cambs, Derbys, Devon, Essex, Gloucs, Herefs, Lancs and other counties, with a few for Germany and Austria 15th-18th cent; wills, settlements, inquisitions, bonds and related legal and financial documents 14th-18th cent, Talbot, Scrope of Masham, Stafford of Grafton and other families; abstracts and schedules of deeds 16th-19th cent; manorial records 14th-16th cent, Gloucs, Staffs, Worcs, etc, incl valuations and accounts for various manors 15th cent; Talbot of Grafton household and estate accounts 1565-95; inventory of Grafton and Salwarpe 1570; accounts for benevolences collected in Salop 1499-1500 and nd; Worcs and Salop shrievalty rolls 16th cent; Talbot family papers 15th-19th cent, incl commissions, pardons, licences, recusancy acquittances 1587-1603 and papers of Sir Gilbert Talbot as deputy lieutenant of Calais *c*1495-1513; Talbot pedigrees 18th-19th cent; misc Troutbeck (of Mobberley, Cheshire) and Wellys (of Hoar Cross, Staffs) family papers 15th-17th cent; coucher book of honour of Tutbury early 16th cent.

British Library, Manuscript Collections (Add Ch 72121-74194, Add MSS 46454-64, Seals CXCII 4-8). Given 1937 by Viscount Fitzalan of Derwent, to whom they had been bequeathed by the 17th Earl of Shrewsbury. (For related estate records with the Duke of Norfolk's muniments see no 37.) HMC *First Report, App*, 1870, p50; *Various Collections II* (1903), pp289-336.

[l] Additional Talbot charters 13th-17th cent, mainly Cheshire and Salop; trust deeds 1638-59.

British Library, Manuscript Collections (Add Ch 75069-75320, 75428-33). Apparently detached from the preceding collection for legal purposes in the 19th century. Presented by EE Barker 1954-5.

[m] Burghfield deeds 16th-19th cent, court rolls 15th-17th cent, leases 1649-1869 and other estate records 1789-1870; misc papers 16th-17th cent, incl papers rel to Calais *c*1503.

Berkshire Record Office (D/ESW). Deposited 1950-78. NRA 98. (Most of these records were withdrawn in 1995 and are now in private possession. Enquiries to Berkshire Record Office.)

[n] Cheshire estate papers (Oxton, etc) 17th-20th cent, incl leases, surveys *c*1850 and maps 1788-19th cent.

Cheshire Record Office (DSH). *Guide*, 1991, p108.

[o] Deeds and legal papers rel to Little Neston (Cheshire) 1800-29.

Cheshire Record Office. Deposited by Withers, solicitors, London, through the British Records Association 1994.

[p] Deeds 1239, 16th-19th cent (164 items), mainly Bampton, etc (Oxon).

Bodleian Library, Oxford (MSS DD. Shrewsbury c.1-5). Deposited by the 21st Earl of Shrewsbury through Berkshire Record Office 1950. NRA 97.

[q] Oxon deeds 1626-1776, Bampton, Heythrop, Chipping Norton, etc.

Oxfordshire Archives. Deposited by Withers, solicitors, London, through the British Records Association 1994.

[r] Heythrop, Bampton and Hook Norton estate records 1796-1870, incl valuations, rentals and accounts.

Oxfordshire Archives (Shrew. I-X). Transferred from Staffordshire Record Office 1976.

[s] Heythrop survey 1759.

Oxfordshire Archives (E 103). Purchased 1983 (Phillips, 13 Jan, lot 391).

[t] Salop deeds (Albrighton, etc) 16th-19th cent; estate records 18th-20th cent, incl mining leases 1708-1829 and maps 18th-19th cent.

Shropshire Record Office. Deposited 1949-68 by the 21st Earl of Shrewsbury and others. *Guide*, 1952, pp 113-14; Accession Lists Sept-Dec 1952, Jan-May 1963, June-Sept 1968.

[u] Worcs deeds (Grafton, etc) 16th-20th cent; misc legal papers 16th-17th cent; Worcs court rolls (Grafton, Upton Warren) 15th-17th cent; rentals 1453/4-1490/1; Worcs estate records 19th-20th cent, incl maps and rentals.

Hereford and Worcester Record Office, Worcester (BA 881, 962, 963, 1120, 8181). Deposited 1949-78, mainly through other record offices. NRA 1489.

[v] Worcs deeds 1394, 1500-1918; Cooksey manor survey 1650; Huddington manor plan and terrier 1790, 1809.

Hereford and Worcester Record Office, Worcester. Deposited by Withers, solicitors, London, through the British Records Association 1994.

[w] Accounts and papers of John Parsons as agent for the Salwarpe estate 1773-85.

Hereford and Worcester Record Office, Worcester (Worcester City Library collection, 899:749, parcel 82). NRA 1111.

[x] Abstract of title, Alton, etc c1825.

Public Record Office (C 108/35).

[y] Talbot family papers 1654-1779, incl letters to the 1st Earl Talbot 1731-6.

Lambeth Palace Library (MS 3129). Purchased 1980 (Christie's, 16 Apr, lot 56).

Related collections: Fitzalan-Howard, Dukes of Norfolk (no 37); Barons Dinevor (Glamorgan Record Office D/DD, NRA 1343).

[21] CHICHESTER-CONSTABLE of Burton Constable

The Constable family was established in the East Riding of Yorkshire in the twelfth century, resided at Burton Constable from the late fifteenth century and purchased the seignory of Holderness in 1560. In 1620 Sir Henry Constable was created Viscount Dunbar. On the death of the fourth Viscount in 1718 the peerage became dormant and the Constable estates passed to his nephew Cuthbert Tunstall of Wycliffe (Yorkshire, North Riding) who assumed the name of Constable. His son William died without issue in 1790 and was succeeded by his nephew Edward Sheldon, afterwards Constable, who in turn was succeeded by his brother Francis. Upon the death of the last-named in 1821 the Constable estates descended to his cousin Sir Thomas Clifford, first Bt, of Tixall (Staffordshire), whose mother had inherited property there from her father Lord Aston of Forfar. Sir Thomas took the name of Constable. His grandson Sir Frederick Constable, third Bt, died in 1894 and was succeeded by his cousin Walter George Raleigh Chichester. The latter, who in turn took the additional name of Constable, was the son of Charles Raleigh Chichester by Mary Balfe of Runnamoat (County Roscommon), the grandson of Sir Charles Chichester by Mary Barbara Constable and the great-grandson of Charles Chichester of Calverleigh Court (Devon).

Estates in 1883: Constable: Yorks ER 10,981 acres, Yorks NR 7,685 acres, Co Durham 25 acres, Middlesex 15 acres, Staffs 8 acres, total 18,714 acres worth £24,381 a year; Balfe: Co Roscommon 6,024 acres, Co Galway 376 acres, total 6,400 acres, worth £5,158 a year.

[a] Deeds 12th-20th cent (c240 medieval), mainly Yorks ER but also Yorks NR, Yorks WR, Lincs and other counties; cartulary c1270; wills, settlements, trust papers and executorship papers 13th-19th cent, Constable, Tunstall, Clifford and other families; abstracts of title, legal and case papers, bonds, etc 17th-20th cent; manorial court rolls, court files, account rolls and other records 14th-20th cent (c65 medieval rolls), mainly Yorks ER, incl Burstwick court rolls 1368-1925, but also Lincs, incl Barrow-upon-Humber court rolls 1350-1613, Staffs and Sussex; Seignory of Holderness court rolls, account rolls and other records 14th-19th cent.

Yorks ER estate records 14th-20th cent, incl leases late 16th-early 17th cent, surveys and valuations from 17th cent, maps and plans from 18th cent, rentals 17th-20th cent, accounts and vouchers 17th-20th cent, corresp 18th-20th cent, tithe papers 17th-19th cent, enclosure papers 18th-19th cent, drainage papers 14th-19th cent, Humber foreshore and Spurn Point lighthouse papers 18th-20th cent, and papers rel to Cherry Cob Sands 18th-19th cent; estate records rel to Yorks NR (Wycliffe, etc) 18th-20th cent, Yorks WR (Kirk Deighton, etc) 16th-19th cent, Devon (Chichester family) 19th cent, Herts (Standon: Aston family) mid 18th cent, Lincs and Notts (Markham family) 1673-1776 and Staffs (Tixall, etc) 17th-19th cent; inventories 18th-20th cent, incl Burton Constable, Tixall and Wycliffe; household papers 18th-19th cent, incl accounts 18th-19th cent and cellar books 1771-1861; garden and stable accounts 19th cent; labourers' accounts 1747-1805; coachman's accounts c1830-52; Halsham mausoleum accounts 1792-1807; Tixall building accounts and papers 1827-32.

Papers rel to East Riding county, borough and parish affairs 16th-20th cent, incl coronership papers 1586-1832, Hedon corporation books 1657-1797 (2 vols), Aldbrough parish book 1650-1823 and Holderness Hunt papers 19th-20th cent; appointments, commissions, grants of arms, etc 16th-19th cent; family corresp and papers 16th-20th cent, Constable, Tunstall, Clifford, Chichester and Chichester-Constable, incl corresp and papers of William Constable 1757-90, the Hon Thomas Clifford 1761-87 and Sir Thomas Clifford-Constable 1779-1820; misc papers 14th-20th cent, incl pedigrees and genealogical papers from c1500, Forest of Pickering receiver's roll 1334, survey of the Duke of Buckingham's estates 1521 with receivership account 1538-9, account roll for the Duke of Norfolk's manors in Yorks and Lincs 1517-18, Wardrobe account of Sir Ralph Sadleir 1552-3 and account for the Army in the North 1571.

Humberside County Archives Service (DDCC). Deposited by Brigadier RCJ Chichester-Constable and JR Chichester-Constable 1955-84 and purchased 1992. Further estate and family papers 19th-20th cent were deposited from Burton Constable 1993. NRA 6491.

[b] Seignory of Holderness, court records 1704-1834.

Humberside County Archives Service (DDIV/7, 34). Deposited by Messrs Iveson, West & Wilkinson, solicitors, Hull 1958, 1970. NRA 7411.

[c] Seignory of Holderness, accounts of fines 1741-1840.

Hull University, Brynmor Jones Library (DSJ). Deposited by Messrs Stamp, Jackson & Sons, solicitors, Hull. NRA 10607.

[d] Seignory of Holderness case papers (claim to foreshore) 1879, with other legal papers 19th-20th cent.

Hull University, Brynmor Jones Library (DCC). ?From the office of Messrs Stamp, Jackson & Sons. NRA 10952.

[e] Misc papers, incl cartulary 14th cent and survey of Sir John Constable's estate 1578 (1 vol); papers rel to Lancelot Brown late 18th cent, plans by Thomas White and other architectural drawings late 18th cent.

In private possession. Enquiries to the Curator, Burton Constable Hall, Hull.

[f] Aston of Tixall settlements and related papers 1698-1825.

Staffordshire Record Office (D 4295). Deposited by Williams & James, solicitors, London, through the British Records Association 1986. NRA 6133.

[g] Deeds and papers 12th-17th cent (mostly non-archival), mainly Yorks but also Lancs, Lincs and other counties.

West Yorkshire Archive Service, Yorkshire Archaeological Society (DD 53/III). Purchased by Lord Grantley at the Burton Constable sale (Sotheby's, 24-26 June 1889). NRA 5783. (The sale comprised family deeds and papers as well as material collected in the eighteenth century (including documents purchased from the antiquary John Burton in 1771). The following eight groups of papers also relate to MSS sold in 1889.)

[h] Yorks deeds and papers 13th-18th cent.

West Yorkshire Archive Service, Yorkshire Archaeological Society (MD 37). Purchased by JS Earle 1889. *Catalogue*, 1931, p69.

[i] Papers rel to Abraham Woodhead, Roman Catholic controversialist 17th-18th cent.

West Yorkshire Archive Service, Yorkshire Archaeological Society (MS 43-59). *Catalogue*, 1931, pp5-7.

[j] Holderness Middle Bailiwick papers 17th cent.

West Yorkshire Archive Service, Yorkshire Archaeological Society (MS 321). *Catalogue*, 1931, p38.

[k] Deeds 13th-18th cent, mainly Yorks, with papers 14th-17th cent.

West Yorkshire Archive Service, Leeds (Acc 1731). Purchased by JEF Chambers 1889. Presented to Leeds District Archives by HJDM Jowitt 1972. NRA 19413.

[l] Papers and corresp of Sir Ralph Sadleir 1554-85.

British Library, Manuscript Collections (Add MSS 33591-4).

[m] Tixall deeds, estate papers and local papers 16th-18th cent, with some antiquarian papers of Arthur Clifford early 19th cent.

William Salt Library, Stafford (WSL 45/57). NRA 6133.

[n] Further misc Aston of Tixall papers mainly late 17th cent.

Bodleian Library, Oxford (MS Eng.misc.c.291). Probably collected by WH Black. Purchased 1947.

[o] Papers rel to the history of Yorkshire collected by John Burton.

Bodleian Library, Oxford (MSS Top.Yorks.a.1, b.3-17, d.4-7, e.7-29). Purchased by Lord Herries 1889, subsequently repurchased by RCJ Chichester-Constable and sold again at Sotheby's 1937. NRA 20306. (See also Fitzalan-Howard, Dukes of Norfolk, no 37, for material retained in the Constable-Maxwell papers.)

[p] Cartulary of Easby Abbey (Yorks) 13th cent.

British Library, Manuscript Collections (Eg MS 2827). Sold from Tixall 1899.

Related collections: Chichester family (Hull University, Brynmor Jones Library DDCH, NRA 6800), including Irish (Balfe) estate papers 1847-70; Aston of Tixall (William Salt Library, Stafford HM Aston, NRA 8253, and WSL 45/57, NRA 6133; Staffordshire Record Office D 4295, NRA 6133).

[22] CHOLMONDELEY, Marquesses of Cholmondeley

The Cholmondeley family was established at Cholmondeley (Cheshire) in the thirteenth century, and acquired further estates in Cheshire, Denbighshire and Flintshire by marriage and purchase. The Vale Royal (Cheshire) estate was acquired through the marriage of Sir Hugh Cholmondeley to Mary Holford in the late sixteenth century but passed to a junior branch of the family (later Barons Delamere). On the death of the Hon James Cholmondeley in 1775 the Clifton or Rocksavage estate near Runcorn (Cheshire), which he had acquired through his first wife, heiress of the Savage family, Earls Rivers, passed to his great-nephew the fourth Earl (later first Marquess) of Cholmondeley.

The first Marquess of Cholmondeley (so created 1815), whose grandfather the third Earl had married Mary, daughter of Sir Robert Walpole (1676-1745), first Earl of Orford, inherited the Walpole estate of Houghton (Norfolk) on the death of the fourth Earl of Orford in 1797. The Walpole family, settled at Houghton since the thirteenth century, had acquired property in Norfolk by marriage and purchase, including the Pell family's

Dersingham and West Winch estate, bought in 1697. Hessett and Rougham (Suffolk), acquired through the marriage of Robert Walpole (d1700) and Mary, daughter and heir of Sir Jeffrey Burwell of Rougham, had been sold by the first Earl of Orford, who, however, had extended the Norfolk estate by purchase and built Houghton Hall.

Property in Dorset (Puddletown), Devon and elsewhere in the west country was acquired by the second Earl of Orford (d1751) through his marriage in 1724 to Margaret, Baroness Clinton, daughter and heir of Samuel Rolle of Heanton Satchville (Devon). On the death of the third Earl of Orford in 1791 the barony of Clinton and a portion of this estate devolved upon the Trefusis family, Barons Clinton of Heanton Satchville, but Puddletown passed to the fourth Earl of Orford and on his death to his cousin Horatio Walpole, Baron Walpole of Wolterton, who was created Earl of Orford in 1806.

Estates in 1883: Cheshire 16,992 acres, Norfolk 16,995 acres, Devon 4 acres, total 33,991 acres worth £41,228 a year.

[a] Cheshire, Denbighshire and Flintshire deeds 12th-19th cent (over 1,000 medieval); deeds for London, Lancs, Salop, Surrey, Suffolk and Yorks 13th-18th cent; Savage and Cholmondeley wills, settlements and related papers 16th-19th cent; legal papers 16th-19th cent, incl register of Savage deeds 1602; Cheshire manorial records 15th-19th cent, incl Bickley bailiffs' accounts 1415-16 and rental 1486-7, and manor and hundred of Nantwich 1547-1840; misc manorial records for other counties 14th-18th cent, incl Congerstone (Leics) court roll ?1343, Clun (Salop) court roll 1383-4, and accounts of the 1st Earl of Cholmondeley as seneschal of Richmond *alias* West Sheen 1702-26.

Cheshire estate records (Cholmondeley and Rocksavage) 16th-20th cent, incl leases for lives and for years, surveys and maps from 17th cent, rentals and accounts 16th cent (notably for Savage estates early 17th cent), papers for various townships, papers rel to schools 19th-20th cent and corresp 17th-20th cent; Wrenbury tithe accounts 1574-9; Leftwich salt-making accounts 1623-1726; papers rel to Delamere Forest and to Old and New Pale Farms 16th-19th cent; London, Kent, Suffolk and Surrey estate papers 1741-1816; Carmarthenshire rentals 1813-27; Cholmondeley Castle building papers 18th-19th cent, incl accounts 1705-14 and accounts and corresp 1801-21; Cholmondeley Castle inventories 18th-19th cent; Rocksavage household accounts 1627; military corresp and papers 17th-18th cent, incl militia corresp 1745-6; Cholmondeley township records 18th cent; Cholmondeley cattle club, fire brigade and horticultural society records 20th cent.

Commissions and patents 16th-19th cent; Cholmondeley family corresp and papers late 16th-20th cent, incl corresp and accounts of the 1st Earl c1675-1725, pedigrees, and literary and printed items; misc papers from late 14th cent,

incl cartulary of Scrope family of Bolton (Yorks NR) late 14th cent with rental c1516, accounts for Hunts manors of Sir John Paynell 1399-1410, and letters patent 1398 and accounts 1522-3, 1542-3 for Arundel College, with Arundel rental 1558 and bailiffs' account nd.

Cheshire Record Office (DCH). Deposited 1952-78.

[b] Misc Cheshire deeds and papers 1923-41.

Cheshire Record Office (DSW/2224). Deposited by Smith Whittingham, solicitors, Nantwich. NRA 23743.

[c] Norfolk and Suffolk deeds 14th-18th cent; executorship, trust and legal papers 15th-18th cent, Walpole and Pell families, incl executorship papers for the 1st Earl of Orford and trust accounts of Lady Maria Walpole 1743-4; executorship accounts (Marquess of Cholmondeley) 1840-2, 1870-1; financial papers 16th-20th cent, Walpole, Pell and Cholmondeley; Norfolk manorial court records 1553-20th cent, Grimston, West Rudham, West Winch, etc.

Norfolk leases and tenancy papers 17th-20th cent; misc Suffolk leases 17th cent; Norfolk maps, plans, surveys, particulars, valuations, rentals, accounts, vouchers and estate papers 17th-20th cent, incl maps and field books by Thomas Badeslade 1720 and Houghton survey book by Joseph Hume 1800, Castle Rising rent accounts 1703-18 and game books 1833-1964; records of Norfolk farms, cottages, woods and timber 19th-20th cent (extensive), incl Houghton timber survey 1816; misc tithe awards and papers 19th-20th cent; Hessett and Rougham estate accounts and papers c1674-1700, incl rental 1678-9; Littleport parsonage (Cambs) estate papers 16th-17th cent; Devon (Rolle estate) rentals 18th cent; Fremnells in Downham (Essex) survey 1629.

Houghton Hall drawings and plans 18th-20th cent, building records c1721-49; misc household and library inventories and papers 18th-20th cent; cellar accounts 1749, 1914-66; household accounts c1797-1820; visitors' books from 1826; architectural drawings and plans for London houses (Walpole family) and for Heanton Satchville (Devon) 18th cent; London household papers (Cholmondeley family) 20th cent; Houghton parish church plans 18th cent and parish constables' and overseers' records 1738-1835; Houghton social club records 1905-59; Castle Rising burgages book 1714 and electoral map 18th cent; drawings for Swaffham market cross 1782.

Walpole and Pell family corresp and papers 16th-18th cent, incl business papers of Callibut Walpole late 16th-17th cent and Robert Walpole (d1700), bills and receipts of the 1st Earl of Orford mid-18th cent and corresp and financial papers of the 3rd Earl c1756-72; accounts of Thomas Badeslade for surveying and map making 1720; misc Cholmondeley family papers 17th-20th cent, incl appointments from 1689, papers of Sybil, Marchioness of Cholmondeley and corresp of Sir Philip Sassoon, 3rd Bt; misc papers 16th-20th cent, incl pamphlets and engraved maps, Great Massingham antiquarian collections ?18th cent and Cholmondeley genealogical collections 17th cent.

In private possession. Enquiries to the Administrator, Estate Office, Houghton, King's Lynn, Norfolk PE31 6VE. NRA 37395.

[d] Deeds 14th-19th cent (*c*2,000), ? mainly Norfolk; misc legal papers ?16th-18th cent, incl Pell family of Dersingham 17th cent; Norfolk manorial records 14th-18th cent; Norfolk leases, surveys, valuations and rentals 16th-18th cent; Norfolk estate accounts, vouchers and misc papers 1508-1866, many *temp* Sir Robert Walpole, incl bailiffs' accounts 1508-32 and later, tithe account book 1644-69, and timber, granary and farm accounts 18th cent; accounts for west country (Rolle family) manors 1729-31 (3 vols); ? Houghton household accounts 17th-18th cent, with inventory of plate 1756; building accounts for stables 1727-38; Civil War rate assessments 1645-9; family corresp and papers 17th-early 19th cent, incl the 3rd and 4th Earls of Orford but comprising mainly Treasury and other papers of the 1st Earl; papers of the Pell family of Dersingham 1586-1662, incl Civil War and other papers of Sir Valentine Pell; misc MS volumes 16th-18th cent, incl letter book of Sir Francis Walsingham 1570-3 and legal notebook of Jeffrey Burwell 17th cent.

Cambridge University Library (Cholmondeley (Houghton) MSS). Deposited by the 5th Marquess of Cholmondeley 1951 and purchased 1984. GA Chinnery, *A Handlist of the Cholmondeley (Houghton) MSS*, 1953. NRA 7114.

[e] Misc Norfolk manorial records 1657-19th cent.

Norfolk Record Office. Deposited by Standley & Co, solicitors, Norwich 1964. NRA 34852.

[f] Norfolk manor court minutes (Great Massingham, etc) and misc estate papers 18th-20th cent, incl rentals for Grimston 1819-28 and the Norfolk estate 1766-7, 1834.

Norfolk Record Office. Deposited by Pounder, Brown & Gethin, solicitors, King's Lynn 1971. NRA 34853.

[g] Walpole papers 13th-19th cent collected by HL Bradfer-Lawrence, incl misc deeds (Beds, Devon, Norfolk and Somerset) 13th-18th cent, table of reference to a map of the Dersingham estate 1720, rentals for Dersingham *c*1300, 16th cent and Houghton 1773, Crostwight estate accounts 1751-4, Houghton garden plan nd, and letters of James Christie about a valuation of pictures at Houghton 1778.

Norfolk Record Office. Presented 1967 by Lt-Col PL Bradfer-Lawrence and Mrs BE Grey. NRA 27666.

Related collections: Barons Walpole of Wolterton (British Library, Manuscript Collections Dep

9201; Norfolk Record Office NRS 27328, NRA 27664); Barons Delamere (Cheshire Record Office DBC); Puddletown deeds and papers 16th-19th cent (Dorset Record Office D/Pud, NRA 7916).

[23] COKE, Earls of Leicester

The Coke family owned land in Norfolk from the thirteenth century. Sir Edward Coke (1549-1633), Lord Chief Justice, added greatly to the Norfolk estates, inherited Suffolk property through his wife Bridget Paston of Huntingfield, and purchased estates in Buckinghamshire (Farnham Royal), Dorset (Durweston, etc), London (Bevis Marks), Oxfordshire (Minster Lovell), Somerset (Donyatt) and elsewhere. His eldest son married a Berkeley, inheriting the Portbury estate in Somerset. Property in Derbyshire, Lancashire and Suffolk was settled on, or acquired through marriage by, a younger son of Sir Edward Coke, and used again thereafter to provide for a junior branch of the family.

Thomas Coke (1697-1759), created Earl of Leicester in 1744, married Margaret Tufton, co-heir of the sixth Earl of Thanet, and through her acquired the Dungeness lighthouse dues. He was succeeded by his nephew Wenman Roberts, who took the name of Coke, and whose wife was heiress of Chamberlayne property in Oxfordshire and Warwickshire (Wardington and Long Itchington) as well as of the Denton family's estate of Hillesden in Buckinghamshire.

Out-county properties were sold and the estates concentrated in Norfolk between *c*1750 and 1820. On the sales of certain outlying Norfolk parishes on the Holkham estate in 1910-12, deeds, court rolls and papers from the Holkham muniments were transferred to the new owners of the properties.

Estates in 1883: Norfolk 44,090 acres, worth £59,578 a year.

[a] Deeds 12th-20th cent (over 2,000 medieval), mostly Norfolk but incl Bucks, Kent, Oxon, Suffolk, Warwicks, etc; schedules of deeds, etc from early 17th cent; wills, settlements, trust papers and executorship papers 16th-20th cent, incl minutes and accounts for the minority of Thomas Coke, Earl of Leicester 1707-18; manorial records 13th-19th cent, mainly Norfolk but incl misc court rolls, etc for Bucks, Dorset, Kent, Oxon, Somerset and Suffolk mainly 15th-17th cent; Norfolk monastic terriers, rentals, etc 14th-early 16th cent.

Norfolk estate records mainly 16th-20th cent, incl leases 18th-19th cent, maps 16th-20th cent, surveys and valuations, rentals and accounts, wood accounts, building department and brickyard records 19th-20th cent, letter books 1816-1926 and papers rel to sales of property, schools on the estate, etc; estate records for other counties 16th-19th cent, incl Bucks (Hillesden, etc mainly 17th-18th cent), Kent (Kingsdown

18th cent), London (Bevis Marks, etc 17th-19th cent), Oxon (Minster Lovell, etc early 17th-early 19th cent), Somerset and Dorset (Portbury, Durweston, etc mainly 18th cent) and Suffolk (16th-18th cent); records of farms in hand 18th-20th cent.

Architectural drawings for Holkham Hall 18th-19th cent; inventories 17th-20th cent, Holkham, etc; household accounts from late 16th cent, mainly Holkham; library catalogues, catalogues of MSS, etc; meteorological journals 19th-20th cent; misc garden records 18th-20th cent; sheep-shearing accounts 1804-21 (3 vols); Holkham church and parish papers from late 16th cent; papers rel to Wells harbour, etc 19th-20th cent and to the Wells and Fakenham Railway; Norfolk county papers *temp* Sir Edward Coke, incl justices' book 1579-1607 and militia book 1602; Dungeness lighthouse accounts 18th-early 19th cent.

Family papers 16th-20th cent, incl legal papers of Sir Edward Coke early 17th cent, grand tour and other accounts of the Earl of Leicester early 18th cent, political and agricultural corresp of the 1st Earl of Leicester *c*1776-1840, and financial papers of the 2nd Earl (investments, etc) late 19th cent; game books from 1793; genealogical papers; collected MSS; misc items 15th-18th cent, incl survey of diocese of Ely 1497-8, evidence book of Sir Christopher Hatton late 16th cent, account of the Duke of Norfolk's possessions 1543, surveys of Sir Richard Southwell's Norfolk estate 1547, 1558 (2 vols), ?Long Sutton (Lincs) acre book *c*1540, and rental of the Earl of Suffolk's Wilts estate 1796.

In private possession. Enquiries to the Archivist, Estate Office, Holkham Hall, Wells-next-the-Sea, Norfolk. HMC *Ninth Report Part II, App*, 1884, pp357-75; *Various Collections IV*, 1907, pp313-25. NRA 12332.

[b] Ashill and Saham Toney (Norfolk) deeds and papers 14th-17th cent, incl deeds 16th-17th cent and manorial records 1327-1509.

Norfolk Record Office (NRS 15122-52, 21152-21356; MSS 20901-50). Deposited at various dates.

[c] Ashill and Saham Toney manorial records 1588-1916.

Norfolk Record Office. Deposited by WF Smith 1975.

[d] Billingford, Castle Acre, Tittleshall, etc manorial records 1595-early 20th cent.

Norfolk Record Office (MSS 20687-20762). Deposited by Messrs Foster, Calvert & Marriott, solicitors, Norwich 1956. NRA 9306.

[e] Flitcham deeds and papers 13th-19th cent, incl *c*570 medieval deeds, court rolls 1380-1629, maps and other estate records late 16th-early 19th cent, and a building account for New Place 1614.

Norfolk Record Office. Deposited by HM the Queen 1954, 1984. NRA 4636.

[f] Kempstone deeds and papers 14th-20th cent, incl deeds 17th-19th cent, manorial court rolls and accounts 1307-1652, and abstracts of title 19th-early 20th cent.

Norfolk Record Office. Deposited by Messrs Fraser, Woodgate & Beall, solicitors, Wisbech 1956. NRA 5687.

[g] Kempstone reeves' and bailiffs' accounts 1313-98, court book 1593/4-1728.

Norfolk Record Office (R 154 C-D). Deposited by WRB Foster 1970.

[h] Manorial records, Wells, etc 1613-early 20th cent; legal papers 1842-1903, incl draft will of 1st Earl of Leicester 1842 and corresp with 2nd Earl.

Norfolk Record Office (MSS 13949-50, 15441-50, 15498-15505, 19852-69; P 196 A-B). Deposited by Messrs Digby, Watson & Pope, solicitors, Fakenham 1953-4 and by their successors Messrs Hayes & Storr 1974. NRA 9306.

[i] Misc estate records 14th-16th cent, incl Billingford terrier mid-14th cent.

Norfolk Record Office (BRA 833/1-7 [MC 220]). Given by the executors of AW Turner through the British Records Association 1956.

[j] Holkham household accounts 1655 (1 vol).

Norfolk Record Office (box M, P 168 B).

[k] Weasenham deeds and papers 13th-20th cent, incl deeds from *c*1200, court rolls 1307-1631, bailiffs' accounts 15th-early 16th cent, and terriers and rentals from late 13th cent.

In private possession. Enquiries to the Historical Manuscripts Commission. NRA 12332(E).

[l] Holkham Hall building accounts 1757-9 (3 vols).

Public Record Office (C 107/67).

Related collection: Crutchley MSS (John Rylands University Library of Manchester, NRA 10463), including deeds and papers for Coke estates in Derbys, Lancs and Suffolk 12th-19th cent.

[24] COMPTON, Marquesses of Northampton

The Compton family was established at Compton Wynyates (Warwickshire) in the thirteenth century and purchased Castle Ashby (Northamptonshire) in 1512. The second Baron Compton, created Earl of Northampton in 1618, acquired estates in Buckinghamshire (Moulsoe), Middlesex (Canonbury), Somerset (Pitney and Wearne, Long Sutton) and elsewhere through his marriage in 1594 to Elizabeth, daughter and heiress of Sir John Spencer, Lord Mayor of London. The Buckinghamshire estate and property in Warwickshire (Whatcote) was disposed of in the nineteenth century.

Spencer Compton (d1743), second son of the third Earl, was created Earl of Wilmington in 1730, and acquired an estate in Sussex which passed at his death to his brother the fourth Earl of Northampton. This, together with the Somerset property, later descended to Lord George Augustus Henry Cavendish through his marriage in 1782 to Elizabeth, daughter of the seventh Earl (see no 17).

On the death of the fifth Earl in 1754 the barony of Compton, together with some papers, descended to his daughter, *suo jure* Baroness Ferrers, and thence to the Townshend family, Marquesses Townshend. The ninth Earl was created Marquess of Northampton in 1812.

The Torloisk (Mull, Argyllshire) and Kinross-shire estate was acquired through the marriage of the second Marquess of Northampton to Margaret Clephane in 1815, but passed to the fourth Marquess's son Lord Alwyne Compton (d1911). The fourth Marquess (1851-1913) married in 1884 Mary Florence, daughter of William Bingham Baring (1799-1864), second Baron Ashburton, and through her inherited the Ross and Cromarty, Cornwall (Callington) and Devon (Cotleigh) estates. Of these, the English estates were sold by the sixth Marquess in 1919-20.

Estates in 1883: Northampton: Northants 9,649 acres, Warwicks 4,985 acres, Bucks 3 acres, Argyllshire 8,000 acres, Kinross-shire 864 acres, total 23,501 acres worth £23,870 a year; Ashburton: Devon 2,676 acres, Cornwall 1,872 acres, Hants 190 acres, Ross-shire 28,556 acres, total 33,294 acres worth £6,002 a year.

[a] Deeds 12th-20th cent (c300 medieval), mainly Bucks, Northants and Warwicks, with some for Gloucs (Chipping Campden) 13th-15th cent, Kent (Erith) and Somerset 17th cent, etc; misc abstracts 17th-20th cent; settlements 1596-1799; wills and legal papers 16th-20th cent; manorial court records for Bucks (mainly Moulsoe) 1494-1858, Northants 16th cent-1858 and Warwicks 14th-18th cent; court rolls for Fen Stanton and Hilton (Hunts) 1510-1600 and for Hendford, Pitney and Wearne, and Long Sutton (Somerset) c1540-1669; Broad Campden (Gloucs) halimote court estreats 1481.

Northants and Warwicks estate records 14th-20th cent, incl leases 14th-19th cent, surveys, valuations, maps, plans and rentals 16th-20th cent, accounts and vouchers 14th-20th cent (Northants from 17th cent), and corresp and papers 16th-20th cent, with enclosure papers and game books from 18th cent; Bucks leases 1525-1686, surveys, valuations, maps and plans 16th-18th cent, rentals, accounts and vouchers 17th-19th cent and estate papers 16th-19th cent; estate papers for Somerset 16th cent-1710, incl surveys 1610-92 and rentals 1571, 1609-73, and for Middlesex 16th-19th cent, incl leases 16th cent-1792 and accounts 1756-96; misc Hunts rentals 1553-5, 1734-9 and accounts 1476-1508; misc estate papers 16th-18th cent, incl Chipping Campden leases 1593-1756, Hurstborne (Hants) leases 1516-1655 and accounts 1703-4, Wilmington

(Sussex) leases 1626-86 and rental 1583, and Great Dalby (Leics) accounts 1508; valuation of the estates of Lewis, Lord Mordaunt 1602 and papers rel to the Westmorland estates of the 5th Earl of Dorset 17th cent; Torloisk and Kirkness estate accounts and papers 1815-64, incl Kirkness survey and rental 1828.

Plans and papers rel to houses 17th-20th cent, incl William Talman's estimates for Castle Ashby 1695, Castle Ashby great hall plans 1771 and garden papers 1868; architectural drawings and papers of Sir Matthew Digby Wyatt and EW Godwin 1859-77 and Sir Harold Breakspear 1934 rel to Compton Wynyates; inventories 16th-20th cent, mainly Castle Ashby but incl Compton Wynyates 1522 and London (Piccadilly) 1876; misc household accounts 17th-20th cent, Castle Ashby, Compton Wynyates and London, incl wine cellar book 1796-9.

Accounts and papers rel to Northants militia, yeomanry and volunteers 1784-1815; election papers 18th-19th cent, mainly rel to Northampton; Castle Ashby charity school accounts and inventory 1712 and almshouses building accounts 1687-1725; appointments and commissions 16th-19th cent; accounts of the 2nd Earl of Northampton as Master of the King's Robes 1626-30; family, personal, political and financial corresp and papers 16th-20th cent, incl accounts of Sir Henry Compton 1563-8, Civil War and sequestration papers 1642-60, and papers of the 3rd, 4th and 8th Earls and the 2nd Marquess; literary, genealogical and other papers 16th-19th cent, incl some rel to the Mordaunt family 1560-1620.

In private possession. Enquiries to the Marquess of Northampton's Historical Manuscripts, Estate Office, Castle Ashby, Northampton NN7 1LJ. NRA 21088.

[b] Misc Warwicks leases and agreements 1750-1848, rentals 1672-82, 1715, 1750, accounts 1629-76, 1777-97 and corresp 1795-1818; misc Northants and London accounts 1629-35, incl some rel to building at Castle Ashby; rentals of the estates of the 1st Earl of Northampton 1619 and the 2nd Earl c1630-43.

Warwickshire County Record Office (CR 556/274-90). Deposited by Campbell, Brown & Ledbrook, solicitors, Warwick 1958. NRA 11903.

[c] Great Doddington (Northants) deeds, wills and settlements 1693-1845, with manorial court records 1649-75, terriers 1693, 1842 and map 1844; Ecton (Northants) manorial papers 1661-1730; misc papers 14th-18th cent, incl Wroxhill (Beds) court roll 1306-8.

Northamptonshire Record Office (GD 2-174). Deposited by the 6th Marquess of Northampton 1935. NRA 23652.

[d] Northants manorial records 1673-1762; Moulsoe manor court rolls 1731-75.

Northamptonshire Record Office (1941/4, Box 124). Deposited by Markham, Cove & Colpman, solicitors, Northampton 1941.

[e] Marriage settlement (7th Earl and Countess Cowper) 1870 and related Compton family trust papers 1870-99.

Northamptonshire Record Office (ZB 1015). Deposited by Boodle Hatfield, solicitors, London, through the British Records Association 1985.

[f] Ashburton estate corresp and papers 19th cent, incl Callington accounts and papers 1824-44, Manaton and Buckland Filleigh (Devon) accounts 1829-49, misc Melchet Park (Hants) estate papers 1842-62, maps, enclosure particulars and papers rel to Croydon and Addiscombe (Surrey) c1801, and corresp rel to Gloucs, Herefs and Somerset estates; household papers mid-19th cent, incl Addiscombe inventory 1845; corresp and papers of the 1st and 2nd Barons Ashburton, Harriet Mary, Lady Ashburton (1805-57) and Louisa, Lady Ashburton (1827-1903); misc business papers of William Adair, banker 1757-67; Bingham family papers 18th-19th cent, incl executorship and trust papers, and maps, plans, rentals and accounts rel to Maine and Pennsylvania estates c1788-1881; misc family papers.

In private possession. Enquiries to the Historical Manuscripts Commission. NRA 24219.

[g] Cornwall deeds 1591-1927, mainly Callington; Callington manor and borough court baron and leet records 1829-1917, with Callyland manor presentments 1739-1864; misc surveys, maps, particulars and valuations 1793-1918 and rentals 1791, c1800; misc estate corresp and papers 19th-20th cent, incl some rel to tin mining at Callington c1855-1916.

Cornwall Record Office (Acc 34). Deposited by the 6th Marquess of Northampton 1952, 1970. NRA 5010.

[h] Devon deeds 1675-1928 and abstracts 1792-1907; wills and settlements 1680-1906; trust accounts and papers 1860-1910; Trematon (Cornwall) court roll 1730; misc Devon leases, agreements, maps, plans, particulars (incl a few for Cornwall) and valuations 1713-1919; misc estate corresp and papers, incl accounts 1886-9 and papers 1858-93 rel to a dispute with the Plymouth, Devonport & South Western Railway Co; misc family and genealogical papers 18th-20th cent.

Devon Record Office (1860M). Deposited by the 6th and 7th Marquesses of Northampton 1969, 1982. NRA 16369.

[i] Cotleigh (Devon), etc rental and account 1844-7; Devon, etc estate corresp of the 1st Baron Ashburton 1827-31.

Devon Record Office (3720M).

[j] Manorial records for Canonbury 1720-1925 and Clerkenwell 1720-1872; Canonbury and Clerkenwell leases, rentals, accounts, maps and estate papers 18th-20th cent; London sheep skin market books 1754-72.

Greater London Record Office (E/NOR). Deposited by the 6th Marquess of Northampton 1970, 1975. NRA 34922.

[k] Literary and other papers of the 3rd Earl of Northampton 17th cent.

British Library (Add MSS 60273-85). Purchased at Christie's, 8 Mar and 5 July 1978. Formerly at Castle Ashby.

Related collections: Cavendish, Dukes of Devonshire (no 17); Marquesses Townshend (in private possession, NRA 1224), including Middlesex estate papers 17th-18th cent; Vyner of Newby (West Yorkshire Archive Service, Leeds, NRA 5836), including Torloisk estate papers; Maine (USA) estate papers c1792-1831 (Baring Bros & Co MS Collections Dep 3, 85, NRA 30566).

[25] COWPER, Earls Cowper

In the seventeenth century the Cowper family was established at Ratling (Kent), and also acquired interests in Hertfordshire, the estates in Hertingfordbury (including Cole Green and the later seat of Panshanger) and neighbouring parishes being later extended by purchase. Sir William Cowper, third Bt, was Lord Chancellor 1707-10 and 1714-18, and was created Earl Cowper in 1718. He married firstly Judith, daughter of Sir Robert Booth, who brought estates in London and Westmorland, and secondly Mary Clavering of Chopwell (County Durham). Property in Durham and the West Riding of Yorkshire (Potter Newton, etc) was eventually inherited by the second Earl on the death of his uncle John Clavering in 1762. The third Earl inherited the property of Henry Nassau d'Auverquerque, Earl of Grantham, who died in 1754.

In 1805 the fifth Earl Cowper married Emily Lamb, who, on the death of her brother the third Viscount Melbourne in 1853, inherited the Lamb family estates. Sir Matthew Lamb (1705-68) had bought Brocket (Hertfordshire) in 1746, estates in Nottinghamshire (Greasley and Selston) and Lincolnshire (Boothby Graffoe) from Sir Robert Sutton in 1753, Sysonby (Leicestershire) in 1762, and property at Bolsterstone and Langsett (Yorkshire, West Riding). The Lincolnshire and Yorkshire possessions were afterwards sold by the first Viscount Melbourne (1745-1818). Through his marriage to Charlotte, sister and heir of George Lewis Coke (d1750), Lamb had also inherited estates in Derbyshire (Melbourne and Over Haddon), Leicestershire (Baggrave, sold in 1748, and the manors of Castle Donington and Melton Mowbray) and Northamptonshire (Duston). These had been acquired by Sir John Coke (1563-1644) and subsequently enlarged by purchase. When Lady Cowper (who had married secondly the third Viscount Palmerston) died in 1869 her property passed to her grandson the seventh Earl Cowper.

The sixth Earl married in 1833 Anne Florence Robinson, daughter of the second Earl de Grey. In 1859 she succeeded her father as Baroness Lucas, and as heir to his Wrest Park and other Lucas estates (see no 28). On her death in 1880 she was in turn succeeded in these estates by her son the seventh Earl Cowper. On his death without issue in 1905 the Cowper estates passed to his niece Ethel, wife of William Grenfell of Taplow (Buckinghamshire), who was created Baron Desborough. The Lucas estates, however, passed to the seventh Earl's nephew the Hon Auberon Herbert, whilst the Lamb estates passed mostly to Lord Cowper's youngest and only surviving sister Amabel, wife of Lord Walter Kerr. (The Nottinghamshire estates did not pass to the Kerr family, but most of their records were kept at Melbourne rather than at Panshanger.) The Wrest Park estates were always administered separately from the Cowper estates, and are dealt with elsewhere (see no 28). The Lamb estates, however, are dealt with in this entry. (The Brocket estate was administered with that of Panshanger from c1881 until its sale in the 1920s.)

Estates in 1883 (Cowper and Lamb): Herts 10,122 acres, Notts 5,294 acres, Derbys 2,787 acres, Kent 2,078 acres, Northants 1,067 acres, Yorks NR and WR 696 acres, Suffolk 44 acres, total 22,088 acres worth £38,859 a year.

[a] Deeds, Herts 13th-20th cent, Yorks 13th-18th cent, London and Middlesex 16th-19th cent and Co Durham 16th-18th cent, with some for Derbys, Suffolk, etc 16th-17th cent; abstracts of title 16th-19th cent; wills, settlements, executorship and trust papers 16th-20th cent, Cowper, Clavering and Hardwick families, incl executorship papers of the 1st Earl for the Marchioness de Gouvernet (d c1722) and the 2nd Earl for the Earl of Grantham 1754-6; testamentary papers of Peniston Lamb (d1805); will of Pascoe Grenfell 1802 and executorship papers of Lord and Lady Desborough c1944-70; legal and financial papers 16th-20th cent, Cowper and Clavering families; Herts (Hertingfordbury, Tewin, etc) manorial records 14th-20th cent.

Herts estate records 16th-20th cent, incl leases 18th-20th cent, maps, terriers, particulars and valuations 17th-20th cent, surveys, rentals and accounts, vouchers and estate corresp and papers 16th-20th cent, survey of Herts timber 1719 and wood books 1775-99, tithe papers 18th cent, enclosure papers 1801-13 and game books 1899-1953; Kent estate papers 18th-mid-19th cent, incl rentals 1723-1821 and wood accounts late 18th cent; Yorks WR (Potter Newton) estate records 16th-19th cent, incl leases, surveys, maps, rentals and accounts, and papers rel to enclosure and sales of Leeds building land early 19th cent; Westmorland estate papers 17th-mid-18th cent, incl valuations and rentals 1723-39 and map 1740; Co Durham estate papers 16th cent-1829, incl accounts 1702-13, rentals and vouchers 1789-97 and lead and coal mining papers 16th-18th cent; London and

Middlesex estate papers 17th-20th cent, incl Cornhill plans 1748, 1787 and 1801, rentals and agency papers c1720-1801 and accounts c1851-80; Lamb (Herts, etc) estate papers 18th-20th cent, incl Brocket estate maps and valuations from 1752, Brocket rentals and accounts 1881-1905, rental of Sir Matthew Lamb's estates 1767 and Notts and Lincs accounts 1758.

Building records, Cole Green (Herts) 1704 and Panshanger (Herts) c1806-21, 1855; Cole Green household plans c1732-47; red books by Humphry Repton for Tewin Water (Herts) 1798 and Panshanger 1800 (2 vols); misc household inventories 18th-19th cent, incl Cole Green furniture 1799 and Panshanger plate 1837-56; accounts, vouchers and papers 18th-19th cent, mainly for Cole Green and Panshanger house and garden and the London household; Italian household records of the 3rd Earl Cowper 1757-89; household receipts of the 1st Viscount Melbourne 1825-6; papers rel to Herts lieutenancy, militia, elections and county affairs late 17th-20th cent, incl Hertford poll book 1727 and election expenses 1759, plans by James Adam for a new shire hall 1767-8 and Welwyn Rifle Butts accounts 1879-85; accounts and papers rel to Hertingfordbury, Tewin and other Herts schools 19th-early 20th cent; Canterbury (Kent) election accounts (6th Earl Cowper) 1830 and misc Marlow (Bucks) election papers (John Clavering) 1727-31; St Agatha's, Shoreditch, charity accounts early 20th cent.

Cowper family papers 17th-20th cent, incl appointments and commissions, official, legal, political, personal and family papers of the 1st Earl, diaries and papers of his wife, grand tour and Italian papers of the 3rd Earl, papers of the 6th Earl and his wife, corresp and papers of the Hon Edward Spencer Cowper (1779-1823), letters of Spencer Cowper (1713-74), Dean of Durham, and papers of John Clavering of Chopwell (d1762); Lamb family papers 18th-19th cent, incl accounts of Sir Matthew Lamb 1746-68, papers of the 2nd and 3rd Viscounts Melbourne and Lady Caroline Lamb, and letters of George Lamb (1784-1834); Grenfell family papers 19th-20th cent, incl extensive corresp of Lady Desborough (d1952), and papers of Julian Fane (1827-70) and Julian Grenfell (1888-1915); literary, genealogical and misc papers 17th-20th cent, incl letters of the poet William Cowper (1731-1800) and letters and poems of Abraham Cowley (1618-67); Nassau d'Auverquerque papers late 17th-mid-18th cent, incl Netherlands estate papers 1682-1725, Dutch and English household accounts c1689-1753, papers of Count Henry of Nassau (1640-1708) as Master of the Horse to William III, military and official papers of Count William Maurice of Nassau (1679-1753, governor of Sluys and Dutch Flanders), corresp of the Earl of Grantham (d1754), and trusteeship papers for the 3rd Earl of Bath (d1711), with rentals and accounts for his Devon and Cornwall estates 1701-8.

Hertfordshire Record Office (D/EP, D/ELb, E/ERv, D/ENa, D/EFa, D/EX789). Deposited 1952-88

by Monica, Lady Salmond, Mr and Mrs Julian Salmond and Rosemary, Lady Ravensdale, and purchased 1994. NRA 19662, 26283, 26768. The collection includes deeds received in 1954 from the London solicitors Trower, Still & Keeling and manorial records received in 1947 and 1954 from Longmores, solicitors, Hertford. The marriage settlement of George Vernon of Farnham (Surrey) 1676 was transferred to Surrey Record Office 1954.

[b] Brocket (Herts) estate rental 1747-69 and accounts 1772-1835.

Hertfordshire Record Office (Acc 27). Deposited by the County Land Agent 1941. NRA 507.

[c] Kent deeds 15th-19th cent; Cowper settlements 1760-1805, with probate of the 3rd Earl 1790; misc Ratling manorial records 1604-1767; Kent legal and estate papers 16th-19th cent (mainly 19th cent), incl particulars, valuations, maps and accounts; Kent militia and lieutenancy papers 1843-71; appointment of John Finch as Chief Justice 1635.

Centre for Kentish Studies (U 499). Deposited by Monica, Lady Salmond through Hertfordshire Record Office 1954-63. NRA 5470.

[d] Deeds, Leics 12th-18th cent and Derbys 13th-20th cent; misc deeds for Herts, Lincs, London, Middlesex, Yorks, etc 16th-19th cent; abstracts 17th-19th cent; wills, settlements and related papers 16th-20th cent, Coke and Lamb families, incl executors' accounts, Sir Matthew Lamb 1768; legal papers 16th-20th cent, incl Irish estate case papers 1674 and papers rel to Lady Caroline Lamb's separation from Viscount Melbourne 1825; manorial court records for Leics (Castle Donington, Melton Mowbray) 14th-20th cent, Derbys (Barrow-upon-Trent) 17th-18th cent, Hanley Castle (Worcs) 1478 and Ugley (Essex) 1503-1714.

Derbys estate records 15th-20th cent, incl leases and agreements, surveys and maps, particulars and valuations, rentals and accounts, tithe papers from 17th cent, Melbourne mill book 1708-11 and misc timber records c1733-1879; Leics estate records 17th-19th cent, incl leases, maps from 18th cent, rentals, accounts and papers; misc estate records for Herts (incl accounts 1747-53), Lincs (Boothby Graffoe) c1713-69, Yorks WR (Bolsterstone and Langsett) c1754-1802 and Co Wicklow (Coke family) c1666-74; Ugley (Essex) and Thorley (Herts) rentals and accounts (Leventhorpe family) 1645-74; estate papers, Viscounts Fanshawe (Herts timber accounts) 1608-87, Millbanke family (Halnaby, Yorks NR) 1821-43 and Parsloes (Essex) estate ?17th-18th cent.

Papers rel to Melbourne Hall (Derbys) 17th-20th cent, incl building records 1678-1728, architectural drawings by EH Godwin (1833-86), inventories and tenancy papers 18th-20th cent, and household accounts c1633-1753; drawings by James Paine for Wilsford House (Lincs) 1749-51; plans and papers for the Earl of

Berkeley's house at Cranford (Middlesex) c1700 and Monteviot (Roxburghshire) 20th cent; household accounts, Brocket 1826-9 and Leventhorpe family 1661-81; records and papers rel to Melbourne parish and local affairs 16th-20th cent, incl churchwardens' and overseers' records from 1541; Lamb family papers 18th-19th cent, incl political and financial papers of Sir Matthew Lamb (1705-68), election papers 18th-early 19th cent, misc corresp and papers of the 2nd and 3rd Viscounts Melbourne, and diaries and papers of George Lamb (1784-1834); misc Kerr family papers late 19th-20th cent; financial papers of Sir Thomas Leventhorpe 1669-81; genealogical and misc papers 17th-20th cent.

In private possession. The papers are the property of Lord Ralph Kerr at Melbourne Hall, Derbyshire, to whom application should be made for permission to see them. NRA 30228. Included are eighteen boxes of deeds and legal papers 17th-20th cent transferred from the London solicitors Stephenson Harwood 1989.

[e] Northants deeds and leases 15th-20th cent; Duston estate papers 16th-20th cent, incl tenancy papers, maps and plans from 18th cent, terrier 16th cent, particulars and valuations 1857, 1911-12, rentals and accounts from 17th cent, letter books 1893-1913, papers rel to Duston drainage and the Nene navigation 1852-93, and ironstone accounts and papers c1854-1909.

Northamptonshire Record Office. Deposited from Melbourne Hall by Lord Ralph Kerr 1993. NRA 30228.

[f] Notts (Greasley, Selston, etc) deeds 14th-20th cent; Beauvale manor survey 1653; Notts estate records 15th-20th cent, incl leases and agreements, surveys, maps, rentals and accounts; Notts colliery papers 16th-20th cent, tithe papers from 17th cent, enclosure and drainage papers 1850-80 and Greasley church building papers 1759-61; Notts (Annesley, Felley and Selston) parochial accounts and papers c1787-1863; architectural drawings and papers for Beauvale House (Notts) (by EH Godwin) 1864-76.

Nottinghamshire Archives (DD LM). Deposited from Melbourne Hall by Lord Ralph Kerr 1994. NRA 30228.

[g] Kimberley (Notts) deeds 1817-1906 (20 items); abstract of title 1817-71.

Nottinghamshire Archives (DD 46). Deposited through Hertfordshire Record Office by Monica, Lady Salmond 1954, 1957. NRA 6881.

[h] Misc Notts estate agent's papers 1888-1912, incl papers rel to Underwood church 1888-94.

Nottinghamshire Archives (DD 1198, PR 22092-5). Deposited by Ms B Gill 1977. NRA 6885.

[i] Coke family wills, settlements and related trust and legal papers 1647-1755, incl Fanshawe

(of Parsloes) trust papers 1700-17 and executorship papers for the 6th Earl of Thanet (d1729); household accounts and papers (not Melbourne) 17th cent-1748; Cranford (Middlesex) garden papers c1720-3; papers rel to Derbys and Leics local affairs 17th-18th cent, incl election papers for Derbys 1679 and Leics 1698-1703; Coke family papers 16th-18th cent, incl appointments and commissions, and official and political papers of Sir John Coke (1563-1644, Secretary of State) and Thomas Coke (1674-1727); records of Colonel John Coke's troop 1688-90; household accounts and letters of Sir Fulke Greville (1554-1628).

British Library, Manuscript Collections (Add MSS 64870-92, 69868-69935). Purchased from the 12th Marquess of Lothian 1987, 1989. HMC *Twelfth Report, App I-III*, 1888-9. NRA 30228.

[j] Patent of Sir Henry Guildford of Taplow Court 1614; diaries and papers of Lord Desborough.

Buckinghamshire Record Office (AR 7/70; D/X 962). Deposited by Monica, Lady Salmond 1970 (except for the patent which was transferred from Hertfordshire Record Office 1987) and purchased from the executors of Lady Ravensdale 1993. NRA 23171.

[k] Corresp and papers of the 2nd Viscount Melbourne.

Royal Archives, Windsor Castle. Access restricted. Presented to HM the Queen by Monica, Lady Salmond 1954. HMC *Papers of British Cabinet Ministers 1782-1900*, 1982, p36.

[l] Diplomatic and personal corresp and papers of the 3rd Viscount Melbourne.

British Library, Manuscript Collections (Add MSS 60399-60483). Presented by HM the Queen 1978, to whom they had been given by Monica, Lady Salmond 1954. HMC *Private Papers of British Diplomats 1782-1900*, 1985, p37. NRA 23026.

Related collections: De Grey, Barons Lucas (no 28); Grenfell of Taplow Court (Buckinghamshire Record Office D/GR, NRA 2317; Berkshire Record Office D/EG, NRA 4230; University College of Swansea Library, NRA 26521).

[26] CREWE-MILNES, Marquess of Crewe

Sir Ranulph Crewe (1558-1646), Lord Chief Justice 1625-6, purchased the ancestral Crewe estates in Cheshire from the heirs of Sir Christopher Hatton and built Crewe Hall 1615-36. Through his marriage in 1598 to a co-heir of John Clippesby he acquired property in Norfolk, later sold by his grandson John Crewe. On the death of the latter in 1684 the estates passed to his daughter Anne, wife of John Offley of Madeley (Staffordshire), whose eldest son succeeded to the Crewe and Madeley estates and assumed the name of Crewe. The latter's great-grandson, the second Baron Crewe, married in 1807 Henrietta Walker-Hungerford, of

Calne (Wiltshire). The third Baron died without issue in 1893 and the family estates passed to his nephew Robert Milnes, second Baron Houghton, only son of Richard Monckton Milnes, first Baron Houghton (d1885) by Annabella Crewe. The second Baron Houghton took the name of Crewe-Milnes and was created Earl of Crewe in 1895 and Marquess of Crewe in 1911.

Richard Slater Milnes (1759-1804), of Fryston (Yorkshire, West Riding), descended from a Derbyshire family, acquired property at Great Houghton (Yorkshire, West Riding) through his wife. Their son Robert Pemberton Milnes (1784-1858) married in 1808 Henrietta Monckton, daughter of the fourth Viscount Galway and granddaughter of Pemberton Milnes of Bawtry (Yorkshire, West Riding). It was Richard Monckton Milnes (1809-85), son of RP and the Hon Henrietta Milnes, who was created Baron Houghton in 1863.

Estates in 1883: Crewe: Cheshire 10,148 acres, Staffs 5,479 acres, Wilts 907 acres, total 16,534 acres worth £29,016 a year; Houghton: Yorks WR 5,429 acres, Lincs 1,357 acres, Notts 780 acres, Derbys 30 acres, Staffs 3 acres, total 7,599 acres worth £11,787 a year.

[a] Deeds 13th-20th cent (c425 medieval), mainly Cheshire and Staffs but incl Norfolk, Salop, Warwicks and other counties; wills, settlements and related trust and executorship papers 17th-20th cent, Crewe, Offley and Hungerford families; legal and case papers mainly 16th-19th cent, incl Cholmondeley *v* Crewe; manorial records 14th-19th cent, mainly Cheshire and Staffs (Sandbach, Madeley, etc) but incl Radbourne (Warwicks) 14th-17th cent and Timberland (Lincs) 1712-1825.

Crewe (Cheshire) and Madeley (Staffs) estate records 15th-20th cent, incl leases 16th-19th cent (numerous), surveys from 17th cent, maps and plans 19th cent, rentals and accounts from 16th cent, corresp from 17th cent, letter books 19th-20th cent, and papers rel to tithes, enclosure, roads, canals, railways, schools and churches, almshouses, etc; papers rel to Madeley collieries 18th-early 20th cent; Norfolk rental 1642 and account 1638; Leics rental 1689-94; Crewe Hall inventory 1688 and papers 19th cent; Madeley Manor inventory 1851; papers rel to Sandbach and to borough of Nantwich 16th-19th cent; misc Crewe family papers 17th-20th cent; misc papers 15th-18th cent, incl rental of Eastgate, Chester 1426, manorial accounts for Stafford family estates 1531-2, will and inventory of Sir Edward Coke 1634-5 and lease book of Wilbraham Tollemache 1770-8.

Cheshire Record Office (DCR). Deposited 1970 and subsequently by the Marchioness of Crewe, Mary, Duchess of Roxburghe, and the trustees of the O'Neill and Crewe settled estates. NRA 1299.

[b] Misc Madeley estate papers and plans late 19th cent.

William Salt Library, Stafford (WSL 14/45) (BRA 485). Presented by GF Brown & Co, solicitors, Feltham, through the British Records Association 1945. NRA 7959.

[c] Wilts deeds 13th-18th cent; trust and legal papers, Hungerford family 17th-19th cent; misc Wilts estate records, incl leases 16th-19th cent.

Wiltshire Record Office. Transferred from Cheshire Record Office. NRA 1299.

[d] Architectural drawings rel to the interior of Crewe Hall (1 vol); papers rel to Cheshire 16th-17th cent.

Untraced. Sold at Sotheby's, 22 Oct 1956, lots 55, 95. Formerly in the library at Crewe Hall.

[e] Deeds 14th-20th cent, mainly Yorks WR (incl Bawtry and Great Houghton) and Notts but also Derbys and Lincs; wills, settlements, executorship papers, etc 16th-19th cent; manorial records, Derbys and Yorks 17th-20th cent, incl Austerfield manor court books 1724-1939; estate papers 16th-20th cent, mainly Yorks (Fryston estate) but also Lincs (Timberland estate), incl rentals 17th-20th cent, canal and railway papers 1825-47, and embankment and drainage papers 1784-92; inventory of Bawtry Hall 1838; shrievalty papers, Yorks 1650-1, Derbys 1695-6; misc family papers 17th-19th cent, incl corresp and papers of the 1st Baron Houghton 1837-85.

Sheffield Archives (CM). Deposited by the Marchioness of Crewe 1951, with later deposits 1956-7, 1965. *Guide to the Manuscript Collections in the Sheffield City Libraries,* 1956, *Supplements I and II,* 1968; *Sheffield City Libraries Report 1956-57.* NRA 1082 (partial list); NRA 1299 (for papers transferred from Cheshire Record Office).

[f] Misc legal, estate, household and family papers late 16th-mid-20th cent, incl misc deeds 16th-18th cent (Yorks, etc), Tattenhall (Cheshire) court roll 1594-1601, misc Crewe estate papers 19th cent, Yorks estate maps and plans 19th cent, Crewe Hall inventory 1619, papers rel to Crewe Hall fire and rebuilding 1866-71, London household accounts 1872-1948, Crewe family patents and appointments 1604-1913, papers of Sir Ranulph Crewe 1585-1648, other Crewe and Cunliffe-Offley family papers 17th-19th cent, and papers of the 1st Baron Houghton.

In private possession. Enquiries to the Historical Manuscripts Commission.

[g] Papers of the 1st Baron Houghton, with some of his father RP Milnes, 1806-85.

Trinity College, Cambridge. HMC *Papers of British Politicians 1782-1900,* 1989, p70.

[h] Papers of the Marquess of Crewe.

Cambridge University Library. Deposited by the Marchioness of Crewe 1958. HMC *Papers of British Politicians 1782-1900,* 1989, p24.

Related collection: Viscounts Galway (Nottingham University Library, Manuscripts Department Ga,

NRA 6741), including Milnes and Monckton-Milnes family correspondence 19th cent.

[27] **CUST, Earls Brownlow**

The Cust family was settled at Pinchbeck (Lincolnshire) in the fifteenth century, and acquired further Lincolnshire property by marriage and purchase. Sir Richard Cust, second Bt (1680-1734), married in 1717 Anne Brownlow, sister of Sir John Brownlow, fifth Bt, created Viscount Tyrconnel in 1718. Through this marriage the Cust family inherited part of the estates of Sir John Brownlow, third Bt (d1697), of Belton (Lincolnshire). Sir Brownlow Cust, fifth Bt (1744-1807), was created Baron Brownlow in 1776 in recognition of his father's services as Speaker of the House of Commons, and his first marriage, to Jocosa Drury, brought the Arthingworth (Northamptonshire) estate into the family. The Marnham (Nottinghamshire) property had been a late seventeenth-century Brownlow purchase. A borough interest at Clitheroe (Lancashire), purchased in 1802, was sold following the 1832 Reform Act.

John Cust (1779-1853), second Baron and (1815) first Earl Brownlow, married in 1810 Sophia, daughter and co-heir of Sir Abraham Hume. This marriage brought not only Hume property in Lincolnshire (Torksey and South Kyme) but eventually, under the will of her uncle the seventh Earl of Bridgewater, a considerable portion of the Egerton inheritance, comprising the Ellesmere estate in Shropshire, the Ashridge estate in Buckinghamshire, Hertfordshire and Bedfordshire, and properties in County Durham and the North Riding of Yorkshire (see also no 33).

On the death of the first Earl Brownlow the Cust estates were divided, part of the Lincolnshire estates, together with the Northamptonshire and Nottinghamshire properties, passing to his younger son. On the death of the third Earl in 1921 his estates passed to a cousin, Adelbert Salusbury Cust, formerly of Cockayne Hatley, a Bedfordshire estate inherited in the mid-eighteenth century and subsequently used to provide for younger sons.

Estates in 1883: Brownlow: Salop 20,233 acres, Lincs 11,652 acres, Bucks 11,785 acres, Herts 8,551 acres, Beds 2,968 acres, Yorks NR 1,689 acres, Co Durham 920 acres, Berwickshire 536 acres, Flintshire 1 acre, total 58,335 acres worth £86,426 a year; (ERC Cust: Lincs 14,868 acres, Notts 1,993 acres, Northants 226 acres, Lancs 33 acres, Rutland 2 acres, total 17,122 acres worth £25,696 a year;) HFC Cust (of Cockayne Hatley): Beds 1,410 acres worth £1,564 a year.

[a] Deeds, mainly Lincs 16th-19th cent, Cust, Brownlow and Hume, but incl some medieval deeds for Lincs and Salop, and deeds mainly 16th-19th cent for Beds (Cockayne Hatley, etc), Hunts, Lancs, Northants, Notts, etc; wills, marriage settlements and trust and executorship papers, Cust family 16th-19th cent, Brownlow

17th-18th cent; executorship papers, Duke of Ancaster 1747 and Earl of Egmont; legal papers, abstracts, schedules, etc 16th-20th cent; case papers 17th-19th cent, incl Stanground and Farcet (Hunts) tithes late 18th cent, with related documents from 14th cent, and Egerton *v* Brownlow 1853; Lincs manorial records (Gosberton, etc) 14th-17th cent; honour of Berkhamsted, Northants rental 1558-75; Clitheroe borough court papers 17th-18th cent.

Lincs estate records 16th-20th cent, incl leases, agreements, surveys and maps from 17th cent, rentals and accounts mainly from 17th cent, corresp 18th-19th cent, papers rel to fen drainage and enclosure, and Belton farm records 18th-20th cent; papers rel to Drury estates in Cambs and Hunts, etc 18th cent, Hume estates in Herts, Essex and Sussex 18th-19th cent, Clitheroe (Lancs) estate 18th cent, and Ashridge and Berkhamsted (Bucks and Herts) estate early 20th cent; Cockayne Hatley (Beds) legal and estate papers 15th-19th cent; London rental 1681-5, with account of ground rents (Brownlow Buildings, Middlesex) 1722; London (Brooke's Wharf) deeds and papers from 15th cent; Stanground valuation and other papers 16th-18th cent; Salop estate estreat rolls 1598-9, rental 1651-2, plans 19th cent and papers rel to sales 19th-20th cent; Belton House building accounts 1684-8, with corresp and papers rel to alterations late 18th-early 19th cent; inventories late 17th-early 19th cent, Belton House, etc, incl library catalogues *c*1750, 1794 and inventory of pictures 1830; household accounts and vouchers 17th-19th cent, mainly Belton, incl cellar, house and stable books 18th cent; garden accounts *c*1765-82.

Papers rel to Grantham elections, corporation, school, canal, turnpikes, etc 18th-19th cent; other local papers, Lincs, etc, incl Kirton-in-Holland joyce and acre books 1639 (2), Skirbeck wapentake muster book 1650, Marnham (Notts) enclosure agreement 1675 and Lincs militia order book 1760-1; Belton parish records 19th-20th cent; patents, appointments and commissions from 16th cent; Brownlow and Cust family corresp and papers 17th-20th cent, incl account book of Richard Brownlow, prothonotary, 1617, corresp and papers of Sir John Cust (1718-70), Speaker of the House of Commons, corresp and papers of the 1st Earl Brownlow as lord lieutenant of Lincs 1809-52, First World War papers of Harry Cust, corresp of George V with Sir Charles Cust and papers of the 6th Baron Brownlow rel to the abdication of Edward VIII 1936; Savile and Cust of Cockayne Hatley corresp and papers 17th-19th cent; misc Egerton family corresp and papers *c*1590-early 19th cent, incl letters to Lord Keeper Ellesmere and literary notes of the 8th Earl of Bridgewater; misc papers, incl account roll for obsequies of Charles IX in St Paul's Cathedral 1574, pedigree of the Earls of Derby *c*1600, official letter book of the Earl of Southampton rel to Crown lands 1662, and diary of the 5th Baron Berkeley of Stratton 1756-67 (Egerton family copy); printed material from 17th cent, incl Civil War pamphlets.

Lincolnshire Archives (BNL). Deposited 1957-72 and purchased from the 7th Baron Brownlow 1992. NRA 6799, 7193. See also *Records of the Cust Family*, 3 vols, 1898-1927; Lincolnshire Archives Committee, *Archivists' Report* 12 (1960-1), pp63-6.

[b] Architectural drawings, Belton House, etc 19th cent, incl designs by Wyatville and Salvin.

In private possession. Enquiries to the House Manager, Belton House, Grantham, Lincolnshire NG32 2LS.

[c] Deeds 13th-19th cent, mainly Herts; Egerton settlements, executorship papers and related legal papers late 16th-mid-19th cent, incl schedule of purchases 1580-94, 2nd Earl of Uxbridge decd 1769-74, Archdeacon Egerton decd late 18th cent (chancellorship of Hereford Cathedral, etc), 7th Earl of Bridgewater decd 1829-35 and Berkhamsted Common case 1860s (with copies of earlier documents); manorial records, mainly Herts 14th-early 19th cent but incl Dagnall and Studham (Beds, Bucks) 16th cent, Wrexham (Denbighshire) 1504-5 and Bromfield (Salop) 1626-7; honour of Berkhamsted steward's papers, etc 17th-18th cent; misc Ashridge estate papers 16th-19th cent, incl leases, survey 1574, maps 18th-19th cent, rentals and accounts 18th-19th cent and corresp 17th cent; estate papers rel to Salop late 16th-18th cent, Yorks and Co Durham 1748, Chertsey (Surrey) mainly 1724-95 and Worsley (Lancs) 18th-19th cent; valuation of Bridgewater estates 1626-7; papers rel to Little Gaddesden (Herts) church 17th cent and enclosure early 19th cent.

Papers rel to Ashridge building and furnishing 1604-8; licences to empark 17th cent; papers rel to repairs and alterations to Bridgewater House (London) 1796-9; Egerton family papers late 16th-mid-19th cent, incl a few official papers of Lord Ellesmere 1593-1613, papers of Henry Egerton, Bishop of Hereford, and John Egerton, Bishop of Durham 18th cent, and misc business and financial papers of the 3rd Duke and 7th Earl of Bridgewater; misc papers, incl receivers' account for the Countess of Suffolk's estates 1561-2 and rental of St John's chapel, Berkhamsted 1535.

Hertfordshire Record Office (AH). Presented by the 6th Baron Brownlow and otherwise acquired by gift or purchase 1928-60. NRA 9422 (partial list).

[d] Diaries of William Buckingham, Ashridge steward 1813-14, 1820-7 (3 vols).

Hertfordshire Record Office (D/EX 230). Deposited by GG Buckingham 1968. NRA 18327.

[e] Wormley (Herts) estate deeds 16th-19th cent, with related Hume family settlements, legal and financial papers, manorial papers and estate papers 18th-early 19th cent; deeds and related papers for Hume estates in Norfolk, Lincs and London 17th-19th cent.

Hertfordshire Record Office (D/EWb). Deposited by the 6th Baron Brownlow 1964 (formerly Belton House muniments box 33). NRA 10011.

[f] Deeds 17th-20th cent and manorial records 16th-20th cent for Ashridge estates in Herts, Bucks and Beds; manorial records for Halse (Northants) 18th-20th cent and Sibford Gower (Oxon) 18th-19th cent; legal and case papers rel to the Ashridge estate 19th-20th cent, incl legal agents' letter books 1849-97, Berkhamsted Common papers and sale particulars 1923; estate labour book 1850-2.

Hertfordshire Record Office (D/ELS). Deposited by Lovel Smeathman & Co, solicitors, Hemel Hempstead 1960, 1963. NRA 18363.

[g] Bucks deeds *c*13th-19th cent (mainly from 16th cent), legal papers 16th-17th cent and manorial records (Pitstone, Ivinghoe) 15th-18th cent; Bucks estate papers mainly 16th-19th cent, incl surveys and valuations, rentals and accounts 16th-18th cent, papers rel to Pitstone common wood *c*1380 and 16th-early 17th cent, enclosure papers 17th-19th cent, and corresp and plans rel to coprolite workings 1871; misc Ashridge estate (Bucks, Herts, etc) rentals and accounts 16th-18th cent, incl rentals 1687, 1704-24 and accounts 1760-2; Ivinghoe and Edlesborough (Bucks) parochial papers 17th-19th cent.

Buckinghamshire Record Office (AR 24/87, 51/88, 60/88, 16/89, etc). Mainly deposited by the 6th Baron Brownlow with Buckinghamshire Archaeological Society 1928 and subsequently transferred to the record office.

[h] Misc Ivinghoe and Pitstone accounts and papers 17th cent.

Buckinghamshire Record Office. Provenance unrecorded.

[i] Bucks deeds and related papers 16th-early 20th cent, with a few for Beds, Herts, etc 17th-19th cent.

Buckinghamshire Record Office (D 12). Rescued from 'a bombed lawyer's office' and presented to Buckinghamshire Archaeological Society by Mrs Antonia Nightingale 1955. Subsequently transferred to the record office. NRA 16238.

[j] Deeds 15th-19th cent, nearly all Beds (Ashridge and Cockayne Hatley estates); Cockayne and Cust settlements, wills, etc 16th-18th cent; will of Henry, Duke of Kent 1736 and related papers; misc manorial records, Beds and Bucks (Cockayne Hatley, etc) 15th-19th cent; misc Beds estate papers 18th-19th cent, mainly Ashridge estate parishes, incl surveys and maps; ecclesiastical and parochial papers 17th-19th cent; misc Cockayne and Cust family papers 17th-19th cent, incl Beds poll tax papers 1681 and personal accounts 18th cent.

Bedfordshire Record Office (BW). Deposited from Ashridge and Little Gaddesden Reading Room 1928-31 and by the 6th Baron Brownlow or his agents 1951-60. NRA 30112.

[k] Halse manorial records 1718-94; Wollaston (Northants) estreats of fines 1629-50.

Northamptonshire Record Office. Deposited by the 6th Baron Brownlow 1953-4.

[l] Salop deeds from *c*1200, mainly 16th-19th cent; wills, settlements and related papers 16th-19th cent; legal and case papers 16th-early 20th cent; Salop manorial records 14th-early 20th cent, Ellesmere, Whitchurch, etc, incl court rolls, rentals and accounts (many medieval); Salop estate records 16th-20th cent, incl leases 16th-19th cent, surveys and valuations 16th-early 20th cent, maps from *c*1600, rentals and accounts 18th-20th cent, corresp and letter books 19th-20th cent, and papers rel to tenancies 18th-20th cent, purchases and sales 18th-20th cent, timber 16th-18th cent, and enclosure and tithes 17th-19th cent; papers rel to churches, schools and charities 16th-20th cent, the Shropshire Union Canal 18th-20th cent and railways 19th-20th cent; misc papers, incl papers of the 1st Earl of Bridgewater rel to the Marches 1630-40 and register of deeds, Salop commission of the peace 1610.

Shropshire Records and Research Unit, Shropshire Record Office (Records of the Bridgewater estates, SRO 212, 611, etc). Deposited by the 6th Baron Brownlow and others from 1948. NRA 37869. The majority of the medieval deeds, including Buildwas and Haughmond Abbey charters (see *Trans Shropshire Arch Soc*, 4th series xi, 1927-8, pp78-81) are reported to have been accidentally destroyed at Ashridge in 1953.

[m] Ellesmere deeds 1789-1880 (1 bundle); Ellesmere estate records 19th-20th cent, incl agreements and related papers 1861-1939, maps and plans 1840-1966, rentals and accounts 1802, 1899-1949, memoranda, registers, and papers rel to repairs; sale particulars 1972; Ellesmere National Schools accounts 1900-3 (1 vol).

Shropshire Records and Research Unit, Shropshire Record Office (SRO 5872). Deposited 1993. NRA 36453.

[n] Misc papers of the Egerton family, Earls of Bridgewater 16th-19th cent, incl Co Durham and Yorks NR deeds and abstracts 17th-19th cent, rentals 1796-1800, accounts 1803-87, vouchers 1770-99, and Chertsey rent accounts 1732-9; settlements 1691-1765 (3), rental 1692 and other papers 17th-18th cent of the Lowther family, baronets, of Swillington (Yorks WR).

North Yorkshire County Record Office (ZCN). Deposited by the executors of ER Hanby Holmes, Barnard Castle 1983. NRA 37278.

[o] Deeds rel to burgage tenements in Clitheroe 16th-early 19th cent, with associated legal papers; Clitheroe estate papers 1802-36; papers rel to Clitheroe borough 17th cent and elections 1674-1830.

Lancashire Record Office (DDFr). Deposited by Messrs Francis & Co, solicitors, Cambridge, through Cambridgeshire Record Office 1966. NRA 14652.

[p] Corresp of the 8th Earl of Bridgewater 1782-1807, mainly with French and Italian correspondents.

British Library, Manuscript Collections (Eg MSS 60-4, 3043). Acquired 1929 and earlier. For indexes to the Bridgewater MSS bequeathed to the British Museum by the 8th Earl see Eg MSS 3060-85 (acquired 1933).

Related collection: Egerton, Earls of Ellesmere (no 33).

[28] DE GREY, Barons Lucas

Sir Roger de Grey of Ruthin (Denbighshire) had lands in Bedfordshire and other counties in the early fourteenth century, and property in Northamptonshire and Norfolk was acquired later by marriage. Burbage (Leicestershire) was inherited by Reginald, third Lord Grey of Ruthin, as heir general of John Hastings, Earl of Pembroke (d1389). On the death of Henry Grey, eighth Earl of Kent, in 1639 the barony of Grey of Ruthin devolved on a nephew but the earldom of Kent passed to a cousin. The eleventh Earl married in 1663 Mary, daughter of the first Baron Lucas, of Shenfield and Colchester (Essex). She was created Baroness Lucas of Crudwell (Wiltshire), another Lucas family property, the same year.

When Henry, Duke of Kent died in 1740 he was succeeded in turn by his daughter the Countess of Hardwicke and by her daughter Amabel, Lady Polwarth, created Countess De Grey in 1816. Lady De Grey died in 1833, being succeeded by her nephew Thomas Robinson (later De Grey) as second Earl De Grey and fifth Baron Lucas. He died in 1859, leaving two daughters, Anne, Baroness Lucas, who married the sixth Earl Cowper (see no 25), and Mary, who married Henry Vyner. Part of the Robinson estates in Yorkshire descended to Lady Mary Vyner (Newby, etc) and her cousin the second Earl of Ripon (Studley Royal, etc); but the Wrest Park and other Lucas estates, together with Robinson property in the North and West Ridings of Yorkshire (the Clifton and Craven estates), passed to Lady Cowper. On her death in 1880 the Lucas estates were inherited by her son the seventh Earl Cowper, and on his death in 1905 by his nephew the Hon Auberon Herbert, who also succeeded to the barony of Lucas. He died in 1916, and Wrest Park was sold the following year. The Craven estates passed in 1880 to the Hon HF Cowper, Lady Cowper's younger son, who died without issue in 1887. Both the Clifton and Craven estates continued to be held in trust for Lady Cowper's descendants until their sales following the First World War.

Estates in 1883: Earl Cowper: Beds 9,105 acres, Essex 3,227 acres, Wilts 2,536 acres, Leics 913 acres, total 15,781 acres worth £21,533 a year; Hon HF Cowper: Yorks WR 5,720 acres worth £6,333 a year.

[a] Deeds for Beds 12th-20th cent (over 350 medieval), Essex 16th-19th cent, Leics 15th-20th cent and Wilts 18th-20th cent, with deeds for Yorks (Robinson estates) 17th-20th cent and for Middlesex (St James's Square) and other counties 13th-20th cent; wills 17th-19th cent, Grey, Yorke, Hume-Campbell, Robinson and Cowper;

settlements and related papers late 15th-20th cent, incl Weddell and Robinson 17th-19th cent; legal and case papers from late 15th cent, incl papers rel to sales 19th-20th cent; Vallance feodary ?14th cent; manorial court records 14th-19th cent, incl Beds 14th-18th cent, Essex 14th-19th cent, Leics 15th-18th cent, Wilts 16th-18th cent and Yorks WR 19th cent; court rolls, honour of Leicester 1439-40 and honour of Ampthill (Beds) 1587-8.

Leases, surveys, maps, rentals, accounts and other records of the Beds estate 14th-20th cent, incl estate survey *c*1719 and papers rel to enclosure, tithes, poor law and parish affairs, churches and schools; Essex estate records 17th-20th cent, incl leases, surveys, maps, rentals and enclosure papers; Leics estate papers 16th-20th cent, incl leases, survey and rental late 17th cent and enclosure papers; Wilts estate papers 17th-20th cent, incl leases 18th-19th cent and Crudwell rentals late 18th cent; Yorks NR and WR estate papers 18th-20th cent, incl leases, Robinson rentals late 18th cent, De Grey estate accounts 1849-54, enclosure papers 18th cent and papers rel to Clifton and Craven estates (Cowper, later Lucas) 19th-20th cent; misc estate papers 15th-18th cent, incl Cheshire rental 1417, Earl of Kent estate accounts late 15th cent, account roll for the Earl of Derby's estates 1550-1, valor of the Earl of Kent's estates 1573, papers rel to Denbighshire estate 1604-5 and to Herefs and Gloucs properties 17th-early 18th cent, and Suffolk rental 1792.

Papers rel to building and alterations at Wrest Park 17th-19th cent, incl architectural drawings and accounts for house and garden 1672-1730; Wrest Park inventories, household accounts, etc 16th-19th cent; papers rel to London houses 16th-19th cent, Newby Hall (Yorks WR) and Southill (Beds) late 18th cent and Putney Heath (Surrey) late 18th-early 19th cent; papers rel to Beds lieutenancy and commission of peace 16th-18th cent; patents, appointments and commissions 15th-19th cent; corresp and papers 17th-20th cent, De Grey and related families, incl Civil War papers of the 10th Earl of Kent, personal accounts late 17th cent, papers of the Duke of Kent early 18th cent, diplomatic and political papers of the 2nd Baron Grantham, political corresp and papers of the 2nd Earl De Grey, corresp, etc of the 2nd Earl of Hardwicke *c*1740-87 and corresp of Lord Polwarth 1772-81; genealogical, literary, artistic and misc papers, incl journals of Catherine Talbot (1721-70), author.

Bedfordshire Record Office (L 1-33). Deposited by the 9th and 10th Baronesses Lucas 1936-85, accepted in lieu of tax on the estate of the 10th Baroness and allocated to the record office 1993. NRA 6283. For HMC-reported MSS, mostly sold between 1922 and 1978, see HMC *Guide to the Location of Collections*, 1982, p15. A few genealogical and other MSS remain in family possession.

[b] Beds manorial court records 1699-1936.

Bedfordshire Record Office (HF 81; DDX 192, 338). Deposited by Hooper & Fletcher, solicitors, Biggleswade 1951, 1966. NRA 960.

[c] Beds manorial court minutes 1603-1744; Harrold (Beds) leases, terriers and estate papers 1542-1612.

Bedfordshire Record Office (HA 5, 9-11, 13). Deposited by Hawkins & Co, solicitors, Hitchin 1932. NRA 5672.

[d] Abstract of Wrest Park building expenses 1834-40; De Grey family epitaphs 1545-1790.

Bedfordshire Record Office (DDX 219). Deposited 1954 by the executors of JG Murray, a subsequent owner of Wrest Park. NRA 6970.

[e] Fordham Hall (Essex) court roll 1711.

Essex Record Office (D/DXB 50). Transferred from Bedfordshire Record Office 1936. NRA 3505.

[f] Colchester Abbey cartulary *c*1250-1415 and ledger book *c*1315-1530.

Essex Record Office, Colchester and North-East Essex branch. Deposited by Colchester Borough Council 1985. Formerly Wrest Park MSS 56, 57 (see HMC *Second Report, App*, 1871, p7).

[g] Burbage and Sketchley (Leics) manorial court records 1696-1925.

Leicestershire Record Office (12D 32/1-5, DE 319). Deposited by Pilgrim & Griffiths, solicitors, Hinckley 1932, 1958. NRA 36384.

[h] West Woodyates (Dorset) estate papers 1828-73 (12 items).

Dorset Record Office (D 353). Deposited by Baroness Lucas 1970. NRA 7828.

[i] Agency papers of John Selden for the 8th Earl of Kent and his wife Elizabeth Talbot 1619-50, incl rentals and surveys of Talbot estates in Notts (Worksop) and Yorks WR (Sheffield, Whiston, etc) 1636-7, 1650.

Bodleian Library, Oxford (MSS Selden supra 113-15). Purchased 1947. NRA 17153.

[j] Diplomatic papers of the 2nd Baron Grantham 1771-9.

British Library, Manuscript Collections (Add MSS 24157-79). Presented by Anne, Countess Cowper 1861.

Related collections: Cowper, Earls Cowper (no 25); Earls of Kent, Goodrich estate records 16th-early 19th cent (Hereford Record Office O 68, NRA 32656); Vyner of Newby (West Yorkshire Archive Service, Leeds, NRA 5836); Vyner, formerly Robinson, of Studley Royal (West Yorkshire Archive Service, Leeds, NRA 6160); Clifton estate papers 16th-18th cent (York City Archives Department YC/AE, NRA 11988); Earls of Hardwicke, family papers (British Library, Manuscript Collections Add MSS 35349-36278); Earls of Ripon, family papers (British Library, Manuscript Collections Add MSS 40862-80, 43510-43644).

[29] DOUGLAS, Earls of Morton

In the Middle Ages the Douglas family owned extensive estates in Fife (Aberdour), Midlothian (Dalkeith), Berwickshire, Peeblesshire and elsewhere, and were created Earls of Morton in 1458. The third Earl of Morton (d1550) was succeeded in his estates and title by his son-in-law James Douglas of Pittendriech, Regent of Scotland 1572-8, but in 1588 they reverted to the Douglases of Loch Leven (Kinross-shire).

Considerable sales of land took place in the seventeenth century, including Dalkeith to the Earl of Buccleuch in 1642 and Loch Leven to Sir William Bruce of Balcaskie (Fife) *c*1670. The islands of Orkney and Shetland, however, were granted to the family in 1643. They were annexed by the Crown in 1669, regranted in 1707 and finally sold to the Dundas family, later Earls of Zetland, in 1766 (see no 32). The Dalmahoy (Midlothian) estate was acquired in the mid-eighteenth century, and the Conaglen (Argyllshire) and Loddington (Leicestershire) estates probably for sporting purposes in the later nineteenth century.

Earlier but temporary accessions of property had come through marriages with the Hay family of Smithfield (Peeblesshire) in 1649 and the Halyburton family of Pitcur (Forfarshire) *c*1730. The marriage of the eighteenth Earl to Helen Watson in 1844 explains the presence in the Morton archive of Watson of Saughton (Midlothian) records.

Estates in 1883: Argyllshire 49,814 acres, Midlothian 10,411 acres, Berwickshire 2,551 acres, Fife 1,644 acres, W Lothian 91 acres, Leics 650 acres, total 65,161 acres worth £22,288 a year.

[a] Writs 13th-19th cent, mainly Fife and Midlothian, but incl Berwickshire, Dumfriesshire, Kinross-shire and Peeblesshire 14th-18th cent and Roxburghshire (Melrose Abbey) 1524-1618; cartulary 16th cent, protocol books 1525-1658 (3) and inventories of writs 15th-18th cent; legal and case papers 16th-19th cent, incl some rel to Orkney and Shetland *c*1669-1766; wills, settlements and related papers 14th-19th cent, incl executry papers of Christian, Countess of Buchan 1506-1606, curatory papers of Laurence, 5th Lord Oliphant 1588-1626 and sederunt books for the 14th Earl of Morton 1744-68 (2); judicial and financial papers 16th-19th cent; sheriff and barony court records 16th cent (fragments).

Fife and Midlothian tacks 15th-19th cent, surveys, maps, particulars and valuations 18th-19th cent, rentals 15th-20th cent and accounts 17th-20th cent, incl Bellfield (Fife) estate accounts 1716-73; Conaglen estate accounts 1872-1905; papers rel to limeworks in Fife 1788-1822, Dalmahoy quarry 1787-93, Aberdour teinds 16th-19th cent and the Pitcur estate 18th cent, etc; Auchterhouse (Forfarshire) rental 1580 and rental of the 7th Earl of Galloway's lands 1757; household papers 16th-20th cent, mainly accounts and vouchers for Aberdour 1657-1797 and Dalmahoy 1606-1949, but incl inventories of Aberdour and Banff castles 1580.

Commissions and appointments 16th-19th cent; papers rel to the shrievalty of Kinross 1539-1615, the Civil War, the risings of 1715 and 1745, shipping and fisheries 17th-19th cent, the Midlothian Yeomanry Cavalry 1709-1807, the Fifeshire Yeomanry Cavalry and Militia 1808-24, the county valuation of Fife 1695-6 and other Fife and Midlothian affairs; family and political corresp and papers 15th-20th cent, incl papers of the 4th Earl of Morton and the Douglases of Loch Leven 16th cent, personal inventories 16th-18th cent, corresp rel to Orkney and Shetland and other business matters 17th-18th cent, and papers about the representative peerage 1714-1822; official papers of Adam Keltie, Clerk of the Exchequer 16th-17th cent; other papers 16th-19th cent, incl royal household books 1650-1 (2), Melrose Abbey tithe and estate account books 1527-8 (3), and Coldingham Priory (Berwickshire) tithe books 1546-7.

Papers of the Watson family of Saughton 16th-early 20th cent, incl deeds, legal papers, wills and settlements, financial, business and estate accounts and papers, and personal corresp and papers.

Scottish Record Office (GD 150). Deposited on loan by the 21st Earl of Morton 1936 and purchased 1981. NRA 32338.

[b] Writs, Argyllshire 16th-19th cent, Berwickshire 18th-19th cent, Fife and Midlothian 16th-20th cent and the superiority of Westcraigs (W Lothian) 1647-1841; inventories of writs 18th-19th cent; probate and executry papers of the 18th Earl of Morton (d1858); legal and case papers 16th-20th cent; Dalmahoy estate papers 18th-20th cent, incl tacks 19th cent, valuations and plans 18th-20th cent, rentals 1852-93, factory accounts and vouchers 1854-62 and papers rel to mineral exploration c1855-92; Aberdour estate papers 18th-20th cent, incl valuations and plans 18th-20th cent, rentals 1857-93 and papers rel to Aberdour harbour 19th cent; papers rel to Aberdour teinds 1647-1894; misc Argyllshire estate papers 19th-20th cent; misc papers rel to the Berwickshire estates of the Watson family of Saughton and the Swinton family of Swinton 17th-19th cent.

Dalmahoy House, inventory and valuation 1858 and garden accounts 1842-55; accounts of work at Inverscaddle House (Argyllshire) 1861-4; other papers 18th-19th cent, incl some rel to James Short's bursaries to the University of Edinburgh 18th-19th cent and accounts of the Earl of Morton with Dalgleish & Bell, solicitors 1890-7.

Scottish Record Office (GD 236, NRA(S) 2710). Deposited by Dundas & Wilson, solicitors, Edinburgh 1977. NRA 30684.

[c] Fife and Midlothian estate plans 18th-20th cent, incl Saughton 1795.

Scottish Record Office (GD 253). Deposited by D & JH Campbell, solicitors, Edinburgh 1951. NRA 13863.

[d] Writs 16th-20th cent, mainly Fife and Midlothian; inventories of writs 19th cent; executry and settlement papers c1755-1859; trust accounts and papers c1829-63, c1927-61; legal and case papers 18th-20th cent; Fife and Midlothian tacks 19th cent; rentals 19th cent, mainly of the Aberdour estate but incl Applegarth (Dumfriesshire) 1827-9; Fife and Midlothian estate accounts, vouchers and papers 18th-20th cent, incl papers rel to mineral exploration at Dalmahoy late 19th cent; misc papers 18th-20th cent, incl letters rel to the sale of Melrose charters to the Lord Clerk Register 1827-32.

Papers of the Watson family of Saughton 18th-19th cent, incl Saughton survey 1795, factory accounts and vouchers c1820-49, estate corresp 1804-89 and accounts of James Watson with James Hope WS 1804-12.

In private possession. Enquiries to the National Register of Archives (Scotland) (NRA(S) 467). NRA 13863.

[e] Cartulary of the Douglas family of Loch Leven (Kinross-shire) 14th cent; family and political corresp and papers of the Douglas family of Loch Leven and the Earls of Morton 15th-17th cent, incl corresp of the 6th and 7th Earls, and letters of James VI and I (1566-1625), the 1st Earl of Kinnoull and the 1st Earl of Traquair 1605-36; rolls of Argyllshire men enlisted for the relief of La Rochelle 1627.

National Library of Scotland (MSS 72-84). Purchased from the 20th Earl of Morton 1927. HMC *Second Report, App*, 1871, pp183-5.

[f] Orkney and Shetland letter book of John Ewing, agent to the Earl of Morton 1715-36.

National Library of Scotland (Advocates' MS 31.2.9).

[g] Orkney writs, inventories of writs, wills and legal papers 16th-18th cent, incl will of Robert, Earl of Orkney 1593 and papers rel to Crown and bishopric rents 1696-1761; suit rolls of the bishopric of Orkney 1621-36; Orkney estate records 17th-18th cent, incl tacks 1641-1759, rentals, accounts and vouchers 1629-1769, factory corresp 1651-1767 and inventories of the Northwall estate 1738-9; household accounts and vouchers 1648-1769 and inventories 1716-41; misc personal inventories 17th-18th cent, incl one of the lands of Patrick, Earl of Orkney 1608; local and misc papers 17th-18th cent, incl election papers 1713-61, papers rel to wrecks 1651-1764 and to ecclesiastical affairs 1615-1764, and papers rel to the rebellions in Orkney 1715-47.

Orkney Archives (GD 150). Transferred from the Scottish Record Office 1982. NRA 25647.

[h] Shetland writs, legal papers and estate records 17th-18th cent, incl suit roll 1709, rentals 1652-1765, household and estate accounts and papers 1614-1757, corresp 1720-1802, Tingwall teind papers 1719-21, and papers rel to wrecks 1664-1744 and to ecclesiastical patronage 18th cent.

Shetland Archives (GD 150). Transferred from the Scottish Record Office 1982. NRA 25549.

[30] DOUGLAS-HAMILTON, Dukes of Hamilton and Brandon

The Hamilton family (created Lords Hamilton 1445, Earls of Arran 1503, Marquesses of Hamilton 1559 and Dukes of Hamilton 1643) were landholders in Buteshire (Arran), Lanarkshire and West Lothian by the fourteenth century. Forfeited estates of the Douglas family were acquired in 1455 (see also no 31), and lands in Arran were granted to the second Lord Hamilton with the earldom of Arran in 1503. Estates in Forfarshire (Arbroath Abbey, granted 1597) and elsewhere in Scotland were acquired subsequently, but by the eighteenth century the family's principal estates remained those in Arran (Brodick), Lanarkshire (Hamilton) and West Lothian (Kinneil), the Kinneil estate extending into the neighbouring county of Stirlingshire at Polmont. Some Lanarkshire property, including Crawford, had passed in the late seventeenth century to the Douglas family, Earls of Selkirk.

The fourth Duke (1658-1712), further created Duke of Brandon in 1711, acquired estates in Lancashire (Ashton Hall) and Staffordshire (Gerard's Bromley and Sandon) through his marriage to Elizabeth, daughter and heir of the fifth Baron Gerard and co-heir of the first Earl of Macclesfield. Sandon was sold in 1776 (to the first Baron Harrowby) and Ashton Hall in 1853; and by the mid-nineteenth century the remaining Staffordshire property had also been alienated. Anne (d1771), widow of the fifth Duke and co-heir of Edward Spencer of Rendlesham (Suffolk), married in 1751 Richard Nassau of Easton (Suffolk), brother of the fourth Earl of Rochford, and had a son William Henry Nassau (1754-1830), later fifth Earl of Rochford. Her Spencer property was inherited by the ninth Duke in 1771, and the Rochford estate in Suffolk eventually passed to the tenth Duke (d1852) on the death of the fifth Earl of Rochford in 1830. The tenth Duke married Susan, daughter and co-heir of the author William Beckford of Fonthill (Wiltshire) (d1844), whose papers and collections she inherited.

Hamilton Palace was given up in 1947, when Lennoxlove (East Lothian), the former seat of the Stewart family, Barons Blantyre, was acquired. The fifth Baron Blantyre had bought it with a fortune inherited from Frances, Duchess of Richmond and Lennox (d1702). The Dundonald papers were inherited by the sixth Duke of Hamilton through his mother (sister of the fifth Earl of Dundonald and heir to his unentailed estates). In 1761, on the death of the Duke of Douglas, the marquessate of Douglas passed to the seventh Duke of Hamilton, but the Douglas estates passed to a nephew of the Duke of Douglas (see no 31).

Estates in 1883: Buteshire 102,210 acres, Lanarkshire 45,731 acres, W Lothian 3,694 acres, Stirlingshire 810 acres, Suffolk 4,939 acres, Berks 2 acres, total 157,386 acres worth £73,638 a year, exclusive of a mineral rent of £67,006.

[a] Writs 14th-20th cent, mainly Buteshire, Lanarkshire and W Lothian, with some for Ayrshire, Renfrewshire and Stirlingshire, etc; papal bulls rel to Lismore bishopric and the archbishopric of Arbroath 1450-1557; deeds, Lancs 13th-19th cent and Staffs 14th-18th cent; misc deeds for Berks, Wilts, etc 16th-20th cent; inventories and abstracts of title 16th-20th cent, Scottish and English estates; wills, settlements, executorship and trust papers 16th-20th cent, Hamilton, Gerard and Nassau, incl executorship accounts for William Beckford 1844-8, and trust papers for the 5th Duke of Atholl 1817-53 and the Lindsell family of Holme (Beds) 18th-20th cent; legal and financial papers 16th-20th cent, incl papers rel to the duchy of Châtellerault 17th-20th cent, the Douglas cause 18th cent and the estate of the 5th Earl of Rochford; Avondale (Lanarkshire) barony court minutes 1596-7; presentments for Ashton and Scotforth (Lancs) manors 18th cent; Nether Wyresdale (Lancs) manor call books 1748-62; Holbrook (Suffolk) manor court rolls 1603-27.

Buteshire, Lanarkshire, W Lothian and Stirlingshire estate records 16th-20th cent, incl tacks 16th-20th cent, maps, plans, surveys and valuations 17th-20th cent, rentals and accounts 16th-20th cent, corresp 18th-20th cent, journals of John Burrell (land agent) *c*1747-92, memorandum books 19th-20th cent, papers rel to teinds 16th-19th cent, and papers rel to Lanarkshire estate improvements and railways mid-19th cent and emigration from Arran 19th cent; extensive Lanarkshire, W Lothian and Stirlingshire coal, salt, ironstone and mineral working papers 17th-20th cent, incl leases, accounts and corresp, with records of particular undertakings 18th-19th cent; papers rel to other Hamilton estates in Scotland 16th-20th cent, incl rentals and accounts for Arbroath 16th-17th cent and Dunbartonshire and Renfrewshire 1746-57, and North Uist (Inverness-shire) estate papers 20th cent; estate papers for the Douglas family, Marquesses of Douglas *c*1607-88 (mainly Roxburghshire and Selkirkshire, but incl Saltoun, E Lothian, rentals 1685-8) and for the Cochrane family, Earls of Dundonald 17th-18th cent (Renfrewshire); rentals of Galloway lordship 1621 and of the Earl of Leven and Melville's Fife estate 1799; Clanranald (Inverness-shire) rentals and accounts 1797-1811 (Macdonald family); Lewis (Ross and Cromarty) factory papers (Earl of Seaforth) 1806-16; Lancs leases 16th-19th cent, maps, valuations and surveys 17th-19th cent and rentals, accounts and papers 15th-19th cent; Staffs rentals and estate papers 17th-19th cent; Suffolk rentals, accounts and estate papers 17th-20th cent, incl timber valuations 1831-8; misc Somerset and Wilts (Beckford estate) papers 18th-20th cent, incl survey 1831; Chelsea (Middlesex) map, rentals and papers *c*1638-60; misc Holme (Lindsell family) leases and estate papers 17th-19th cent.

Architectural drawings 17th-20th cent, mainly for Hamilton Palace 1693-19th cent, with some for Kinneil 1703-7 and Ashton Hall late 18th cent, etc; records of house building and repair 17th-19th cent, incl accounts for work by John and William Adam at Hamilton, Holyrood House, Kinneil House and Bo'ness (W Lothian) 1731-62, and for work at Chelsea 1627-40, Crawford Castle 1675-92, Ashton Hall, and Butley and Rendlesham (Suffolk) 18th-early 19th cent; papers rel to Brodick Castle restoration 1808-45 and a house at Weddicar (Cumberland) 1765; household inventories 17th-20th cent, mainly Hamilton and Holyrood, but incl Sandon 1651-2, London 18th-19th cent, Paisley (Earl of Dundonald) 1711-14 and Bothwell Castle (Earl and Countess of Forfar) 1715-23; Scottish and English household accounts and papers 17th-20th cent, incl Hamilton, Holyrood House, Kinneil, Ashton Hall, Sandon c1670-80, Bothwell Castle c1688-1741; household accounts of the Marquess of Douglas 1638-49, the Earl of Dundonald 1703-20, the Earl of Rochford early 19th cent and William Beckford c1832-47.

Papers rel to Hamilton burgh and Lanarkshire elections, lieutenancy and county affairs 17th-20th cent, incl excise accounts 1667-85, minutes of the commissioners of supply 1655-1702 and Royal Lanarkshire Militia records late 18th-mid-19th cent; papers rel to Buteshire, W Lothian and Stirlingshire affairs 17th-19th cent, incl Polmont militia accounts 1678-86, Bo'ness ale duty records 1707-10 and W Lothian election corresp 1740; election expenses, Lanark, etc 1741; Lancaster election papers c1784-6.

Patents and commissions 16th-19th cent; family and political papers 16th-20th cent, incl personal inventories 16th-19th cent and accounts from 17th cent, Thirty Years' War papers of the 1st Duke (d1649), account books of collectors-general of taxes 1633-83 and Darien scheme papers c1697-1703; papers of the 5th, 9th and 10th Dukes, Charles Hamilton (collector of customs in Jamaica) 1779-98, Brigadier-General RM Poore (1866-1938), the Barons Gerard c1600-1702, the Earls of Dundonald 1656-1739, the 5th Earl of Rochford and William Beckford; accounts and corresp of the 1st Earl and Countess of Forfar 1680-1740; literary and misc papers 16th-20th cent, incl papers of Gilbert Burnet (d1715), author of Memoirs . . . of the Dukes of Hamilton (1676), and log book of HMS Pallas 1878-9.

Papers of the Stewart family, Barons Blantyre 17th-19th cent, incl papers rel to the inheritance from the Duchess of Richmond and Lennox 1696-1727, legal and financial papers 17th-19th cent, E Lothian and Renfrewshire tacks, rentals and estate papers 17th-20th cent, Lennoxlove architectural drawings and household papers 18th-20th cent, Indian papers of the Hon Charles Stewart c1770-80, papers rel to publication of the poetry of Robert Burns 1802-25, and other political and family papers 17th-19th cent.

In private possession. Enquiries to the National Register of Archives (Scotland) (NRA(S) 2177).

HMC *First Report, App,* 1870, pp112-14; *Eleventh Report, App VI,* 1887; *Supplementary Report,* 1932. NRA 10979.

[b] Bonds of manrent 1457-1607; papers rel to prosecutions at Lanark sheriff court 1640-1783 and to actions against Covenanters 1671-87; official, political and family correspondence and papers 1563-1858, mainly 17th cent, incl commissions and appointments, inventory of jewels of Mary, Queen of Scots 1556, royal corresp of the 1st Marquess (d1604), royal household accounts 1623-4, other royal financial papers 17th cent, and extensive political corresp of the 1st, 2nd and 3rd Dukes; extent rolls of Scottish burghs 1597-1631 (2); records of the Royal Regiment of Horse c1685-9; Gerard family and estate corresp c1663-94, mainly of the 4th Baron and his wife.

Scottish Record Office (GD 406). Purchased from the 15th Duke of Hamilton 1983. NRA 10979.

[c] Legal papers 16th-19th cent, incl some rel to the Douglas cause; estate papers 16th-19th cent, mainly Lanarks, incl Hamilton rentals 16th cent, Douglas lordship rentals and accounts 1632-8, Hamilton lordship accounts 1640-50 and Arran factory accounts 1647-9; papers of Charles Hamilton 1785-99, incl accounts for work at the Duke of Hamilton's Holyrood House lodgings; accounts and vouchers of Robert Hamilton, writer in the service of the 1st Duke 1643-9.

Scottish Record Office (GD 237). Deposited by Tods, Murray & Jamieson, solicitors, Edinburgh. NRA 32483.

[d] Factor's accounts, Dunbartonshire, Lanarkshire and Renfrewshire 1728-52.

Scottish Record Office (CS 96/3271).

[e] Arran estate records 18th-20th cent, incl tacks, tenancy papers, maps, plans, valuations and rentals 18th-19th cent, factory accounts and vouchers c1774-1942, corresp 1812-1942, estate journals of John Burrell 1766-82, forest and sawmill records 1793-1938, Stronach quarry sales book 1882-90, papers rel to improvements 1881-1917, kelp manufactory papers 19th cent, and pier and steamer accounts 1872-1914; Brodick Castle household accounts and vouchers 1855-1906; papers rel to local affairs 1797-20th cent, incl volunteer roll 1804, records of the Arran branch of the Royal National Lifeboat Institution c1870-1909, and Arran district committee records 1875-1930.

In private possession. Enquiries to the National Register of Archives (Scotland) (NRA(S) 331). NRA 10978.

[f] Legal and trust papers 16th-20th cent; Kinneil barony court book 1657-69; Lanarkshire estate records 17th-20th cent, incl rentals and accounts from 17th cent, journals and letter books 18th-20th cent and feu and teind books 18th-19th cent; W Lothian and Stirlingshire estate papers 17th-19th cent, incl rentals and vouchers 1670-99; records of coal and mineral

working 16th-20th cent, Lanarkshire, W Lothian and Stirlingshire; rentals, Arran 1816 and Lewis (Lord Seaforth's estate) 1807; Wyresdale (Lancs) rental and accounts 1708-9; Lancs and Suffolk estate accounts 1811-20; Wilts (Milford and Woodford) rentals and papers c1820-56.

Hamilton mausoleum and Dungarvel Lodge (Lanarkshire) building accounts 19th cent; inventories for Hamilton 18th-20th cent, incl library catalogue 1816, and for Holyrood and Dungarvel late 19th-early 20th cent; Scottish household accounts 1705-6, 1813-1915, mainly Hamilton Palace but with some for Holyrood, Dungarvel, etc; Portman Square household accounts 1810-40; misc papers 17th-19th cent, incl accounts of the West Lothian Fencibles 1796 and Lanarkshire Militia 1798-9.

Hamilton District Libraries (Hamilton Estates). Deposited from the Hamilton Estate Office, Hamilton c1962. NRA 36701.

[g] Renfrewshire titles and related legal papers 1680-20th cent.

In private possession. Enquiries to the National Register of Archives (Scotland) (NRA(S) 576). NRA 14815.

[h] Lanarkshire titles 1545-1634.

British Library, Manuscript Collections (Add Ch 19086-7, 19089, 19091-3). Purchased 1870.

[i] Papers of Andrew Stuart of Torrance (d1801) as agent to the Dukes of Hamilton, incl Douglas cause and other legal papers 16th-18th cent, financial papers 17th-18th cent, papers rel to repairs at Holyrood Abbey church 1757-8, corresp and papers rel to estate, business and political affairs 18th cent, and papers of the 6th Duke of Hamilton 1747-62.

National Library of Scotland (MSS 5346-71, 8262-76; Ch 4689-4736, 8412-29). Presented by Madam Stuart Stevenson 1940, 1961.

[j] Agency papers of Davidson & Warrender, WS, rel to the Dukes of Hamilton c1772-1836, incl writs, inventories and corresp.

Edinburgh University Library, Special Collections Department (MSS La. II 509 Ham.). Bequeathed by the antiquarian David Laing (1793-1878). *Index to Manuscripts*, 1964, I. 676.

[k] Suffolk (Easton Park) deeds and legal papers 17th-20th cent, abstracts of title 19th cent, rental 1863, plans 1892 and sale papers mainly 1919-22; misc papers 18th-20th cent, incl Beckford (?Worcs) manor court roll c1768 and Great Glemham (Suffolk) household inventory 1905.

Suffolk Record Office, Ipswich branch (HA 222). Deposited by Lady Jean Fforde 1969. NRA 29033.

[l] Suffolk manorial court records (Easton, etc) 1855-1932.

Suffolk Record Office, Ipswich branch (HB 18). Deposited by Hill & Abbot, solicitors, Chelmsford 1949. NRA 27651.

[m] Lancs (Gerard) tenancy agreements 1661-78 (1 vol).

Public Record Office (C 103/175).

[n] Cartularies, Furness Abbey (Lancs) 15th cent and Arbroath Abbey 16th cent; English state papers 1532-85, mainly rel to Sir Ralph Sadler's embassy to Scotland 1543; other misc and library MSS, incl MSS of the *Gesta Cnutonis* 11th cent, the *Brut* 15th cent, and Robert Hawes's history of Framlingham 1712.

British Library, Manuscript Collections (Add MSS 32646-57, 33241-69). Bought 1886-7 from the government of Prussia, which had acquired them from the collections of the 10th Duke and William Beckford, sold at Sotheby's 1882. Ninety-one other MSS resold by the Prussian government at Sotheby's, 23 May 1889, are now widely dispersed. HMC *Guide to the Location of Collections*, 1982, pp28-9.

[o] Corresp and papers c1632-1809, mainly letters from the 2nd, 3rd and 4th Dukes to the 2nd Earl of Selkirk, with corresp of the 1st Duke rel to the duchy of Châtellerault.

National Library of Scotland (MSS 1031-3). Presented 1931 by the trustees of Sir William Fraser. HMC *Eleventh Report, App VI*, 1887.

[p] Corresp and papers of William Beckford, incl letters of the 10th Duke of Hamilton and inventories of Hamilton Palace mid-19th cent.

Bodleian Library, Oxford (MSS Beckford). Purchased by BH Blackwell Ltd from the 15th Duke of Hamilton at Sotheby's, 5 July 1977, and presented 1984.

Related collections: Earls of Selkirk (in private possession, NRA 10180, NRA(S) 76; Scottish Record Office GD 253); Barons Blantyre (in private possession, NRA 19457, NRA(S) 1244), including Lanarkshire estate papers 17th-19th cent.

[31] DOUGLAS-HOME, Earls of Home

By the seventeenth century the Home family had added considerable estates in Berwickshire, East Lothian (Dunglass), Roxburghshire and elsewhere to their ancestral Home (Berwickshire) lands through marriage, purchase and royal grant. Alexander Home (d1619) was granted Coldingham (Berwickshire) in 1592 and was created Earl of Home in 1605. By the mid-eighteenth century, however, these lands had been much reduced by sale to a core of Berwickshire estates, of which the most important was that at The Hirsel, near Coldstream. Dunglass (East Lothian), gained by marriage in the fifteenth century, passed out of the family in the seventeenth, whilst Home was sold to the first Earl of Marchmont in the early eighteenth century. Clippesby (Norfolk), acquired through the ninth Earl's marriage in 1768 to Abigail, coheir of John Ramey of Yarmouth, was sold by the tenth Earl c1830.

George Douglas, twenty-first Earl of Angus, acquired much of the forfeited property of his kinsman, James, Earl of Douglas, who was attainted in 1455 (see also no 30). His descendant was created Marquess of Douglas in 1633. The third Marquess, created Duke of Douglas in 1703, inherited large estates in Lanarkshire, including Bothwell and Douglas, and Roxburghshire (Jedburgh Forest), with Bunkle and Preston (Berwickshire) and lands in Ayrshire, Forfarshire and Renfrewshire. (Tantallon (Lanarkshire), however, had been sold by the second Marquess.) On the Duke's death in 1761 his estates devolved on his nephew Archibald Stewart (1748-1827), who took the name of Douglas and was created Baron Douglas of Douglas in 1790. When the fourth Baron Douglas died without issue in 1857 the title was extinguished, but the family estates were inherited by the first Baron's granddaughter Lucy, daughter of the second Baron Montagu of Boughton and wife of the eleventh Earl of Home.

Estates in 1883: Lanarkshire 61,943 acres, Roxburghshire 25,380 acres, Berwickshire 10,422 acres, Forfarshire 5,209 acres, Ayrshire 2,271 acres, Renfrewshire 1,325 acres, total 106,550 acres worth £56,632 a year, exclusive of minerals valued at £5,916.

[a] Writs 15th-20th cent, mainly Berwickshire, Lanarkshire and Roxburghshire but incl some for Fife, E Lothian, Peeblesshire, Perthshire, etc 15th-18th cent; inventories of writs 16th-19th cent; misc marriage contracts 17th-19th cent and executry and trust papers 18th-20th cent, Douglas and Home families, incl executry papers of Charles Baillie-Hamilton, MP (1800-65); legal and financial papers 15th-20th cent, Douglas and Home, incl Douglas and Angus peerage case papers 1762-1822 and misc legal accounts c1730-19th cent; Kirriemuir (Forfarshire) court roll 1564; barony court books for Coldingham (Berwickshire) 1611-54 and Douglas (Lanarkshire) 1671-6; court book of the earldom of March (Berwickshire) 1647-9.

Tacks 16th-20th cent, mainly Bunkle and Preston (Berwickshire) from 16th cent and Lanarkshire from 18th cent; Douglas estate papers 16th-20th cent, incl maps and plans 18th-20th cent, valuations, rentals, accounts, vouchers, corresp and papers, with Tantallon accounts and papers c1582-1722, rental of the earldom of Angus 1612-42, taxation roll of the Douglas estates 1665, accounts of Jedburgh Forest improvements 1772-1808, papers rel to Bothwell teinds 18th-19th cent and Douglas game books 1824-66; papers rel to Lanarkshire minerals 19th-20th cent, incl coal leases and Happenden quarry ledger 1832-6; misc leases, rentals, factory accounts, vouchers, corresp and papers for the Home estates from 16th cent, mainly Berwickshire, incl papers rel to Berwickshire and Dunglass teinds 16th-19th cent and game, shooting and fishing records from c1811; rentals, accounts, corresp and other records of the Douglas-Home estates from 1857; papers rel to the Clippesby estate c1814-30; Duke of Queensberry, Amesbury (Wilts) estate valuation 1812; George Keith, Earl Marischal, Aberdeenshire and Banffshire rental c1681.

Architectural drawings of The Hirsel 19th cent and misc building papers and inventories 18th-20th cent, mainly for The Hirsel; valuations of Bothwell and Douglas castles 1844, 1857; Coldstream household book 1592; misc household accounts and papers 17th-20th cent, Home and Douglas, incl garden accounts for The Hirsel 1722-3, Douglas parks stock books 1880-1935 and chapel records for The Hirsel and Douglas Castle 1877-1920; misc papers rel to Forfarshire and Lanarkshire freeholders and politics 17th-19th cent; accounts of the 10th Earl of Home as colonel of the Berwickshire militia 1803-16; Elvanfoot (Lanarkshire) road trustees' accounts 1792-1811 and letter book 1814-19; Douglas (Lanarkshire) local authority minute book 1888-90; patents, commissions and family corresp and papers of the Douglas and Home families 15th-20th cent, incl misc accounts, vouchers and personal inventories from 16th cent, diaries of the 12th Earl 1850-1908, diaries and corresp of Lady Mary Coke (1727-1811) and Elizabeth, Duchess of Buccleuch (d1827), and corresp and literary papers of Lady Louisa Stuart (1757-1851); letters of the Duke and Duchess of Queensberry 1766-78; papers rel to Lord James Douglas's regiment in France 1633-65; military accounts of the Earl of Home's company 1747-50; misc papers 15th-20th cent, incl indenture of the Earl of Angus and Henry VI 1462, MS narrative of the Duke of Argyll's campaign 1715-16 and MS and printed sermons and theological tracts c1738-1826.

Writs, legal, financial and estate corresp and papers of the Robertson family of Lude (Perthshire) c1598-1714, incl legal notebooks of Duncan Robertson 1676-87, Rosneath (Dunbartonshire) household inventory 1678 and misc accounts of the Campbell family, Earls of Argyll 1663-86; deeds and papers for the Blythswood (Renfrewshire) estate of the Campbell family, Barons Blythswood 16th-19th cent.

In private possession. Enquiries to the National Register of Archives (Scotland) (NRA(S) 859). HMC *Twelfth Report, App VIII*, 1891, pp78-185. NRA 10169. The collection includes records previously in the custody of Strathern & Blair, the family's Edinburgh solicitors (see NRA(S) 400, NRA 12629).

[b] Writs 1390-1693 (4).

Scottish Record Office (GD 1/180). Presented by the 13th Earl of Home 1935.

[c] Misc papers rel to the Clippesby estate 1814-31; vouchers of Abigail, Countess of Home and her executors 1813-14.

Norfolk Record Office (MC 372). Purchased 1966.

[d] Clippesby extent 1769; plan of the Earl of Home's Hickling (Norfolk) estate c1769.

Norfolk Record Office (MC 253). Purchased 1989.

[e] Papers of and rel to James Douglas (1671-92), styled Earl of Angus; misc papers of the Douglas family, Marquesses and Dukes of Douglas 1592-1759.

National Library of Scotland (MSS 973-4). Presented by AO Curle 1933.

Related collections: Milne-Home of Wedderburn (Scottish Record Office GD 267, NRA 11620), including Berwickshire rentals and accounts for the 8th Earl of Home 1736-44 (GD 267/18/10, 267/23/6, 267/25/45-6, 55); Robertson of Lude (Scottish Record Office GD 132, NRA 32025); Blair-Oliphant of Ardblair (in private possession, NRA 22823, NRA(S) 1915), including further Robertson of Lude papers; Blythswood estate papers 16th-20th cent (Strathclyde Regional Archives TD 234, NRA 14874).

[32] DUNDAS, Marquesses of Zetland

Sir Lawrence Dundas, first Bt (d1781), a younger son of Thomas Dundas of Fingask (Perthshire), was Commissary-General and contractor to the army 1748-59, and made extensive purchases of land. By 1770 he had acquired estates in the North Riding of Yorkshire (Aske, near Richmond, and Marske, in Cleveland) from the Darcy and Lowther families respectively, the Hope estate (Kerse, etc) in Stirlingshire and Clackmannanshire, the Ballinbreich (Fife) lands of the Earls of Rothes, and the Orkney and Shetland estates of the Earls of Morton (see no 29). Other estates, sold by 1883, included property in Surrey, Hertfordshire (Moor Park, acquired 1763, re-sold 1788), Ireland and the West Indies. His son was created Baron Dundas, of Aske, in 1794, and his grandson Earl of Zetland in 1838. The third Earl was created Marquess of Zetland in 1892.

Estates in 1883: Yorks NR 11,614 acres, Fife 5,566 acres, Stirlingshire 4,656 acres, Clackmannanshire 2,726 acres, Dunbartonshire 162 acres, Orkney 29,846 acres, Shetland 13,600 acres, total 68,170 acres worth £49,324 a year exclusive of minerals.

[a] Deeds late 15th-20th cent, mainly Yorks NR but incl a few for Herts, Middlesex, Notts and Surrey 17th-19th cent; wills, settlements and legal papers, Dundas 18th-19th cent and Lowther 17th-18th cent; Yorks manorial records 16th-20th cent, incl Marske and Loftus; North Riding estate records (Richmond and Cleveland estates) 17th-20th cent, incl leases, surveys, plans, rentals, accounts, vouchers, corresp and papers rel to enclosure and schools; records rel to Loftus alum works 1634-1867 and Cleveland (Upleatham) ironstone mining 1849-1935; misc papers for Moor Park estate (incl sale 1784-8), Scottish estates c1751-1813, Irish estate 1762-1860 and West Indies estate c1755-1833; plans of Aske Hall by John Carr 1767; household papers mainly *temp* Sir Lawrence Dundas (Aske, Kerse, Moor Park, London house); Richmond (Yorks) burgage books 1679, 1773 and theatre deeds 1816; Dundas family corresp and papers 18th-20th cent, incl army and other papers of Sir Lawrence Dundas, corresp of the 1st Baron, papers of the 1st and 2nd Earls of Zetland and of John Charles Dundas, MP (1808-66), and Indian corresp and papers of the 2nd Marquess.

North Yorkshire County Record Office (ZNK). Deposited by the 3rd Marquess of Zetland from 1965. NRA 16269 (partial list).

[b] Stirlingshire and Clackmannanshire estate records 18th-20th cent, incl tacks, tack books from 1749, plans and drawings, rentals and accounts, estate minute books 1847-78 (2 vols), letter books 1806-1952, and papers rel to minerals, roads, bridges, Grangemouth harbour, etc; papers rel to Kerse House 19th cent, incl inventories 1845-98; Fife estate papers 18th-20th cent, incl rentals and accounts from 1772 and maps 19th-20th cent; misc Orkney and Shetland estate papers 18th-mid-19th cent, incl Orkney estate papers and accounts, Shetland accounts early 19th cent and Orkney kelp accounts 1796-1801; misc legal and financial papers rel to all Scottish estates 18th-19th cent, with a few references to the Yorks estates; Earl of Erroll, estate, etc accounts 1758-71 (1 vol).

Scottish Record Office (GD 173; RHP 6100-36, 48002-48486, 80001-80863, 83361-4). Deposited by the 3rd Marquess of Zetland 1966 and by Lord Ronaldshay's Children's Trust 1986. Keeper's *Report* (1986), p26; NRA 10745.

[c] Scottish writs 1594-1764; papers rel to Orkney estate 1765-1834.

Scottish Record Office (GD 236/1/18-24, 29). Deposited by Dundas & Wilson, CS, Edinburgh 1965. Keeper's *Report* (1965), p19.

[d] Ballinbreich (Fife) charters c1250-1517 (8 items).

Untraced. HMC *Fourth Report, App*, 1874, pp503-4.

[e] Orkney writs and titles 1581-1794 (a few only); Orkney legal papers 18th-20th cent, mainly rel to divisions of commonty and mining; Orkney and Shetland estate records 16th-20th cent, mainly Orkney, incl tacks, surveys, valuations, plans, rentals and accounts from 1598 (earldom and bishopric of Orkney, etc), reports and corresp, and kelp accounts and papers 1727-38, 1781-1872; papers rel to local administration 17th-20th cent, incl Kirkwall burgh affairs, Orkney and Shetland elections 1734-1872, commissions of supply, baillie and admiralty court proceedings 1666-1812 and militia and parochial affairs (apparently not all of Dundas provenance).

Orkney Archives. Acquired from the Earldom of Orkney estate office c1920, with later additions from various sources. NRA 15343.

[f] Shetland rental 1772-8; rent and feu duty ledgers c1850-80.

Shetland Archives (Hay & Co collection).

[g] Factor's instructions, rent ledger and letter book 1785-8.

Shetland Archives (Bruce of Sumburgh collection). NRA 13555.

[h] Shetland rental 1792; factor's letter book 1876-81.

Shetland Archives. Deposited by Messrs Malakoff, Ltd, Lerwick. NRA 13554 (NRA(S) 449).

[i] Orkney estate map c1776.

National Library of Scotland (Acc 10541). Acquired 1992.

[j] Letter book of Sir Lawrence Dundas 1761-2.

National Library of Scotland (Acc 8425). Acquired 1983. HMC *Accessions to Repositories 1983.*

[k] Corresp and papers of the 2nd Marquess rel to India and Burma 1899-1958, incl papers as Secretary of State for India 1935-40.

British Library, Oriental and India Office Collections (MSS Eur.D 609). Deposited by the 3rd Marquess of Zetland 1961, 1973. NRA 20539.

[33] EGERTON, Earls of Ellesmere

Thomas Egerton (1540-1617), natural son of Sir Richard Egerton of Ridley (Cheshire), was Lord Chancellor 1603-17, and was created Baron Ellesmere in 1603 and Viscount Brackley in 1616. He built up considerable estates in Cheshire and adjoining counties, including the Ellesmere estate in Shropshire (purchased from the feoffees of the sixth Earl of Derby) and properties in Denbighshire and Flintshire. In 1598 he inherited Tatton (Cheshire) and Worsley (Lancashire) from his brother-in-law Richard Brereton. (Tatton later passed to a younger son of the second Earl of Bridgewater.) In 1604 he was granted Ashridge (Hertfordshire), which became the nucleus of a large estate in Hertfordshire, Buckinghamshire and Bedfordshire.

John Egerton (d1649) succeeded his father as second Viscount Brackley, and in the same year was created Earl of Bridgewater. He married c1601 Frances, daughter and co-heir of the fifth Earl of Derby (d1594), and purchased the Brackley estate in Northamptonshire (like Ellesmere a property that had passed to the Earls of Derby from the family of Strange). He also acquired property in Lincolnshire that had passed to the Earls of Derby through the marriage of the fourth Earl to a granddaughter of Charles Brandon, Duke of Suffolk. (These estates were alienated in the eighteenth century.) The fourth Earl was created Duke of Bridgewater in 1720.

On the death of the third Duke of Bridgewater in 1803 his Ashridge and Ellesmere estates passed to a cousin as seventh Earl of Bridgewater (see no 27), but the Brackley and Worsley estates, together with the canal property and Bridgewater House (London) passed to his nephew Lord Gower, later first Duke of Sutherland, with remainder to his second son Francis Leveson-Gower (later Egerton), created Earl of Ellesmere in 1846. The Bridgewater Canal was sold in 1887, and the Worsley estate, to the Bridgewater Estates Company, in 1923. The Stetchworth (Cambridgeshire) estate, near Newmarket, was acquired by the third Earl of Ellesmere, and the Mertoun (Berwickshire) estate by the fourth Earl

(as Viscount Brackley) in 1912. The fifth Earl succeeded a cousin as sixth Duke of Sutherland in 1963.

Estates in 1883: Lancs 10,080 acres, Northants 2,839 acres, Cheshire 303 acres, Staffs c100 acres, total c13,300 acres worth £71,290 a year.

[a] Deeds 12th-17th cent, mainly Cheshire but incl Lancs, Lincs and Northants 16th-17th cent, London and Middlesex 14th-18th cent, Staffs and Warwicks 13th-18th cent, and Denbighshire and Flintshire 16th-17th cent; settlements, wills, trust deeds and related Egerton family papers late 16th-early 18th cent; legal and case papers 16th-early 19th cent, incl papers rel to the Brereton and Downes families 16th cent, the Earls of Derby and their estates 16th-17th cent, the Salusbury, Cecil, Herbert, Vaughan, Spencer and Cranfield families 17th cent, the 1st Duke of Bolton decd 1694-1705, the Wrey family (of Drayton Beauchamp (Bucks) and Chelsea) 17th-18th cent, Waldegrave trust papers late 18th cent and Bridgewater Trust papers (Lord Francis Egerton *v* James Sothern) early 19th cent; roll of extracts from Whithorn Priory cartulary (rel to Isle of Man) 1504; abstracts of deeds 18th cent; misc manorial records 14th-18th cent, mainly 16th-17th cent, incl Bromfield and Yale (Denbighshire and Flintshire) 14th-17th cent, Lincs 16th-17th cent, Cheshire and Salop 17th cent, and Wollaston (Northants) 16th-18th cent.

Misc leases, surveys, rentals, accounts and other estate papers for Egerton estates 16th-18th cent, incl Cheshire (Tatton, etc) 16th-17th cent, Lincs 16th-18th cent, Northants (Brackley, Wollaston, etc) 17th cent, Lancs 17th cent (incl Worsley rental 1679), Salop 16th-18th cent, Flintshire and Denbighshire 16th-17th cent, and Westmorland (lead mines) 18th cent; Earls of Derby estate papers 16th-early 17th cent, incl Isle of Man valor 1512-13, Derby valor 1593 and accounts 1599-1606; other estate papers 16th-18th cent, incl the Astley (Warwicks) estate 16th cent, the Herbert estates in Wales 1598-1637, the Cheyne estates 17th-18th cent, the Wrey estates in Cornwall, Devon, etc late 17th-early 18th cent and the Waldegrave estates in Essex and Somerset 18th cent; Dunrobin (Sutherland) estate and farm papers 1787-97; building accounts and papers (Bridgewater House, Ashridge, etc) 17th-18th cent; inventories of plate, furniture etc late 16th-18th cent; household accounts and vouchers late 16th-18th cent; Dunrobin and Trentham (Staffs) library catalogues.

Bucks county and lieutenancy papers late 16th-early 18th cent, incl muster book 1673 and militia order book 1677-1715; papers rel to Cheshire and Lancs taxation and lieutenancy 1580s; commissions, appointments, etc mainly 16th-17th cent; Egerton family corresp and papers 16th-early 19th cent, incl legal, official, political, business and personal corresp and papers of Lord Chancellor Ellesmere *c*1578-1617, papers of the 1st Earl of Bridge-water as President of the Council of Wales 1631-42 and lord lieutenant of Salop, papers of the 2nd Earl rel to Tangier 1679-80 and the lieu-tenancy of Herts 1680s, papers of the 3rd Earl as a Commissioner of Trade 1694-7 and 1st Lord of the Admiralty 1699-1701, papers of the 1st Duke as Master of the Horse, and canal papers of the 3rd Duke; misc Downes and Sherington (of Wardley, Lancs) papers 16th-17th cent; misc Cheyne family papers 16th-18th cent, incl Bucks shrievalty account of Francis Cheyne 1589-90, accounts of Lord Cheyne (2nd Viscount New-haven) as Clerk of the Pipe 1703-20, Bucks election papers 1713-14 and Duke of Kingston's trust minutes 1725-7; misc Leveson-Gower papers 18th-early 19th cent, incl Privy Seal war-rants (1st Marquess of Stafford) 1755-7, 1784-94 and Sutherland Volunteers papers 1793-7; diplomatic corresp, Benjamin Keene and others with Duke of Bedford and others 1748, 1751 (2 vols); genealogical, heraldic, literary, his-torical and other MSS and papers, incl the Ellesmere Chaucer, Shakespeare forgeries by J Payne Collier, legal and other works by Francis Thynne and a journal of Sir Kenelm Digby 1627-9.

Huntington Library, San Marino, California. Pur-chased 1917, the papers having previously been kept at Bridgewater House. *Guide to British His-torical Manuscripts in the Huntington Library*, 1982, pp21-77; HMC *Eleventh Report, App VII*, 1888, pp126-67. NRA 24601. Other papers, not sold in 1917, may remain in private possession (not available for research).

[b] Letters to John Halsey, steward to the 2nd Earl of Bridgewater, from agents in Salop and Cheshire 1651-62 (7 bundles).

Shropshire Records and Research Unit, Shropshire Record Office (JRW Whitfield collection, SRO 3607). Deposited by Mrs RJ Nash 1976. NRA 21443.

[c] Deeds, mainly Northants 13th-20th cent but incl Lancs 14th-19th cent, Cambs ?18th-20th cent, Middlesex 18th-19th cent and Hants (Southampton) 18th-20th cent; settlements and trust papers late 16th-20th cent, incl papers rel to the Derby inheritance 16th-17th cent and Bridgewater Trust papers 19th-20th cent; legal and case papers 17th-20th cent, incl abstracts of Worsley deeds and papers rel to acquisition of Bridgewater House 1700; Northants manorial records 16th-19th cent, incl manor and borough of Brackley; Northants estate records 16th-20th cent, incl leases and agreements, surveys, maps, rentals and accounts, corresp and papers; Lancs estate records 17th-20th cent, incl leases 1653-1795, survey *c*1722, papers rel to schools 1710-1922 and mining leases 1790-1841; canal papers 18th-19th cent, incl accounts, valuations, commissioners' minutes (1823-71) and appoint-ments; papers rel to wharves and collieries 20th cent; Mertoun estate papers *c*1912-17; papers rel to Derby estates 16th cent, incl valuation 1574

and accounts 1535-94; papers rel to Bridgewater House 1897-1927; papers rel to the borough of Brackley *c*1535-1836, incl burgess rolls, registers of oaths, election records and papers rel to fairs; misc personal and family papers 16th-19th cent, incl pedigree *c*1598, letters to the 1st Earl of Bridgewater, business and charitable corresp of Lord Francis Egerton 1837-46, misc Brereton papers 16th cent, and further Privy Seal papers of the Marquess of Stafford 1742-92.

Northamptonshire Record Office (EB). Deposited 1954. NRA 4357.

[d] Stetchworth and Wood Ditton (Cambs) man-orial records 16th-20th cent.

Cambridgeshire County Record Office. Deposited by the 5th Earl of Ellesmere 1952 and by WJ Taylor 1956.

[e] Bridgewater Trust (later Bridgewater Estates Ltd) records mainly mid-19th-20th cent, incl duplicate deeds (Lancs) 1784-1923, leases 19th-20th cent, maps and plans 19th-20th cent, rentals and accounts 18th cent-1980s and other papers 19th-20th cent.

Salford Archives Centre. Deposited by Bridgewater Estates plc, Walkden, 1983-91. In course of cat-aloguing 1994: prior notice required for production.

[f] Bridgewater canal accounts 1770-1 (1 vol).

Salford Archives Centre. Purchased 1981.

[g] Abstracts of deeds 1761, 1798; misc legal and trust papers 19th cent; canal accounts and papers *c*1759-1811, incl papers rel to the pur-chase and leasing of land, and Liverpool dock papers mid-18th-mid-19th cent; misc estate papers 18th cent; cellar books 1785-96 (2 vols); personal and family corresp of the 3rd Duke of Bridgewater 1737-1803, with related papers.

Salford University Library. Deposited by the 6th Duke of Sutherland 1985. NRA 28500.

[h] Bridgewater Trust (later Bridgewater Estates Ltd), Lancs estate corresp 1895-1960s.

Salford University Library. Deposited by Bridgewater Estates plc 1977, 1983.

[i] Worsley Hall (Lancs) building accounts 1839-46.

British Architectural Library (Edward Blore papers BIE/1). NRA 34275.

Related collections: Cust, Earls Brownlow (no 27); Egerton of Tatton (John Rylands University Library of Manchester, NRA 30541), including papers relating to the minority of the 3rd Duke of Bridgewater; Cartwright of Aynho (Northamptonshire Record Office Acc 1960/23, etc, NRA 21333), including Brackley estate accounts 1779-97; National Coal Board (Lan-cashire Record Office NcBW, NRA 12638), including Bridgewater Colliery records *c*1764-1935; Manchester Ship Canal Co (in pri-vate possession), including records of the Bridgewater Department; Dukes of Sutherland

(Staffordshire Record Office D 593, 868, etc, NRA 10699).

[34] FANE, Earls of Westmorland

The Fane family held land at Tudeley and elsewhere in Kent by the late Middle Ages. Sir Thomas Fane married Mary Nevill (d1626), daughter and heir of the sixth Lord Abergavenny and Baroness Le Despenser in her own right. She inherited the Nevill estates of Mereworth (Kent) and Althorne (Essex). Their son Francis Fane (1583-1628) married in 1599 Mary, daughter and heir of Sir Anthony Mildmay (d1617), through whom he acquired the Apethorpe (Northamptonshire) estate and property in Wiltshire that Mildmay had inherited through his marriage to a co-heir of Sir Henry Sherrington of Lacock (Wiltshire). Francis Fane was created Earl of Westmorland in 1624. An estate at Sharlston (Yorkshire, West Riding) entered the family through the sixth Earl's marriage in 1707 to Catherine, daughter and heir of Thomas Stringer of Sharlston. The Apethorpe estate was sold in 1904 to Henry Brassey, later Baron Brassey.

On the death of the seventh Earl in 1762 the Kent estates passed to descendants of his sisters (see below), but the earldom and the other estates were inherited by his cousin Thomas Fane (1707-71), the son of Henry Fane of Redland (Gloucestershire) and grandson of Sir Francis Fane of Fulbeck (Lincolnshire), the second Earl's brother. Before his accession as eighth Earl, Thomas Fane had already inherited his father's estate at Brympton (Somerset) and other property from his mother, sister and co-heir in her issue of John Scrope of Wormsley (Buckinghamshire). Brympton subsequently passed to a daughter of the eleventh Earl, Lady Rose Weigall (1834-1921), to whom certain family papers, including the correspondence of Priscilla, Countess of Westmorland, also descended.

Mary, a sister of the seventh Earl, married Sir Francis Dashwood, first Bt, of West Wycombe (Buckinghamshire) in 1705. Her sister Catherine married William Paul and had a daughter Catherine, her heir, who married Sir William Stapleton, fourth Bt, of Rotherfield Greys (Oxfordshire), to which family the Kent estate and barony of Le Despenser ultimately passed, together with the Fane family papers and Kent estate muniments kept at Mereworth Castle.

Estates in 1883: Northants 5,973 acres, Yorks WR 1,401 acres, total 7,374 acres worth £11,142 a year.

[a] Deeds, Cambs, Hunts and Northants 12th-19th cent, incl medieval charters of Thorney Abbey (Cambs); deeds for other counties 12th-17th cent, incl Essex 12th-16th cent, Kent and Wilts 13th-17th cent, and Bucks 16th-17th cent; abstracts of title 17th-18th cent; inquisitions *post mortem* 15th-17th cent; wills and settlements 16th-19th cent; executorship

accounts and papers 18th-19th cent; legal papers 16th-19th cent, incl many rel to the barony of Abergavenny; manorial records, Northants 15th-18th cent, incl Oundle accounts 1471-1511, and Farcet and Stanground (Hunts) 15th-17th cent; Kingston Lisle (Berks) manor court roll 1609; Thornbury (?Gloucs) manorial accounts 1406; Chippenham (Wilts) hundred accounts 1582-8; Willibrook (Northants) hundred survey 1652.

Leases 16th-18th cent, mainly Northants and Wilts; misc Northants estate records 16th-20th cent, incl maps, terriers, particulars and surveys, rentals, vouchers, accounts, estate corresp and papers, wood and timber accounts 1649-1791, accounts of sales 1666, farm accounts 1747-52, survey and valuation of enclosures 1777, and game books 1858-1915; Kent estate extent 1589, with rentals, vouchers and accounts *c*1703-30; Crayford (Kent) accounts 1612; Wilts estate terrier *c*1737; Yorks estate rental 1761-2 and misc rentals, accounts and papers 1884-1900; misc Bucks (Medmenham, etc) estate papers 17th-19th cent; Rottingdean (Sussex) estate surveys 16th cent; estate accounts of Thomas Wingfield of Kimbolton (Hunts) 1560-2; extent of the Hants estate of Richard Dowse (d1603); papers rel to property in Sackville Street (Middlesex) 18th cent; misc Apethorpe household records 16th-20th cent, incl inventories of plate 1721-1852, library and muniment room catalogues *c*1837-1904, and household accounts 16th-19th cent.

Papers rel to Rockingham Forest (Northants) 16th-18th cent, to Emmanuel College, Cambridge 17th-18th cent and to the River Nene navigation 1724-30; Northants election papers 1730; Lyme Regis (Dorset) election papers 1781; appointments and commissions 16th-19th cent; personal inventories 17th cent; family accounts and financial papers 16th-19th cent, incl accounts of Sir Anthony Mildmay 1593-6; family and political papers 17th-20th cent, incl diplomatic letters and literary papers of the 11th Earl; misc papers of the 6th Earl as Deputy Warden of the Cinque Ports 1700-7; accounts and papers of Sir Walter Mildmay as Under-Treasurer of England 1567-89 and of John Scrope (d1752), Secretary to the Treasury; letters of Grenville Murray, journalist (1824-81); genealogical, literary and misc papers 14th-19th cent, incl Kent lay subsidy roll 1382-3, religious meditations of Henry Thorne, canon of Peterborough, *c*1600, sermons and commonplace books 17th cent, Thorney Abbey account roll 1441-2, household account book of Edward, Duke of York 1409-10 and Fotheringhay College (Northants) accounts 1469-1535.

Northamptonshire Record Office (Westmorland (Apethorpe) MSS, Acc 1950/88, 1951/147, 1952/1). Deposited by the 15th Earl of Westmorland 1950-2. NRA 36056. The family papers described in HMC *Tenth Report, App IV*, 1885, pp1-59 have been dispersed by sale (see HMC *Guide to the Location of Collections*, 1982, p65; *Private Papers of British Diplomats 1782-1900*, 1985, p23).

[b] Yorks deeds 14th-18th cent; abstract of deeds 1818; wills and settlements 1633-1704, Stringer family; misc legal papers, incl accounts of the losses of the Stringer family in the Civil War *c*1660; Sharlston estate records 17th-20th cent, incl coal leases, maps, surveys, rentals, colliery and estate accounts 1719-99, and corresp 1719-1818; Sharlston Hall inventory 1737; patents and appointments 16th-18th cent, Stringer family; other papers, incl a personal inventory of Thomas Stringer 1550.

West Yorkshire Archives Services, Leeds (WS). Transferred from Northamptonshire Record Office 1975. NRA 35464.

[c] Legal case papers rel to the barony of Abergavenny *c*1598 (3 vols).

British Library, Manuscript Collections (Harleian MSS 4749, 4768, 4798).

[d] Survey of Northants and Rutland forests 1564; misc legal and other papers rel to the Kent and Northants estates early 17th cent; catalogue of Apethorpe books *c*1700; Exchequer accounts and papers of Sir Walter Mildmay 1572-80; literary and other papers of the 2nd Earl of Westmorland (d1665), incl MS autobiography and Northants lieutenancy letter book 1660-5; MS autobiography of the 6th Earl (1680-1736); misc family and other papers, incl household account book of Anne, Duchess of Buckingham 1465-6, political treatises *c*1600 (2) and transcripts of state papers, letters and tracts 16th-17th cent.

British Library, Manuscript Collections (Add MSS 34213-23, 34251). Purchased at Christie's 1892.

[e] Kent deeds (Badsell, etc) 1533-1637.

Public Record Office (C 108/155, 351).

[f] Papers of the 10th Earl of Westmorland 1789-1806, mainly as Lord Lieutenant of Ireland.

National Archives of Ireland, Dublin. Presented by Sir Spencer Ponsonby-Fane 1883. NRA 22312. Other political papers of the 10th Earl, sold at Christie's 16 July 1892, are untraced (HMC *Papers of British Cabinet Ministers 1782-1900*, 1982, p20).

[g] Fane and Weigall family papers 18th-20th cent, incl official and other corresp and papers of the 11th Earl and papers of Priscilla, Countess of Westmorland (1793-1879), Julian Fane, diplomat (1827-70), Lady Rose Weigall (1834-1921), and Henry Weigall, painter (1829-1925); notebook of Admiral John Forbes (1714-96).

Centre for Kentish Studies (U 1371). Deposited by the Revd AF Weigall 1968. HMC *Private Papers of British Diplomats 1782-1900*, 1985, p23. NRA 15266. Other papers were sold by Miss Rachel Weigall at Sotheby's 1965 (2 Mar, lots 452-67).

[h] Diplomatic and military papers of the 11th Earl 1814-50 (4 vols).

Bodleian Library, Oxford (MSS Eng. c. 4861-3, Eng.d. 2577). Bought at Christie's, 29 June 1994, lot 98.

Related collections: Northants manorial records 17th-20th cent (Northamptonshire Record Office Acc 1965/218, 1985/245); Stapleton of Rotherfield Greys (Centre for Kentish Studies U 282, NRA 7749), including deeds, Kent estate records and Fane family papers 14th-18th cent; Dashwood of West Wycombe (Bodleian Library, Oxford MS D.D. Dashwood, NRA 892), including Fane papers 17th-18th cent; Fane of Fulbeck (Lincolnshire Archives FANE, NRA 10303); Fane of Wormsley (Oxfordshire Archives E 4, NRA 36398).

[35] FINCH of Burley-on-the-Hill

Sir Moyle Finch, first Bt, of Eastwell (Kent), married in 1572 Elizabeth, daughter of Sir Thomas Heneage, of Copt Hall (Essex). She was created Countess of Winchilsea in 1628, and the descendants of their eldest son held the earldom of Winchilsea and the Eastwell estate until 1729. Their third son, Sir Heneage Finch (1580-1631), of Kensington (Middlesex), Speaker of the House of Commons, was father of Sir Heneage Finch, Lord Chancellor 1675-82, who inherited estates at Ravenstone (Buckinghamshire) and Daventry (Northamptonshire) from his grandmother, and was created Earl of Nottingham in 1681. A further Buckinghamshire property, Milton Keynes, was purchased in 1677.

The second Earl of Nottingham (1647-1730), Secretary of State 1689-93 and 1702-4, purchased an estate in Rutland from the second Duke of Buckingham in 1694 and built Burley-on-the-Hill between 1694 and 1708. Through his first wife, Lady Essex Rich, the Essex estates of the Rich family, Earls of Warwick, came to the Finch family. His second wife was Anne, only daughter of Viscount Hatton (see no 36). The Hatton estates, however, were never held with the Burley estates, but passed to a younger son of the second Earl in 1764.

On the death of his second cousin the sixth Earl of Winchilsea in 1729, the second Earl of Nottingham inherited the earldom of Winchilsea and the Kent estates. The Kent estates, however, passed on the death of the eighth Earl in 1769 to his brother Edward Finch-Hatton, and the earldoms of Winchilsea and Nottingham passed on the death of the ninth Earl in 1826 to George Finch-Hatton, grandson of Edward. The Rutland, Buckinghamshire and Essex estates, however, passed in 1826 to a natural son of the ninth Earl, George Finch, and on the death of WHM Finch in 1939 to his great-nephew JR Hanbury.

Estates in 1883: Rutland 9,183 acres, Essex 4,318 acres, Bucks 3,657 acres, Northants 174 acres, total 17,332 acres worth £28,443 a year.

[a] Deeds, Rutland from 13th cent, Essex from 16th cent and Bucks from 17th cent; wills, settlements and trust papers 17th-19th cent; legal

papers 17th-20th cent, incl Bermuda estate
1619-83 (Rich family) and debts of the 2nd
Duke of Buckingham 1680-93; court books for
Rutland manors 1791-1808; Rutland estate
records 14th-20th cent, mainly late 17th cent
onwards, incl surveys from 16th cent, Oakham
rental 14th cent, accounts mainly from 17th cent
and misc papers; estate papers for Essex (Foulness, etc) 16th-early 20th cent, Bucks
(Ravenstone, Milton Keynes) mid-17th-20th
cent and Norfolk (Countess of Warwick's estates)
1623-74; Owston (Leics) surveys late 18th cent;
Daventry (Northants) rentals, etc 18th cent;
accounts and papers rel to the building of
Burley-on-the-Hill 1694-1714 and to restoration
after a fire 1909-11; Burley household inventories, accounts, etc from late 17th cent;
inventories for Kensington House 1664-76 and
Rufford Abbey (Notts) (Marquess of Halifax)
1696; papers rel to Rutland county business and
politics 18th-19th cent.

Heneage and Finch family papers 16th-20th
cent, incl corresp of Sir Thomas Heneage
1569-83 and Sir Moyle Finch 1585-c1612, legal
papers of Speaker Finch, parliamentary and legal
papers of the 1st Earl of Nottingham 1670-82,
extensive corresp and papers of the 2nd Earl as
Secretary of State, etc, corresp and papers of the
3rd Earl of Winchilsea and Sir John Finch
(brother of the 1st Earl of Nottingham) as
ambassadors to Turkey 1660-82, corresp and
diaries of Henrietta, Lady Pomfret and her
daughter Lady Charlotte Finch 18th cent, and
papers of the 9th Earl of Winchilsea as Groom of
the Stole (1812-20) and lord lieutenant of Rutland; literary papers of the 1st Marquess of
Halifax; commonplace book of Sir Henry
Wotton; misc medical and literary papers,
printed pamphlets, maps, etc.

Leicestershire Record Office (DG 7, DE 3443).
Deposited from Burley-on-the-Hill 1964-89.
HMC *Seventh Report, App*, 1879, pp511-18,
Finch I-IV, 1913-65, *V* (in preparation). NRA
9845 (partial list). 43 autograph letters were sold
from the collection in 1966 and were mostly
bought by the Osborn Collection, Beinecke
Library, Yale University. About 44 royal warrants
were sold at Christie's between 1981 and 1986.
Legal and literary MSS noticed in 1879 are (with
the exception of Sir Henry Wotton's commonplace book) thought to have been destroyed by
fire in 1908.

[b] Foulness and Shoebury (Essex) manorial
records 16th-20th cent.

Essex Record Office. Deposited by Gregson, Saul
& Goulding, solicitors, Southend 1939, 1944.
NRA 20165.

[c] Foulness manorial and other records
1576-1918.

Essex Record Office (D/DU 514). Deposited by D
Frith of Foulness 1962-3. NRA 3505.

[d] Misc Essex manorial and estate papers
15th-18th cent, incl Foulness accounts 1424,

1486, Hawkwell court roll 1632-59, Hockley or
Hockley Hall court rolls 1713-49 and rental
1687.

Essex Record Office (D/DK M35-6, 134-6, E1).
Purchased 1942. NRA 8733.

[e] Rayleigh, Hockley, etc manorial court rolls,
rentals, etc 1599-1879.

Essex Record Office (D/DCf M 1-24, 27). Deposited by Crick & Freeman, solicitors, Maldon
1965-73. NRA 24577.

[f] Foulness account c1400; marsh rental 1500-1;
Eastwood Bury survey 1589.

Essex Record Office (D/DHt M 42, 45-6). Deposited by the Essex Archaeological Society 1953-7.
NRA 6036.

[g] Foulness compotus 1498-9; Eastwood, etc
rental 1770.

Essex Record Office (Avery Collection D/DQs
184/1, 189). NRA 5380.

[h] Legal entry book of Lord Chancellor Finch
1673-82.

British Library, Manuscript Collections (Add MS
29800). Acquired 1875.

Related collection: Finch-Hatton, Earls of Winchilsea and Nottingham (no 36).

[36] FINCH-HATTON, Earls of Winchilsea and Nottingham

Henry Hatton acquired the manor of Holdenby
(Northamptonshire) by marriage in the early sixteenth century. His grandson, Sir Christopher
Hatton (1540-91), Lord Chancellor, entailed his
estates in Northamptonshire and elsewhere on his
nephew, Sir William Newport (d1597), and then
on his cousin Sir Christopher Hatton (d1619), of
Clay Hall (Essex) and later of Kirby
(Northamptonshire), who married Alice Fanshawe. Their son was created Baron Hatton in
1643 and their grandson Viscount Hatton in 1683.
The first Viscount married in 1685 Elizabeth,
daughter of Sir William Haslewood, of Maidwell
(Northamptonshire), through whom he appears to
have acquired the muniments of the Haslewood
family. On the death of the third Viscount Hatton
in 1764 the Northamptonshire estates passed to
Edward Finch (later Finch-Hatton), a younger son
of the second Earl of Nottingham (see no 35).
Edward Finch-Hatton also succeeded to the Eastwell (Kent) estate, a Finch property, on the death
of the eighth Earl of Winchilsea in 1769, and his
grandson George William Finch-Hatton became
tenth Earl of Winchilsea in 1826.

Property in Nottinghamshire (Newark) and Lincolnshire (Haverholme Priory) was inherited by
the tenth Earl on the death of Sir William Jenison
Gordon, second Bt, in 1831. The Newark property
passed to the eleventh Earl of Winchilsea but the
Lincolnshire estate to a younger son, Murray
Edward Gordon Finch-Hatton, who however succeeded his half-brother as twelfth Earl in 1887.

Eastwell was sold in 1892, and (Kirby having been long since abandoned) Haverholme Priory became for a time the family seat.

Estates in 1883: Earl of Winchilsea: Kent 6,581 acres, Northants 5,114 acres, Notts 741 acres, Leics 355 acres, Lincs 78 acres, Rutland 13 acres, total 12,882 acres, worth £18,216 a year; Hon MEG Finch-Hatton: Lincs 3,632 acres, worth £4,694 a year.

[a] Deeds 13th-18th cent, mainly Northants but incl Lincs and Leics (Haslewood estates) 15th-17th cent, London (Hatton House) 16th-17th cent, Kent ?16th-17th cent, Notts (Newark) 17th-18th cent, Essex (Foulness) 18th cent and a few for Beds, Cambs and Oxon 16th-17th cent; wills, settlements, executorship and trusteeship papers mainly 16th-19th cent, incl Hatton, Finch-Hatton, Haslewood and Jenison Gordon families; legal papers 16th-19th cent, mainly Northants and Hatton family (especially 17th cent) but incl Fanshawe family 17th cent, papers rel to sequestration of Hatton and Haslewood estates 1643-51, papers rel to the manor of Wye (Kent) 18th cent and papers rel to the Newark estate mainly 18th cent; manorial records, Northants 13th-18th cent, Lincs 15th-16th cent, and other counties (Cambs, Essex, Kent, Oxon) 15th-17th cent.

Northants (Holdenby and Kirby) estate records 16th-20th cent, incl leases, maps, surveys, rentals, accounts, Weldon quarry papers 19th-20th cent, etc; misc Haslewood (Northants, Lincs, etc) estate records 14th-17th cent; Kent (Eastwell, etc) estate records 16th-19th cent; misc Lincs and Notts (Jenison Gordon) estate papers 18th-19th cent; Lincs (Wray of Glentworth) estate papers *c*1665-82; Hatton (Kirby, London, etc) inventories and household accounts 17th-early 18th cent; Kirby garden papers 17th cent; papers rel to Northants county affairs (lieutenancy, shrievalty, taxation, politics, etc) 16th-17th cent, Hatton and Haslewood; papers rel to Northants and other forests mainly 17th cent; papers rel to Ely House (London) hospital 1656-7, Billing (Northants) almshouses 17th-19th cent, Eastwell church 1841 and Wye grammar school and college late 19th cent.

Hatton and Finch-Hatton family corresp and papers 17th-20th cent, incl summonses and commissions 17th-18th cent, papers rel to the governorship of Guernsey 15th-early 18th cent, corresp of the 1st Viscount Hatton, and corresp of the 10th Earl of Winchilsea on Catholic Emancipation 1828-9; Jenison and Gordon corresp and papers 18th-early 19th cent; Fanshawe papers 17th cent, incl papers rel to the office of King's Remembrancer of the Exchequer; Finch papers 17th-18th cent, incl legal notes of the 1st Earl of Nottingham and letter books of the 2nd Earl as Secretary of State 1702-4; Saville (Marquess of Halifax) trusteeship accounts 1711-16; genealogical, literary and other papers, incl historical and other collections of Sir Christopher Hatton; misc papers, incl Sempringham Priory

(Lincs) estreat roll 1421, cartulary of St Mary's Abbey, York 13th cent, and copy of register of Pipewell Abbey (Northants).

Northamptonshire Record Office. Deposited by the 14th Earl of Winchilsea and others 1930-71. HMC *First Report, App*, 1870, pp30-4. NRA 4485.

[b] Gretton (Northants) court rolls 1592-1761.

Northamptonshire Record Office (Acc 1943/32). Deposited by Lawrence Graham & Co, solicitors, London 1943.

[c] Gretton and Little Weldon manorial records 17th-20th cent.

Northamptonshire Record Office (Acc 1971/36). Deposited by Lamb & Holmes, solicitors, Kettering 1971, 1983.

[d] Wye manorial court rolls 1611-1705; legal papers early 17th cent.

Wye College, Kent. Transferred from Northamptonshire Record Office 1962 (see NRA 4485: FH 301-2, 3831, 4072).

[e] Kent manorial records 17th-20th cent, incl lesser manors in Wye.

Centre for Kentish Studies (U 55). Presented as part of the Knocker collection 1940-5. NRA 5406.

[f] Lincs estate tenant-right papers 1920; Hants (Sherfield-upon-Loddon) estate papers 1927-42.

Lincolnshire Archives (James Martin & Co 5/3, 7/3). Deposited 1968. NRA 14274.

[g] Charters of monastic and other lands in England 7th-18th cent, mainly collected by the Hatton family but a few from their own archive; Finch and Hatton family papers 16th-18th cent, chiefly corresp and papers of the 1st Viscount Hatton and further papers of the 2nd Earl of Nottingham as Secretary of State, with a few items rel to the Haslewood and Fanshawe families.

British Library, Manuscript Collections (Add Ch 19788-22613, Add MSS 29548-96). Purchased from the 11th Earl of Winchilsea 1873-4. HMC *First Report, App*, 1870, pp14-30. (For further Finch and Saville papers see also Add MS 28569.)

[h] Dugdale's Book of Monuments.

British Library, Manuscript Collections (MS Loan 38). Deposited by the Trustees of the Winchilsea Settled Estate. Purchased 1994.

[i] Medieval historical and religious MSS.

Bodleian Library, Oxford (Summary Catalogue of Western Manuscripts, vol II, part II, 1937, nos 4026-4136, 5134-6, 5210). From the library of the 1st Baron Hatton. Purchased 1671 and given by Lord Hatton 1675.

Related collection: Finch of Burley-on-the-Hill (no 35).

[37] FITZALAN-HOWARD, Dukes of Norfolk

Sir John Howard (d1485), from an old Norfolk family, became in right of his mother a co-heir of the vast Mowbray estates (see also no 7), and was created Duke of Norfolk in 1483. The East Anglian properties were extended in the time of the third Duke (d1554) but forfeited on the attainder of the fourth Duke in 1572. Partially restored in the early seventeenth century, they were thereafter much reduced by sale.

The fourth Duke married in 1556 Lady Mary Fitzalan, daughter and heiress of the twelfth Earl of Arundel, through whom Arundel Castle and the Sussex, Surrey and other estates of the Fitzalan family descended to the Howards. The Sussex estates were later enlarged and consolidated, notably by the eleventh and twelfth Dukes in the late eighteenth and early nineteenth centuries.

Thomas, Earl of Arundel (grandson of the fourth Duke) married in 1606 Alathea, daughter and eventual heiress of the seventh Earl of Shrewsbury (see no 20), bringing valuable estates in the West Riding of Yorkshire (Sheffield), Derbyshire (Glossop) and Nottinghamshire (Worksop) into the Howard family. Worksop later descended to a younger son of the sixth Duke, Lord Thomas Howard (d1689), who married Mary Savile of Copley (Yorkshire, West Riding), but their son Thomas (1683-1732) succeeded his uncle as eighth Duke in 1701 and brought Worksop back into the senior line. It was the principal family seat in the eighteenth century but was sold to the fourth Duke of Newcastle in 1839. The Glossop estate was settled from time to time on younger sons. Edward George Howard, younger son of the thirteenth Duke, was created Baron Howard of Glossop in 1869.

The Cumberland (Greystoke) estate was inherited from Lord Dacre of Gilsland in the late sixteenth century, but descended in a junior line. Charles Howard, of The Deepdene (Surrey) and Greystoke, succeeded a cousin as tenth Duke of Norfolk in 1777, but on the death of the eleventh Duke in 1815 the Greystoke estate again passed to a junior branch. The eleventh Duke married in 1771 Frances, daughter and heir of Charles Fitzroy-Scudamore of Holme Lacy (Herefordshire).

Through the marriage of the fifteenth Duke to Gwendolen Constable-Maxwell, Baroness Herries, in 1904, the Dukes of Norfolk acquired former Constable estates in the East Riding of Yorkshire and Lincolnshire (Everingham and West Rasen) and former Maxwell estates in Dumfriesshire and Kirkcudbrightshire (Caerlaverock and Kinharvie). The Terregles (Dumfriesshire) estate of the Herries family, however, had passed to a junior branch of the Constable-Maxwell family, afterwards the Constable-Maxwell-Stuarts of Traquair.

On the death of the sixteenth Duke in 1975 he was succeeded in the dukedom and the Arundel Castle estates by his kinsman the fourth Baron Howard of Glossop, son of the third Baron by Mona Stapleton, *suo jure* Baroness Beaumont, of Carlton Towers (Yorkshire, West Riding). The Howard of Glossop and Beaumont estates, however, fall outside the scope of this volume.

Estates in 1883: Duke of Norfolk: Sussex 21,446 acres, Yorks WR 19,440 acres, Norfolk 4,460 acres, Surrey 3,172 acres, Derbys 1,274 acres, Suffolk 47 acres, Staffs 25 acres, Notts 2 acres, total 49,866 acres worth £75,596 a year; Lord Herries: Yorks ER 6,858 acres, Lincs 2,800 acres, Dumfriesshire 5,814 acres, Kirkcudbrightshire 3,423 acres, total 18,895 acres worth £19,152 a year.

[a] Deeds 12th-20th cent, mainly Sussex and Surrey estates but incl Norfolk and Suffolk 12th-19th cent, Yorks and Derbys 12th-19th cent, Cumberland and Westmorland 12th-18th cent, Beds, Oxon and Salop 14th-16th cent, and Middlesex (the Strand estate) 16th-19th cent; charters of Rufford Abbey (Notts) (a former Shrewsbury property) 13th-15th cent; settlements, wills and related trust papers 15th-20th cent, mainly Dukes of Norfolk but incl Constable-Maxwell family 19th-20th cent, trusteeship for Lord Donington 19th-20th cent and descent of Shrewsbury estates 18th-19th cent; legal papers from 16th cent, incl extensive papers deposited from solicitors 19th-20th cent; manorial records 13th-20th cent, various counties, incl Sussex (honour of Arundel, Lewes, New Shoreham, etc), Surrey (Dorking, etc), Hants (Hayling), Norfolk and Suffolk (Bungay priory and soke, etc) and Cumberland (Brackenthwaite, etc).

Sussex and Surrey estate records 14th-20th cent, incl surveys, maps and plans, rentals and accounts, letter books, and papers rel to building and repairs, roads and railways, and charities; Hants estate papers c16th-18th cent; Norfolk and Suffolk estate accounts and papers 14th-early 20th cent, incl papers rel to sales; Yorks WR and Derbys estate papers 14th-20th cent, incl Sheffield leases 19th-20th cent; Notts estate papers mainly 16th-18th cent; misc Cumberland and Westmorland estate papers from mid-17th cent; Welsh and Salop surveys, accounts and rentals 14th-17th cent, with Shifnal (Salop) papers late 19th-early 20th cent; Middlesex estate papers 16th-20th cent, incl Strand estate building papers and rentals and papers rel to Kilburn and Notting Hill estates 19th-20th cent; misc papers rel to Scudamore estates (Herefs, etc) 18th cent, Shrewsbury estates (Berks, Cheshire, Oxon, Salop, Staffs and Worcs) 17th-19th cent, Donington estates (Leics and Derbys) early 20th cent, Lincs (West Rasen) estate 19th-20th cent and Scottish estate early 20th cent.

Building papers 18th-20th cent, incl Arundel Castle (drawings by CA Buckler, etc), Norfolk House, Arundel Cathedral and church of St John the Baptist, Norwich; inventories and catalogues, Arundel Castle, Norfolk House, Everingham, etc 17th-20th cent; household accounts of the 1st Duke of Norfolk c1464-6; household accounts and papers 18th-20th cent for Arundel Castle, Norfolk House, Worksop Manor, etc; collegiate church of Holy Trinity, Arundel, accounts, inventories, etc 1395-1551; Fitzalan chapel case papers 19th cent; Arundel almshouse accounts 15th-16th cent; papers rel to the borough of Horsham 16th-19th cent, incl deeds of burgage properties, borough court books 1650-1770 and election papers; rolls, etc rel to the borough of King's Lynn 13th-17th cent; election papers, Sussex 18th-19th cent and Norfolk 1730s; accounts of the Earls of Arundel as receivers for the New Forest 17th cent (7 rolls); Earl Marshal's papers mainly 17th-20th cent, incl papers rel to the Court of Chivalry, College of Arms, coronations, funerals, peerages, etc; shrievalty papers mainly Sussex 16th-18th cent.

Letters patent, commissions, appointments, etc 15th-20th cent, mainly Howard family; family corresp and papers 16th-20th cent, incl the Talbot Earls of Shrewsbury 1513-1617 and the 11th, 14th, 15th, 16th and 17th Dukes of Norfolk; naval, diplomatic and other papers of the 1st Baron Lyons and Viscount Lyons 19th cent; business corresp and papers of John Aylward (merchant, grandfather of the 10th Duke) 1672-1717; corresp and literary papers of Canon MA Tierney 19th cent; letters from Cardinal Newman to the Revd SL Pope 1824-51 (1 vol); minutes, etc of the Catholic Association 1808-29; genealogical, heraldic, historical and misc MSS, incl papers of Sir CG Young (*ex*-Phillipps collection) and the Norris collection (purchased 1888); Norfolk deeds 12th-17th cent (purchased 1786); estate and other accounts of the Earls of Stafford 14th-16th cent.

In private possession. Enquiries to the Librarian, Arundel Castle, Sussex. Documents less than 100 years old are closed to research. Francis W Steer, ed, *Arundel Castle Archives*, vols 1-4, 1968-80; Francis W Steer, *A Catalogue of the Earl Marshal's Papers at Arundel Castle*, Harleian Soc CXV, CXVI, 1964; HMC *Various Collections II*, 1903, *VII*, 1914. NRA 12614.

[b] Maps and surveyor's papers rel to a survey of the Surrey estates 1838.

Surrey Record Office (436). Deposited by Capt AJGC Peachey through the Historical Manuscripts Commission 1956. NRA 3518.

[c] Surrey (Dorking-cum-Capel and Shellwood) manorial records and related papers 1540-1962.

Surrey Record Office (196). Deposited by Holmes, Campbell & Co, solicitors, Arundel 1955, Hart, Scales & Hodges, solicitors, Dorking, and Sir Algar Howard. NRA 17921. Other manorial records held by Holmes, Campbell & Co have been transferred to the Arundel Castle muniments (see NRA 1234).

[d] Further Dorking and Shellwood manorial records 17th-19th cent.

West Sussex Record Office. Deposited by Holmes, Campbell & Co [?1955]. NRA 1234.

[e] Norfolk and Suffolk estate papers 19th-20th cent, incl abstracts of settlements 1839-1904, manorial rentals 1859-62 (Forncett (Norfolk)) and 1928-45, enfranchisement papers 1863-7, report 1861 and rentals and accounts mainly 20th cent.

Norfolk Record Office. Deposited by Smiths Gore, Newmarket, on behalf of the 17th Duke of Norfolk 1978, 1980. NRA 30024.

[f] Fersfield, Shelfanger, Seymer and Bressingham (Norfolk) manorial records 13th-20th cent.

Norfolk Record Office. Among records formerly in the custody of Messrs Harold Warnes & Co, solicitors, Eye, deposited by Messrs Dawson, Butters & Rubery, solicitors, Ipswich, through Ipswich and East Suffolk Record Office 1968, 1969. NRA 34850.

[g] Manorial records for Lopham, Shelfanger, etc (Norfolk) 17th-20th cent.

Norfolk Record Office. Deposited by Lyus, Burne & Lyus, solicitors, Diss 1974. NRA 34849.

[h] Misc deeds and accounts late 13th-early 16th cent, mainly East Anglian estates, incl Norfolk manorial accounts (Bressingham, etc) 14th-15th cent and household account 1462-6.

Norfolk Record Office (MS 21878). Purchased 1967, 1982 (formerly in the collection of Sir Thomas Phillipps). NRA 28421.

[i] Suffolk estate accounts 16th cent.

Suffolk Record Office, Ipswich branch (Iveagh (formerly Phillipps) MSS, nos 40, 103, 225). Purchased 1985. NRA 4134.

[j] Mowbray and Howard cartulary late 15th cent, with schedule of Norfolk House and Arundel Castle muniments 19th cent.

British Library, Manuscript Collections (Add MS 24688). Acquired 1862.

[k] Misc deeds, account rolls, etc rel to the Mowbray and Howard estates 14th-16th cent.

British Library, Manuscript Collections (Add Ch 16531-79 *passim*). Acquired 1866. Formerly in the collection of Sir John Fenn.

[l] Account and memorandum book of Sir John Howard, later 1st Duke of Norfolk 1462-9.

British Library, Manuscript Collections (Add MS 46349). Purchased at Sotheby's, 11 Nov 1946, lot 552 (formerly Phillipps MS 3790).

[m] Household account book of the Earl of Surrey (later 3rd Duke of Norfolk) 1523-4.

University of California Library, Berkeley, California (MS Ac 523). Formerly Phillipps MS 3841. WH Bond, *Supplement to the Census of Medieval and Renaissance Manuscripts in the United States and Canada*, 1962, p2.

[n] Deeds for Yorks WR (Sheffield, etc) 14th-19th cent, Notts (Worksop and Shireoaks (previously Hewett) estates) 13th-19th cent and

Derbys (Glossop, etc) 14th-19th cent; Worksop Priory cartulary *c*1500; Furnivall, Talbot, Savile (of Copley) and Howard settlements and related papers 14th-19th cent; legal papers 17th-20th cent, incl draft deeds, leases, papers rel to sales, Savile of Copley papers 17th-18th cent and solicitors' papers 19th-20th cent; manorial records 13th-19th cent, incl Sheffield 14th-19th cent, Worksop 17th-18th cent, Glossop late 16th cent and Hartington (Derbys) 1275-1595; Sheffield court baron (small debts court) order books, etc 19th cent.

Yorks, Notts and Derbys estate papers 14th-20th cent, mainly 17th cent onwards, incl surveys, maps and plans, rentals and accounts, agents' corresp and papers from 16th cent, and papers rel to collieries and mineral rights 18th-19th cent, quarries 19th-20th cent and woods 17th-19th cent; Staffs, Salop, etc (Earls of Shrewsbury) rentals 1581-4, 1587-92; Yorks (Shireburn family) rentals 1719, etc; building papers for Worksop Manor 18th cent, The Farm (Sheffield) 19th cent and Derwent Hall (Derbys) 19th cent; Worksop Manor inventories 1591-1838 and household accounts 1727-9; Sheffield Castle household accounts 1598-9; papers rel to Sheffield affairs 17th-20th cent, incl market 1784-1899, Shrewsbury Hospital 17th-20th cent, and Corporation Acts early 20th cent; Glossop turnpike trust papers 19th cent; Sherwood Forest roll 1357; patents, commissions, etc 16th-19th cent; corresp of the 15th Duke rel to Sheffield affairs.

Sheffield Archives (Arundel Castle MSS). Deposited by the 16th Duke of Norfolk from Arundel Castle and Sheffield Estate Office 1960, and at various dates by the 17th Duke. Documents less than 100 years old are closed to research. *Catalogue of the Arundel Castle manuscripts*, 1965; HMC *Accessions to Repositories 1970*. NRA 839.

[o] Misc legal and estate papers 18th-19th cent, incl schedules of Sheffield and Worksop deeds 1771-1819, survey of Wheston (Derbys) 1809 and drawings rel to Derwent Hall and grounds 1833, nd.

Sheffield Archives (Bagshawe collection 261-3, 273, 3420, 3475). NRA 7871.

[p] Worksop Manor household account 1727-9.

Sheffield Archives (MD 3398). NRA 23246.

[q] Papers of William Wrightson as steward of the manor of Sheffield 1748-59.

Doncaster Archives Department (Battie-Wrightson papers, DD.BW). *Guide to the Archives Department*, 2nd edn 1981, p 44.

[r] Ministers' accounts for estates of the 5th Earl of Shrewsbury in Yorks, Notts and Derbys 1558-9.

Nottinghamshire Archives (DP 67). Purchased 1956.

[s] Steward's memorandum book 1739-58.

Nottinghamshire Archives (Craven-Smith Milnes papers, DDCW 4/4). NRA 6898.

[t] Sheffield estate papers 16th-18th cent, incl Sheffield and Rotherham (Yorks WR) bailiffs' accounts 1579-82, surveys 17th cent and agents' papers 17th-18th cent; misc estate papers, incl Mowbray receiver-general's account 1422-3 and items rel to Thornbury (Gloucs) 17th cent; household account of the Countess of Norfolk 1385-7.

British Library, Manuscript Collections (Add MSS 27532-8, Add Ch 17208-12). Acquired 1866.

[u] Corresp and papers of Nicholas Williamson of Sawley (Yorks WR), Shrewsbury steward late 16th cent.

Public Record Office (SP 46/47-9). NRA 30828.

[v] Talbot family corresp and papers 15th-early 17th cent (15 vols).

Lambeth Palace Library. Presented by the 6th Duke of Norfolk to the College of Arms *c*1677; purchased by Lambeth Palace Library 1983. See GR Batho, ed, *A Calendar of the Shrewsbury and Talbot Papers, vol II, Talbot papers in the College of Arms*, 1971. Other papers passed into the collection of the antiquary Nathaniel Johnston, and are now to be found in Lambeth Palace Library (see Catherine Jamieson and EGW Bill, eds, *A Calendar of the Shrewsbury and Talbot Papers, vol I, Shrewsbury MSS in Lambeth Palace Library*, 1966), the MSS of the Marquess of Bath at Longleat (see HMC *Bath V, Talbot, Dudley and Devereux papers 1533-1659*, 1980), and the Bacon Frank MSS (see HMC *Sixth Report, App*, 1877, pp448ff; *Catalogue of the Arundel Castle Manuscripts*, 1965, pp181-222; NRA 839, 4883). MSS collected by Thomas, Earl of Arundel (d1646) were given by the 6th Duke of Norfolk to the College of Arms and the Royal Society, the latter collection being acquired by the British Museum in 1831.

[w] Shrewsbury corresp and papers 1548-1619, incl letters to Elizabeth, Countess of Shrewsbury, and accounts of the 1st Earl of Devonshire 1598, 1610.

Folger Shakespeare Library, Washington DC. The papers passed from John Staniforth, a steward, to John Wilson of Broomhead (Yorks) and later to Sir Thomas Phillipps. Purchased 1961. NRA 20633.

[x] Letters to the Howard family from FW Faber, Anthony Hutchinson and other Oratorians 1849-99 (3 vols).

The Oratory, London. NRA 16631.

[y] Deeds 12th-19th cent (*c*280 medieval), mainly Yorks and Lincs but incl a few for Gloucs, Wilts and other counties; Constable and Constable-Maxwell wills, settlements and related papers 16th-20th cent, with inquisitions *post mortem* 14th-17th cent; legal and financial papers (Constable) 16th-20th cent, incl schedules of deeds, sequestration papers 1650s and recusancy papers 17th-18th cent; Sherburne of Stonyhurst (Lancs) legal and financial papers 1627-77; manorial records 15th-20th cent, mainly Yorks ER.

Yorks ER estate records 16th-20th cent, incl leases and agreements, surveys, maps and plans, rentals and accounts; Lincs estate records 16th-20th cent, incl leases, surveys, rentals and accounts; ?Stonyhurst account 1671-5; rental for Seaton Ross (Yorks ER) (Duke of Leeds's estate) 1737; papers rel to Yorks affairs 16th-20th cent, incl shrievalty 1532-1691 and 1830s, Market Weighton navigation and drainage 16th-20th cent (with earlier drainage papers 1399-1400), Market Weighton tithes and rectory 17th-19th cent, Everingham yeomanry cavalry 1803-13 and Everingham church, school and parish affairs mainly 19th cent; accounts for building and alterations at Everingham Park 1757-64, 1844-8; household accounts and papers, Everingham 17th-20th cent, West Rasen 1633-40; Yorks household inventories 1537-20th cent and cellar books 19th cent; catalogues of books 17th-19th cent.

Patents, commissions, etc, mainly Constable family from 16th cent; Constable, Sherburne and Constable-Maxwell family papers 17th-20th cent, incl corresp of the Earls of Nithsdale 17th cent, corresp rel to English and Scottish estates 18th-19th cent, accounts, pedigrees, etc; papers rel to Roman Catholicism 16th-20th cent, incl Everingham register of baptisms, etc 1777-1801, and papers rel to the Sufferings of the Catholicks 1558-1654 (purchased at the Chichester-Constable sale 1889).

Records of the Maxwell estates in Scotland (some formerly kept at Terregles), incl writs 13th-18th cent, legal papers 16th-early 20th cent (tacks, bonds, letters of horning, etc, mostly Maxwell but some rel to Terregles and Traquair), estate records (valuations, plans, accounts, etc) 17th-early 20th cent, Terregles inventories 19th cent and garden account 1921, family corresp from late 16th cent (Earls of Nithsdale, etc), misc family papers, inventories and transcripts, and antiquarian papers of George Chalmers early 19th cent.

Hull University, Brynmor Jones Library (DDEV). Deposited by the 16th Duke of Norfolk 1960-5 in the East Riding Record Office and transferred to Hull University Library 1974, with modern legal papers deposited by the 17th Duke of Norfolk from Carlton Towers 1989. Rentals and accounts less than 100 years old and other records less than 50 years old are not open to research. NRA 11211. For MSS at Everingham Park in 1870 (HMC *First Report, App*, 1870, pp45-6) see HMC *Guide to the Location of Collections*, 1982, p30.

[z] Everingham and Seaton Ross manorial papers mainly 1802-85.

Hull University, Brynmor Jones Library (DDCV). Deposited in the East Riding Record Office by Crust, Tod & Mills, solicitors, Beverley, and transferred 1974. NRA 6482.

Related collections: Berkeley, Earls of Berkeley (no 7); Chetwynd-Talbot, Earls of Shrewsbury (no

20); Howard of Greystoke (Cumbria Record Office, Carlisle D/HG, D/HGB, NRA 23768); Thornbury manorial and estate records (Gloucestershire Record Office D 108, NRA 14347); Howard of Glossop (Derbyshire Record Office D 3705/1-45, NRA 8918); Howard of Corby Castle (in private possession, NRA 7034), including personal and executorship papers of the 11th Duke; Constable-Maxwell-Stuart of Traquair (in private possession, NRA (S) 1362, NRA 9765); Barons Stafford (Staffordshire Record Office, D 641/2/L/1-2, NRA 9561), including Sussex and East Anglian estate papers; Scudamore deeds, estate papers and family papers 12th-19th cent (Public Record Office C 115), including Lanthony Priory cartularies 13th-16th cent.

[38] FOLJAMBE of Osberton

The Foljambe family had knightly status in Derbyshire by the thirteenth century, and by 1500 also owned land in Nottinghamshire and Yorkshire. The Aldwarke (Yorkshire, West Riding) estate was acquired through the marriage of Sir James Foljambe (d1558) to Alice Fitzwilliam. Sir Francis Foljambe (d1640) sold the Walton (Derbyshire) and other estates, but Aldwarke and some remaining Derbyshire property passed on his death to his cousin Peter Foljambe of Steeton (Yorkshire, West Riding) (1599-1699), whose son Francis (d1707) married Elizabeth Mountaigne of Westow (Yorkshire, East Riding).

Francis Ferrand Foljambe of Aldwarke (1750-1814) married in 1774 Mary (d1790), daughter and heiress of John Hewett (formerly Thornhagh), through whom descended the Thornhagh estates of Osberton (Nottinghamshire), South Kelsey (Lincolnshire), Skeffington (Leicestershire) and Arley (Warwickshire), and the Hewett estate of Shireoaks (Nottinghamshire). Osberton became the Foljambe family's principal seat, but the other Thornhagh estates were sold in the early nineteenth century. FF Foljambe also inherited Newtown Savile (County Tyrone) from his wife's uncle Sir George Savile, eighth Bt (1726-84), but that estate was sold in 1806-11. In 1792 Foljambe married secondly Mary, daughter of the fourth Earl of Scarbrough by Barbara Savile.

George Savile Foljambe (1800-1869) married as his second wife Selina Charlotte, Viscountess Milton, daughter and co-heir of the third and last Earl of Liverpool of the first creation. Their eldest son by this marriage inherited property from his mother, and was created Earl of Liverpool in 1915, but this property did not descend with the Osberton estates.

Estates in 1883: Notts 9,289 acres, Yorks NR and WR 5,206 acres, Lincs 3 acres, total 14,498 acres worth £20,140 a year.

[a] Deeds 12th-19th cent (c3,000 medieval), mainly Derbys, Notts and Yorks, but incl some

for Kent, Leics, Lincs, Co Tyrone, etc; abstracts
of title 16th-19th cent, incl Newtown Savile
1789-1832; wills and settlements 14th-19th cent,
Foljambe, Thornhagh, Hewett, Lumley and Savile families; executorship accounts and papers
17th-19th cent, incl Sir George Savile 1783-1804
and Captain TC Lumley-Saunderson 1782-92;
papers of John Hewett and Sir George Savile as
executors of AC Stanhope and guardians of the
5th Earl of Chesterfield 1770-7; legal and case
papers 14th-19th cent; manorial records, Yorks
WR 13th-18th cent (incl Mexborough
1292-1580 and honour of Tickhill 1418), Notts
(Mansfield, etc) 15th-17th cent, and Derbys,
Kent and Lincs 14th-15th cent.

Derbys, Notts and Yorks estate records
13th-20th cent, Foljambe, Thornhagh and
Hewett, incl leases, agreements, surveys, maps,
particulars, rentals from c1500, accounts and
vouchers from 17th cent (mainly Notts and
Yorks), corresp from 16th cent and papers
14th-19th cent rel to timber, drainage, tithes,
enclosure, etc (mainly Notts and Yorks); coal,
iron and lead mining papers 17th-19th cent,
Yorks and Derbys, incl Yorks colliery accounts
c1629-1770; South Kelsey estate papers 18th-
early 19th cent, incl surveys and rentals
1715-1807 and accounts and vouchers 1737-92;
Ulceby (Lincs) rentals and surveys 1443-1630;
Great Staughton (Hunts) particulars and rentals
1723-65; Bristol survey 1653; Trowbridge
(Wilts) rental late 13th cent; Savile (Yorks) estate
papers 18th cent, incl valuation 1755; Newtown
Savile estate papers 1732-1832, incl surveys, val-
uations, rentals, accounts and vouchers; misc
Earl of Scarbrough estate papers c1767-83, Co
Durham, Lincs and Yorks WR, incl Lumley (Co
Durham) colliery corresp and accounts 1778-81.

Accounts and papers rel to building at Steeton
1629 and Aldwarke 1706-8; inventories
16th-18th cent, incl Beauchief Abbey (Derbys)
1536 and Aldwarke 16th cent; misc household
accounts and papers 17th-19th cent; shrievalty
papers, Notts and Derbys 1536-7 and Lincs
1610-1746; Yorks election expenses of Sir
George Savile 1780; papers rel to Notts elections
c1679-1774; subsidy assessments and papers
16th-18th cent, mainly Notts but incl Scarsdale
and High Peak (Derbys) subsidy roll 1601-2;
papers rel to the duchy of Lancaster and honour
of Tickhill 14th cent-1539; constables' accounts
and papers 17th-18th cent, Aldwarke and
Wheatcroft (Derbys); Adel cum Eccup,
Arthington and Rotherham (Yorks WR) charity
school accounts 1714-48; misc Yorks militia
(Savile's regiment) accounts and papers
c1762-76.

Misc appointments 14th-18th cent; Foljambe,
Hewett, Thornhagh and Savile family papers
17th-19th cent, incl political corresp and papers
of FF Foljambe and Sir George Savile; accounts
and papers of Sir Thomas Hewett (d1720) as
Surveyor of the King's Works and as surveyor of
Sherwood Forest, incl Sherwood Forest books
and papers 15th-17th cent; accounts of James

Needham 1534-5, 1540 and Sir Christopher
Wren 1682-3 as Surveyors of the King's Works;
literary, genealogical and other papers 13th-19th
cent, incl book of musters and list of crown
offices and fees *temp* Elizabeth I, extent and customs roll of Notts and Derbys estates of the
Dean of Lincoln 1329, papers rel to College of
the Holy Trinity, Pontefract 1386-1491 and
estate accounts, draft will and household account
of Henry de Lacy, Earl of Lincoln late 13th cent.

Nottinghamshire Archives (DD FJ). Deposited
1962-88. HMC *Fifteenth Report, App V*, 1897;
Papers of British Politicians 1782-1900, 1989, p37.
NRA 20442.

[b] Plan of Shafton (Yorks WR) by Christopher
Saxton 1597; letters of James, Duke of York to
William, Prince of Orange 1678-9; genealogical
papers 17th-18th cent.

In private possession. HMC *Fifteenth Report, App
V*, 1897, pp123-41. NRA 20442.

Related collections: Lumley-Savile of Rufford
(Nottinghamshire Archives DD SR, NRA 6119);
Earls of Scarbrough (in private possession, NRA
6155); Earls of Liverpool, miscellaneous papers
1590-1872 (Berkshire Record Office D/EX 183,
NRA 19683), including Foljambe deeds.

[39] **FORTESCUE, Earls Fortescue**

The Fortescue family was settled in south Devon
by the late twelfth century, but the first major
acquisitions of land were made in the time of Sir
John Fortescue, Chief Justice of England (d1479).
By marriage he acquired estates in Somerset
(Norton St Philip) and Wiltshire (sold in 1725);
and in 1457 he purchased land at Ebrington
(Gloucestershire) from the Corbet family. His son
Martin Fortescue acquired by marriage (1454) the
main group of north Devon estates based upon
Weare Giffard and Filleigh (renamed Castle Hill
c1740). Between the sixteenth and the early eight-
eenth centuries additional lands were acquired,
mainly through wardship or purchase, in south
Devon (Lamerton, Tavistock, etc), on Exmoor
(Challacombe, High Bray, etc), and on the north
Devon coast (Georgeham, Mortehoe), as well as in
Somerset (including former estates of Bath Priory
and the Guild of Holy Trinity and St John the
Baptist, Shepton Mallet), Gloucestershire (Hid-
cote, etc) and Leicestershire. The marriage in
1692 of Hugh Fortescue to Bridget Boscawen,
granddaughter and co-heir of the 4th Earl of Lincoln, brought lands in Cornwall and Lincolnshire,
including former Sidney family estates at Tattershall (Lincs) granted to Lord Clinton in 1574.
In 1781, following the death without issue of the
second Lord Fortescue of Credan, the estates of
that family, including the former Aland family
estates in County Waterford, also passed to the
Fortescues of Castle Hill. The third Baron was
created Earl Fortescue in 1789.

Estates in 1883: Devon 20,171 acres, Lincs 5,116
acres, Gloucs 1,071 acres, Cornwall 571 acres,

Co Waterford 3,958 acres, total 30,887 acres worth £28,673 a year.

[a] Deeds, mainly Devon early 12th-19th cent, Cornwall 13th-19th cent, Somerset *c*1200-19th cent, Gloucs late 12th-19th cent and Lincs 16th-19th cent, with some for Co Waterford 17th-19th cent, Leics 17th-18th cent, Worcs 18th cent and Middlesex (London) 18th-19th cent; trust deeds, wills and settlements 17th-19th cent, mainly Fortescue; misc legal papers 17th-19th cent; Devon court rolls, compoti and presentments, Filleigh, etc 13th-19th cent; Cornwall presentments 18th-19th cent; Somerset court rolls and compoti 15th-16th cent.

Devon (Castle Hill and Weare Giffard) estate records 14th-20th cent, incl leases, agreements and related corresp 1325-20th cent, surveys, maps and plans 17th-20th cent, rentals and accounts late 17th-20th cent, papers rel to Devon mining, forestry, quarries, water supply, turnpikes and railways 19th-20th cent, crop and stock books 19th-20th cent, and agents' diaries and corresp 20th cent; Devon (Exmoor) estate records 17th-20th cent, incl leases 17th-20th cent, surveys, valuations, rentals, accounts and corresp 19th-20th cent, Exmoor mining and sheep grazing papers 19th-20th cent, and Challacombe Estates Company minute and share books 1936-47; Cornwall leases 16th-19th cent; Cornish surveys, rentals, accounts, corresp and antimony and tin mining papers 18th-19th cent; Somerset leases and related papers 1306-19th cent, incl Ashwick coal mining papers 1605-1800; Somerset surveys, rentals and corresp 19th-20th cent; Gloucs leases 1485-19th cent; Gloucs estate papers 17th-20th cent, incl surveys, maps, valuations, rentals, accounts and corresp, and notebook of the cultivation of Ebrington great field 1812; Lincs estate papers 18th-20th cent, incl leases 18th-19th cent, surveys and valuations 18th-19th cent, maps 19th-20th cent, accounts and vouchers, corresp, and papers rel to enclosure and fen drainage 1831-80; Co Waterford leases 17th-19th cent, maps 18th-19th cent, and valuations, rentals, accounts and corresp 19th-20th cent; Middlesex leases 19th cent; Leics leases 1928-35.

Building accounts, Castle Hill 1764-87; corresp and plans rel to rebuilding of Castle Hill 1934-7; household inventories 17th-20th cent, incl catalogue of books at Castle Hill 1886 and inventories of 48 Grosvenor Square and 75 Eaton Place, London 19th cent; Castle Hill and London household accounts 17th-20th cent; papers rel to Devon lieutenancy and magistracy 17th-20th cent, incl corresp rel to militia and volunteers 1781-1820 and to the commission of the peace 18th-19th cent; election papers and accounts, incl Barnstaple election accounts 1747-1816; county rate papers 1811-20; papers rel to disturbances 1830-47 and to Devon and Somerset War Agricultural Executive Committee 1913-42; parochial papers 16th-19th cent.

Family corresp and papers 17th-20th cent, incl Boscawen and Clinton corresp and papers 17th

cent, political corresp of the 1st and 2nd Earls 18th cent-1861, papers of the 2nd Earl as Lord Lieutenant of Ireland 1839-41, parliamentary papers of the 3rd and 4th Earls, travel diaries of the 2nd Earl and JW Fortescue, MP 19th cent, diaries of Sir Seymour Fortescue and of the 4th Earl 19th-20th cent, and MS of Sir John Fortescue's *The Empire and the Army*; survey of arms of Sir Gavin Carew and Sir John More 1569.

Devon Record Office (D 1262). Deposited by the 6th Earl Fortescue 1963-4 and by the 7th Earl 1977, 1982-3, 1988. HMC *Third Report, App*, 1872, pp220-1. *County Archivist's Report* 1964-5, pp5-10; 1976-8, pp15-16; 1982-3, p13; 1983-4, p11. NRA 6304.

[b] Court rolls, Lamerton, Weare Gifford and Filleigh 1430-97.

Devon Record Office (867B). Deposited by Michelmore, Loveys & Carter, solicitors, Totnes *c*1975. NRA 8073.

[c] Gloucs deeds 14th-19th cent; estate maps 19th cent; enclosure and tithe papers (Ebrington, etc) 19th cent.

Gloucestershire Record Office (D 13, 481, 2165, 5358). *Handlist*, 1990, p180.

[d] Gloucs manorial court rolls 1777-1819, with lists of inhabitants 1819.

Shakespeare Birthplace Trust Records Office (ER 24/33). Formerly in the possession of Sir Thomas Phillipps; purchased 1932. NRA 4523.

[e] Gloucs court orders (Ebrington, etc) 1777-1800.

Gloucester City Library. Formerly in the possession of Sir Thomas Phillipps and then of JH Edge.

[f] Gloucs rental (Ebrington) 1801.

Bodleian Library, Oxford (MS Phillipps-Robinson c.215). Formerly in the possession of Sir Thomas Phillipps; given by Lionel and Philip Robinson 1958. NRA 26260.

[g] Lincs (Tattershall and Billingborough) estate papers 1782-1908, incl survey and valuation 1794, account of tenants 1830, rentals 1782-1908 and enclosure and drainage papers 19th cent.

Devon Record Office (D 1262 add 7). Transferred from the Bodleian Library, Oxford 1988. NRA 6304.

[h] Lincs (Sempringham and Tattershall) estate papers 17th-19th cent, incl survey of Pointon 1828.

Lincolnshire Archives (4614-76, 4728, 4836). Transferred from Lincoln City Library. *Archivists' Report* 25 (1973-5), p86.

[i] Lincs rental (Tattershall) 1657.

John Rylands University Library of Manchester. Purchased 1929.

[j] Lincs receivers' accounts (Tattershall, Bill-ingborough) 1693-4.

Public Record Office (C 107/21).

Related collection: legal papers of the 2nd Baron Fortescue of Credan 18th cent (British Library, Manuscript Collections Stowe MSS 403, 1011, 1012).

[40] FOX-STRANGWAYS, Earls of Ilchester

Sir Stephen Fox (1627-1716), courtier and politician, acquired property in Wiltshire (Farley, etc), Somerset (Redlynch), Middlesex (Chiswick) and elsewhere. His eldest surviving son Stephen (1704-1776) married in 1735 Elizabeth, daughter of Thomas Strangways Horner of Mells (Somerset) by Susannah, daughter and co-heir of Thomas Strangways of Melbury Sampford (Dorset), and was created Earl of Ilchester in 1756.

The Strangways family had extensive properties in Dorset, Somerset and other counties by the late fifteenth century. In 1547 Sir Giles Strangways married Joan Wadham, through whom in the early seventeenth century a moiety of the Wadham estates in Devon, Dorset and Somerset came to the Strangways family. The Devon properties, however, along with the Wiltshire estates, were reduced by sales in the early nineteenth century.

In 1874 the fifth Earl of Ilchester acquired the reversion of the Holland House estate in Kensington (Middlesex), together with family papers of the Barons Holland (descended from a younger brother of the first Earl of Ilchester), from the widow of the fourth Baron Holland. (She died in 1889.)

Estates in 1883: Dorset 15,981 acres, Somerset 13,169 acres, Wilts 2,133 acres, Devon 1,566 acres, total 32,849 acres worth £42,452 a year.

[a] Deeds for Dorset 10th-20th cent (5 pre-Conquest), Somerset 12th-19th cent, Devon 14th-19th cent and Wilts 15th-19th cent, with smaller quantities for Middlesex (Chiswick, Kensington, etc) 17th-19th cent, Oxon (Strangways) 14th-16th cent, Warwicks (Edwards family) 1590-1652, Yorks NR (Wilton, etc: Earl of Sunderland) 16th-18th cent and other counties; legal papers 15th-19th cent, Fox and Strangways, incl case papers rel to the Fleet river (Dorset) 19th cent; other legal papers 17th-18th cent, mainly acquired through the Fox family, incl papers rel to Ireland 1676-1718 and the Isle of Arran 1727-38; wills, settlements, trust deeds and related papers 16th-19th cent, mainly Fox and Strangways, incl inventory of Sir Giles Strangways 1547, other executorship papers, Wadham family early 17th cent, Sir Archibald Row 1702-26, etc; manorial records, Dorset and Somerset 13th-20th cent (incl Somerton hundred 1617-1863), Devon 17th-18th cent and Wilts 18th-19th cent.

Dorset and Somerset estate records 15th-20th cent, incl leases and schedules of leases 17th-19th cent, surveys and valuations, maps from 17th cent, Strangways estate accounts 1469-1627, rentals from late 15th cent, and papers rel to advowsons, tithes, enclosure, timber, fee farm rents, taxation, roads and railways, and Abbotsbury (Dorset) decoy and swannery 17th-19th cent; surveys, rentals, accounts and other papers for Fox and Strangways estates in Devon and Wilts 17th-early 20th cent and Wadham estates in various southern counties c1580-1605; papers for Fox estates in Middlesex (Chiswick, development of Hungerford Market with Sir Christopher Wren, etc), Berks, Suffolk, etc late 17th-early 18th cent, and Lord Holland's estates in Wilts (Foxley), etc 1760s; papers for Lord Sunderland's Wilton estate 1692-1741 and the Countess of Salisbury's Dorset and Somerset estate 1529-30; corresp rel to the Talbot estates in Glamorganshire 1803-60.

Accounts, etc rel to building work at Melbury House c1692-9, 1736-4, etc, Redlynch 1740-50, 1800-2, Chiswick 1682-4, Maddington (Wilts) 1786-9 and Stinsford (Dorset) 1828; household inventories, accounts and other papers, Melbury, Chiswick, London, etc 1666-19th cent; Abbotsbury cellar book 1858-64 and wages book 1865-7; garden accounts, etc, Melbury 1852-92 and Evershot (Dorset) (Donisthorpe family) 1747-60; Wilts shrievalty roll 1701-2; Hindon (Wilts) election accounts 1733-c1737; papers rel to parish, charitable and other local affairs 16th-19th cent, incl Redlynch highways accounts 1705-49, Farley hospital accounts 1703-67, Ilton (Somerset) almshouse papers c1749-51 and Evershot Co-operative Society records 1877-93.

Bonds, pardons, commissions and appointments 1484-19th cent, Strangways and other families; Strangways and Fox-Strangways family papers 17th-19th cent, incl business and other corresp of Sir John Strangways 1603-66, accounts of the 1st Earl of Ilchester 1722-78, and papers of the 3rd Earl as lord lieutenant of Somerset and (1835-41) Captain of the Yeomen of the Guard; Fox family accounts and papers c1660-1720, incl Royal Household papers of Sir Stephen Fox and papers of Sir Stephen Fox and others rel to the Paymastership of the Forces; other business papers of Sir Stephen Fox, rel to the Duchess of Buccleuch, the Cornwallis family, the 2nd Earl of Sunderland, etc; misc papers of the Carew family early 16th cent, Edwards family 1586-1622 and George Donisthorpe of Evershot mid-18th cent; accounts of the 1st Duke of Ormonde 1664-1700; pedigrees and other genealogical papers 16th-19th cent; Abbotsbury Abbey demesne livestock accounts late 14th cent-1408 (4 rolls), pardons 1378-1509 (3) and debt account 1504 (1 roll); misc papers 16th-19th cent, incl trading accounts with Portugal 1668-1714.

Dorset Record Office (D 124). Deposited mainly by the 7th Earl of Ilchester, his daughter Lady Galway and Strangways Estates Ltd 1959-69. Enquiries to Dorset Record Office.

[b] Somerset rentals 1660-1780.

Public Record Office (C 108/307).

[c] Dorset deeds, leases, etc 14th-early 19th cent (15 items); executorship papers, Sir Stephen and Charles Fox 1713-21, incl Wilts estate account 1713-15 and calendars of charters 1694-1716; wills, settlements, executorship accounts and misc estate papers c1693-1840, Fox family, Barons Holland; appointments, addresses, etc 18th-19th cent; Fox and Fox-Strangways family papers 17th-20th cent, incl Sir Stephen Fox (household expenses of Charles II 1654-5, Chelsea Hospital papers, papers rel to Duchess of Buccleuch and Cornwallis family, etc) and the 1st-7th Earls of Ilchester; Fox (Holland House) papers 18th-19th cent, incl the 1st, 3rd and 4th Barons Holland, CJ Fox, General CR Fox, Caroline Fox and Dr John Allen; Bruton Priory cartulary 13th cent.

British Library, Manuscript Collections (Add Ch 75522-58, Add MSS 51318-52254, 63145, Eg MS 3772). Mainly acquired from the trustees of the 5th Earl of Ilchester 1962.

[d] Deeds, leases and related papers for the Kensington estate 1744-1955, incl lease registers 1824-c1877, 1928; building agreements 1825-65; rentals 1872, 1890-1931; map 1874 with later additions; papers rel to Holland Farm, the West London Railway, etc 19th cent; misc papers for other estates (mainly Dorset and Somerset) 18th-20th cent.

Greater London Record Office (E/HOL). Deposited 1970. NRA 34971.

[e] Deeds, wills, settlements and legal corresp and papers rel to the Kensington, Chertsey (Surrey) and Ampthill (Beds) estates 18th-19th cent; deed rel to Abbotsbury 1874; lists of Kensington copyholders 1751-71 (1 vol); schedule of Kensington leasehold property 1873, with volume of plans *post* 1855; inventories, Holland House 1873, St Ann's Hill, Chertsey 1891.

Greater London Record Office (Acc 1795). Deposited by Stoneham, Langton & Passmore, solicitors, London, through the British Records Association 1982. NRA 27174.

[f] Misc papers rel to Holland House and park 1799-20th cent, incl head gardener's account book 1799-1801, meteorological records 1884-1952 and Holland House inventory 1946-7.

Kensington and Chelsea Libraries and Arts Service (Acc 26384-91, 26394-26514). Deposited from Holland Park 1986, etc.

Related collections: Wyndham of Orchard Wyndham (Somerset Archive and Record Service DD/WY, DD/DEL, NRA 1199), including Wadham estate records; Bunbury of Barton (Suffolk Record Office, Bury St Edmunds branch, NRA 2582), including Fox family papers 1696-1845.

[41] GASCOYNE-CECIL, Marquesses of Salisbury

On the death of William Cecil, Lord Burghley, in 1598 (see no 19) his properties in Hertfordshire,

Middlesex, Surrey and elsewhere passed to Robert Cecil (1563-1612), his son by his second wife, who was created Earl of Salisbury in 1605 and who became, like his father, Lord Treasurer. Hatfield was acquired in 1607, in exchange with James I for Lord Salisbury's earlier seat of Theobalds. The first Earl also acquired estates in Dorset (Cranborne), Cornwall (St Michael's Mount), Kent (following the attainder of his brother-in-law Lord Cobham in 1603), Northamptonshire (Brigstock Parks), Wiltshire and elsewhere; but the bulk of these (except Cranborne) were sold in the seventeenth and early eighteenth centuries.

The marriage of the fourth Earl in 1683 to Frances Bennett of Beachampton (Buckinghamshire) led to the inheritance of estates in Buckinghamshire, Nottinghamshire and the North Riding of Yorkshire, but these, with some other outlying properties, were sold by the first Marquess of Salisbury (1748-1823). In 1821, however, the second Marquess married Frances, daughter of Bamber Gascoyne of Childwall (Lancashire), who brought valuable estates in Lancashire (Liverpool, etc) and Essex (Ilford, Barking, etc). For a time in the mid-nineteenth century the family also owned the Scottish island of Rum.

Estates in 1883: Herts 13,389 acres, Dorset 3,118 acres, Lancs 1,796 acres, Middlesex 960 acres, Essex 758 acres, Beds 89 acres, Norfolk 80 acres, Wilts 12 acres, total 20,202 acres worth £33,413 a year.

[a] Deeds 12th-20th cent, mainly Herts, London and Dorset but incl medieval and later deeds for Bucks, Gloucs, Kent, Lincs, Middlesex, Notts and Rutland; cartularies, Cobham family 13th-14th cent, Priory of St Michael's Mount, Montagu Earls of Salisbury and Adam Fr:

 Frauncey's 14th cent; registers of deeds, abstracts of title, etc mainly 16th-19th cent, incl book of evidences at Salisbury House 1634-5; wills and settlements, incl Cecil family from early 16th cent; legal and case papers mainly from early 16th cent, incl papers rel to the 1st Earl of Salisbury decd, Cranborne, Enfield Chase, St Michael's Mount early 17th cent, the Cobham estate, Arlington St town house 18th-19th cent and the Middlesex (Strand) estate 19th cent.

Manorial court rolls, books, accounts and papers 13th-20th cent, incl Cranborne manor and hundred from late 13th cent, various Herts manors 14th-20th cent, and misc manors in Kent, Middlesex, Notts, Rutland, etc 14th-16th cent; Herts, Middlesex and Dorset estate records 15th-20th cent, incl leases and agreements mainly from 16th cent, lease books 17th-18th cent, surveys, maps and plans from c1570, valuations, rentals and accounts, vouchers mid-16th-early 20th cent, estate memoranda and corresp from early 16th cent, letter books from 1840s, Cranborne agent's corresp c1680-1740, abstract books 19th cent and labour books c1828-early 20th cent; Essex (former Gascoyne) estate records late 18th-20th cent; Bucks, Notts and Yorks NR (former Bennett) rentals, etc 17th-early 19th cent; records of outlying or alienated estates 15th-19th cent, incl Cornwall (St Michael's Mount) early 15th-mid-17th cent, Gloucs 16th-18th cent, Kent (Cobham, etc) 15th-17th cent, Lincs 16th-18th cent, Middlesex (Edmonton estate) 16th-early 17th cent, Northants (Brigstock Parks, etc) early 17th-early 18th cent (with a Burghley estate account 1555), Notts (Selston) 16th cent, Surrey (Bermondsey) 17th-18th cent and Rum mid-19th cent.

Hatfield House building accounts *c*1607-13, with plans of Theobalds and Hatfield House; inventories of plate, pictures, etc and papers rel to pictures 17th-20th cent; library catalogues and other papers 17th-20th cent; household accounts, Theobalds 1570-early 17th cent and Hatfield House, etc 17th-19th cent; Herts lieutenancy and militia papers (1st Marquess, etc); quittance rolls, liberty of St Albans 17th-18th cent; patents and commissions, Cecil family 17th-19th cent; official, political and personal corresp and papers of Lord Burghley *c*1550-98, mainly as Secretary of State and Lord Treasurer, and of the 1st Earl of Salisbury mainly 1595-1612; corresp and papers of later members of the Cecil family early 17th-mid-20th cent, incl Civil War and Herts lieutenancy papers of the 2nd Earl, accounts of the 1st Marquess as Lord Chamberlain, political and personal corresp and papers of the 2nd Marquess, extensive prime ministerial and other corresp and papers of the 3rd Marquess, and corresp and papers of Lord Cecil of Chelwood, Lord Quickswood and other descendants of the 3rd Marquess; Gascoyne and Price family papers *c*1718-1823, incl corresp and accounts of Bamber Gascoyne late 18th-early 19th cent.

State papers 14th-early 17th cent, incl some papers of Lord Hertford (later Duke of Somerset), the 2nd Earl of Essex and Sir Walter Raleigh; calendar of prisoners committed to the Gatehouse, Westminster 1682-4; rental of lordship of Denbigh 1276; Cranborne Priory accounts 14th cent; St Michael's Mount Priory accounts 15th cent; Cobham College accounts 15th cent; Ilford Hospital records 16th-19th cent; misc and collected MSS.

In private possession. Enquiries to the Librarian and Archivist, Hatfield House, Hertfordshire. NRA 32925. The inclusion of manuscripts in this description does not necessarily mean that they are available for research.

[b] Quit rental for Herts manors 1840-2; corresp with Hatfield agent 1839-43.

Hertfordshire Record Office (D/EL/M34, E62). Deposited by Messrs Longmore, solicitors, Hertford 1947. NRA 4464.

[c] Accounts and papers rel to estates in Herts, Dorset, Surrey, Somerset, Gloucs, Bucks, Notts and Yorks, and to household, garden and stable expenses 1768-80.

Public Record Office (C 114/43-49).

[d] Lancs deeds 14th-20th cent (mainly 17th-19th cent); mortgages, legal papers, etc

17th-19th cent, incl papers rel to the partition of the estates 1751; manorial records 1453-1949; leases 18th-19th cent; surveys, rentals and valuations early 17th-early 20th cent; accounts and financial papers 1806-1911; estate and local papers 18th-19th cent, incl West Derby and Wavertree enclosures and Childwall church, tithes, etc; Bamber Gascoyne decd, accounts 1791-1805 (1 vol); copies of letters from Bamber Gascoyne to his steward 1800-6 (2 vols).

Liverpool Record Office and Local History Department (920 SAL). Deposited from Hatfield House by the 5th Marquess of Salisbury and subsequently. NRA 7839.

[e] Memorandum book of Lord Burghley *c*1592.

British Library, Manuscript Collections (Royal MS App. 67).

[f] Private Foreign Office corresp of the 5th Marquess 1915-19 (4 vols).

Public Record Office (FO 800/195-8). NRA 23627.

Related collections: Cecil, Marquesses of Exeter (no 19); Fox-Pitt-Rivers of Rushmore (Dorset Record Office D 396, NRA 635), including Cranborne hundred and Chase papers mainly 17th-early 19th cent; papers of the 1st Baron Burghley (British Library, Manscript Collections Lansdowne MSS).

[42] GORDON-LENNOX, Dukes of Richmond and Gordon

Charles Lennox, a natural son of Charles II, was created Duke of Richmond in 1675 and granted lands in Scotland and Yorkshire (later sold). Through his grandmother the Duchess of Portsmouth (d1734), the second Duke inherited the French estate of Aubigny (divided among members of the family in the 1830s). The Sussex estate, beginning with a small purchase in 1695, was greatly enlarged by the third Duke between 1750 and 1806.

The Gordon (formerly Seton) family rose to prominence in Scottish affairs in the fifteenth and sixteenth centuries. They were created Earls of Huntly *c*1445, Marquesses of Huntly in 1599 and Dukes of Gordon in 1684. On the death of the fifth Duke in 1836 his extensive estates centred on Gordon Castle and Glenlivet (Morayshire and Banffshire), Huntly (Aberdeenshire) and Badenoch and Lochaber (Inverness-shire) passed mainly to his nephew the fifth Duke of Richmond, the dukedom of Gordon being revived for the sixth Duke of Richmond in 1876. The Gordon Castle and other estates were sold to the Crown in 1937.

Estates in 1883: Sussex 17,117 acres, Yorks 2 acres, Banffshire 159,952 acres, Aberdeenshire 69,660 acres, Inverness-shire 27,409 acres, Morayshire 12,271 acres, total 286,411 acres worth £79,683 a year.

[a] Deeds and leases, Sussex 14th-20th cent (mainly 16th-20th cent), with a few for other

counties 1600-1902; wills, settlements and related papers 18th-20th cent; legal papers rel to the Aubigny estate, with other legal papers 17th-19th cent; manorial records, Sussex 16th-20th cent; Sussex estate records 16th-20th cent, incl surveys, valuations, maps and plans, rentals 1765-1919, and accounts, vouchers, corresp and papers 18th-20th cent; misc Scottish estate papers 19th cent, incl rentals 1837-77; misc French estate papers 18th cent-1838; Goodwood home farm accounts 1806-1903 and racecourse papers 19th-20th cent; household accounts late 17th-early 20th cent; plans and inventories, Goodwood House, Gordon Castle, Richmond House (London), etc 18th-20th cent; commissions and appointments 17th-20th cent; corresp and papers of the Duchess of Portsmouth and the Dukes of Richmond 17th-20th cent, incl diplomatic and military papers of the 2nd Duke and political papers of the 3rd, 5th and 6th Dukes; letters from the 1st Duke of Wellington to AF Greville 1829-41 (1 vol); Gordon family papers 1568-1860 (11 vols), incl royal corresp 1568-1746 (1 vol) and letters from the Marquess of Montrose 1645-6 (1 vol).

West Sussex Record Office. Deposited by the 9th Duke of Richmond and his solicitors 1955, 1965. *The Goodwood Estate Archives,* 3 vols, 1970-84. NRA 850. For the 3rd, 5th and 6th Dukes see also HMC *Papers of British Cabinet Ministers 1782-1900,* 1982, p23, and for the 4th Duke, *Private Papers of British Colonial Governors 1782-1900,* 1986, p35.

[b] Scottish writs 14th-19th cent, mainly Aberdeenshire, Banffshire, Inverness-shire and Morayshire; settlements, wardships, etc 15th-19th cent, with trusteeship accounts and papers 1827-41 and misc legal papers 16th-19th cent; bonds of manrent 1444-1625; Huntly regality court records 1696-1726, with various barony court records 1637-1713; Scottish estate records 16th-19th cent, incl tacks 17th-19th cent, maps and plans, rentals 16th-19th cent, factors' accounts 17th-19th cent, petitions 1707-1841, corresp 18th-20th cent, general estate and household accounts 1689-1822, and papers rel to woods 1697-1849, mines 1726-1809, roads and harbours, Spey fishery 1590-1888 and Spey bridge (Fochabers) 1791-1860; Gordon Castle building papers 1729-1845; household accounts and papers 17th-19th cent; farm records 1764-1842; papers rel to Kinrara House (Inverness-shire) 1804-45 and to Glenfiddich Lodge (Banffshire) 1790-1846; papers rel to Harmony Hall estate, Trinidad 1807-20; Scottish ecclesiastical papers (stipends, tithes, etc) 16th-19th cent; papers rel to freehold votes mainly 18th-19th cent; commissions, patents, grants, etc 15th-20th cent; family corresp and papers 15th-19th cent, incl military papers 17th-19th cent and papers of the 4th Duke of Gordon rel to King's College Aberdeen and the Keepership of the Great Seal of Scotland; Aberdeen and Leith merchant's accounts 1756-69.

Scottish Record Office (GD 44, RHP 31699-48913 *passim*). Deposited 1947-78. SRO *List of Gifts*

and Deposits, vol ii, 1976, pp4-10; Keeper's *Report* (1978), p17; HMC *First Report, App,* 1870, pp114-16.

[c] Scottish estate records 18th-19th cent, incl inventories of writs 18th cent (2 vols), Strathavon (Banffshire) and Glenlivet barony court book 1829-30, tacks (Banffshire, Inverness-shire, Morayshire), surveys and plans, rentals 1770-1855, accounts, Spey fishery accounts 1772-1884, Spey bridge papers 1800-32, and letter books 1801-50.

Scottish Record Office (CR 6, CR 8, RHP 1746-55, 1762-1854, 2210-2512). Deposited from the Fochabers and Glenlivet estate offices by the Crown Estates Commissioners 1962-80. SRO *List of Gifts and Deposits,* vol ii, 1976, pp10-11.

[d] Legal and estate papers of the Dukes of Gordon 1683-1879, incl papers rel to Inverness-shire superiorities 1785-1829 and report on Inverness Castle ruins 1783.

Scottish Record Office (Fraser Mackintosh collection, GD 128/6/1-5). Deposited from Inverness Public Library. NRA 10992.

[e] Misc vouchers of the 4th Duke of Gordon and his wife 1793-1803.

Scottish Record Office (GD 241). Deposited by Campbell & Lamond, WS, Edinburgh (incorporating Thomson, Dickson & Shaw). NRA 10441.

[f] Legal and trust papers 17th-20th cent, incl abstracts and inventories, and sederunt books 1814-36 (2 vols); estate papers 18th-20th cent, incl misc plans, rentals 1753, 1827-33 and Huntly sale particulars 1936.

In private possession. Enquiries to the National Register of Archives (Scotland) (NRA(S) 212). NRA 10747.

Related collection: Bathurst papers (British Library, Manuscript Collections Loan 57, NRA 20952), including Lennox family papers 1721-1826.

[43] **GRAHAM, Dukes of Montrose**

The Graham family was an important landowner in medieval Scotland and by the sixteenth century owned estates in Perthshire (Abernethy, Callander, Kincardine, etc), Stirlingshire (Dundaff, Mugdock, etc) and elsewhere, including East Kilpatrick (Dunbartonshire) and Montrose (Forfarshire). Patrick Graham was created Lord Graham in 1445 and his grandson William Earl of Montrose in 1503. The estates were forfeited on the execution of the first Marquess of Montrose in 1650, but restored in 1660 to the second Marquess, who, however, was obliged to sell his Forfarshire property. In 1680 the third Marquess bought Buchanan (Stirlingshire). His son the fourth Marquess (1682-1742), created Duke of Montrose in 1707, inherited Braco (Perthshire)

from Sir James Graham in 1689 and the estates of
the second earl of Airth and Monteith, including
Aberfoyle (Perthshire) and Drymen (Stirlingshire), in 1694. In 1703 the first Duke bought
the Lennox and Darnley estates in Dunbartonshire, Perthshire, Renfrewshire and Stirlingshire, formerly held by Frances Stuart,
Duchess of Lennox and Richmond. He also
acquired the forfeited lands of Rob Roy near Loch
Lomond (Stirlingshire). The second Duke
(1712-90) sold the lordships of Darnley
(Renfrewshire) and Kincardine (Perthshire) but
bought extensively in Stirlingshire.

Together with the Lennox and Menteith estates a
quantity of family papers of the Stuart Dukes of
Lennox and the Graham Earls of Airth and Menteith passed to the first Duke of Montrose. Other
Menteith papers entered the possession of the
second Earl of Airth and Menteith's executor Sir
James Graham of Gartmore (Perthshire) and his
descendants.

Estates in 1883: Stirlingshire 68,565 acres,
Perthshire 32,294 acres, Dunbartonshire 2,588
acres, total 103,447 acres worth £24,872 a year,
exclusive of £20 for a quarry.

[a] Dunbartonshire, Perthshire and Stirlingshire
writs 12th-20th cent; earldom of Lennox writs
12th-17th cent and cartulary 15th cent; misc
writs 15th-18th cent, incl some for Argyllshire, E
and W Lothian, etc; bonds of manrent 16th cent;
inventories of writs 17th-18th cent; wills, settlements, executry and trust papers 16th-19th cent,
incl curatory accounts for the 1st Duke of Montrose 1684-1721; legal and financial papers
16th-20th cent, incl papers rel to admiralty rights
claimed by the Dukes of Lennox 1608-1702;
regality court records, Montrose and Menteith
1684-1748, Lennox 1677, 1705, Darnley
1717-48 and Tarbolton (Ayrshire) 1705; records
of barony courts of Kincardine 1661-1732 and
Dundaff 1676.

Dunbartonshire, Perthshire and Stirlingshire
estate records 16th-20th cent, incl tacks
17th-20th cent, maps 19th-20th cent, rentals,
accounts and vouchers 17th-19th cent, tenants'
ledgers 1742-1858 and wages books 1738-98;
estate corresp 16th-19th cent, incl extensive corresp of the Duke of Montrose's agent Mungo
Graham of Gorthie 1701-49; estate memorandum book (Mungo Graham) 1740-51; Buchanan
(Stirlingshire) farm records 1794-1805; papers
rel to teinds, stipends and ecclesiastical affairs
16th-20th cent, woodlands c1647-1809, and
losses by tenants in the rising of 1745-6; factory
accounts of the Stuart Dukes of Lennox
1599-1694 and related estate papers 16th
cent-1702, incl rentals of St Andrews archbishopric 1589 and priory c1603, 1622, Partick
(Lanarks) late 16th cent, and Glasgow lordship
1639-40; lordship of Linlithgow (W Lothian)
accounts 1715-34; rental of Cromarty barony
1681.

Records of building at Buchanan Castle and
church (Stirlingshire) and at Aberuthven (Perthshire) church and mausoleum 18th cent, incl

Buchanan Castle plan by William Adam 1745;
Glasgow house building accounts 1680s, early
18th cent; household inventories 17th-18th cent,
mainly for Buchanan Castle but incl some for
Mugdock Castle 1666-9, Edinburgh and
Glasgow 1684, c1702-36, and London early 18th
cent; household accounts and papers 1628-19th
cent, mainly for Mugdock Castle and Buchanan
Castle but incl misc accounts of other houses
(Edinburgh, Glasgow, London) 18th-19th cent
and Bath 1719; accounts and vouchers of the 1st
Duke's chamberlain c1700-30; Glasgow Castle
smith's accounts 1599; Floors Castle (Roxburghshire) inventory 1650; household accounts
of the 2nd Earl of Airth and Menteith 1668-73.

Papers rel to Inversnaid (Stirlingshire) garrison
18th-19th cent; minute book of Stirlingshire road
trustees (western district) 1790-9; personal
inventory, 3rd Marquess 1679; misc appointments 17th cent; family papers 17th-20th cent,
incl personal accounts 1666-18th cent; papers of
the 1st Marquess (1612-50), incl letters of
Charles I and II; extensive corresp and papers of
the 1st Duke (1682-1742), incl solicitor's corresp
and accounts 1710-38 (George Robertson, WS);
journal 1742-72 and corresp of the 2nd Duke
(1712-90); accounts of the Laird of Buchanan's
troop 1643-9 and the Marquess of Montrose's
troop 1677-9; misc papers of the Stuart family,
Dukes of Lennox 15th cent-1603, incl personal
accounts c1598-1600 and letters of Mary, Queen
of Scots and James VI; political and other corresp
and papers of the 1st and 2nd Earls of Airth and
Menteith 1628-81; misc papers, incl inventory of
Montrose manuscripts 1741 and transcript of the
Lennox cartulary 18th cent.

Scottish Record Office (GD 220). Deposited by the
7th Duke of Montrose 1966, 1971. HMC *Second
Report, App,* 1871, pp165-7; *Third Report, App,*
1872, pp368-402. NRA 32572. Further family
and estate papers, not inspected by the National
Register of Archives (Scotland), remain in private
possession.

[b] Rentals and tutory accounts 1678-1702.

Scottish Record Office (GD 236/2/55). Deposited
by Dundas & Wilson, solicitors, Edinburgh 1974.
NRA 32486.

Related collections: Bontine Cunninghame Graham
of Gartmore and Ardoch (Scottish Record Office
GD 22, NRA 29364; National Library of
Scotland Dep 205, 280, NRA 29076); estate
papers of the 2nd Earl of Airth and Menteith
(National Library of Scotland Acc 7055).

[44] GRENVILLE, Dukes of Buckingham and Chandos

The Grenville family was established at Wotton
Underwood (Buckinghamshire) in the eleventh
century. Richard Grenville (1677-1727) married
in 1710 Hester, daughter of Sir Richard Temple,
third Bt, of Stowe (Buckinghamshire), whose family also owned estates in Oxfordshire (Finmere),

Northamptonshire and Warwickshire (Burton Dassett). She succeeded her brother as Viscountess Cobham and was created Countess Temple in 1749: on her death in 1752 the Stowe estates passed to her son Richard Grenville-Temple (1711-79) as second Earl Temple. He also inherited the Eastbury (Dorset) estate from his cousin George Bubb Doddington, Baron Melcombe (d1762).

The second Earl Temple was succeeded as third Earl by his nephew George Nugent-Temple-Grenville (son of George Grenville, the Prime Minister), who married Mary Elizabeth, daughter and heir of Robert Craggs Nugent, Earl Nugent (d1788), bringing estates in Cornwall (St Mawes), Essex (Gosfield, formerly owned by the Knight family) and Ireland. He was created Marquess of Buckingham in 1784. On his wife's death in 1812 the Irish estates passed to her second son (who also succeeded her as second Baron Nugent) but the English estates descended to her eldest son, who succeeded his father the following year as second Marquess of Buckingham.

Richard Temple-Nugent-Brydges-Chandos-Grenville, second Marquess of Buckingham (1776-1839) married in 1796 Anna Elizabeth Brydges (d1836), daughter and heir of the third Duke of Chandos (d1789), through whom the Grenvilles inherited estates in Middlesex (Canons, formerly held by the Lake family), Hampshire and Wiltshire (Avington, etc), Somerset (Keynsham, etc) and Derbyshire, as well as plantations in Jamaica (from the wife of the third Duke). He was created Duke of Buckingham and Chandos in 1822.

His son the second Duke (1797-1861), who married a daughter of the first Marquess of Breadalbane (see no 14), was bankrupted in 1848. Many outlying estates in Buckinghamshire, Dorset, Hampshire, Somerset and elsewhere were sold, together with the manuscript collections and some family papers from Stowe itself. On the death of the third Duke in 1889 his estates passed to his daughter Mary Morgan (later Morgan-Grenville), Baroness Kinloss (1852-1944), who sold the archive from Stowe in the early 1920s.

Estates in 1883: Bucks 9,511 acres, Cornwall 498 acres, Oxon 236 acres, Middlesex 232 acres, Somerset 5 acres, total 10,482 acres worth £18,080 a year.

[a] Deeds 12th-19th cent, mainly Grenville and Temple properties in Bucks 12th-19th cent but incl Temple properties in Gloucs 17th-18th cent, Leics 16th-18th cent, Northants 16th-19th cent, Oxon 15th-19th cent and Warwicks 13th-19th cent, Nugent estates in Cornwall 14th-19th cent, Essex 16th-19th cent and Ireland 16th-19th cent, and Brydges estates in Derbys 18th-19th cent, Hants and Wilts 16th-19th cent, Middlesex 16th-19th cent, Somerset 16th-19th cent, Radnorshire 16th-18th cent, London 16th-19th cent and Jamaica 18th-19th cent; wills, settlements, inquisitions and related papers, Grenville 15th-19th cent, Temple 16th-18th cent, Nugent 17th-early 19th cent and Brydges 16th-19th cent

(mainly 18th cent); legal papers 16th-20th cent, incl cartularies, schedules, case papers, papers rel to bankruptcy of the 2nd Duke 1848, and corresp with solicitors; manorial records, mainly Bucks 13th-19th cent (Wotton Underwood, etc) but incl Kent (Godmersham) 14th-15th cent, Hants 14th-17th cent, Middlesex (Great and Little Stanmore) 18th cent, Cornwall 17th-19th cent, and other counties.

Bucks (Wotton and Stowe) estate records 15th-20th cent, incl Stowe lease book 1619-35, surveys and maps, rentals and accounts, vouchers, corresp, stewards' letter books, and papers rel to wool (Temple family 16th-17th cent), buildings, labour, timber, etc; papers (rentals, accounts, etc) rel to estates in Warwicks 16th-19th cent, Oxon 15th-19th cent, Dorset mainly 18th cent and Yorks NR 16th-17th cent; papers rel to estates in Cornwall and Ireland 17th-19th cent and to Essex (Gosfield estate) 18th-19th cent; papers rel to Brydges estates in Hants, Middlesex, Somerset and elsewhere mainly 16th-19th cent, incl contract books 1760-71, farm accounts 18th cent, account of Mendip mines 15th cent and papers rel to Derbys mines 18th-19th cent; misc estate papers, incl rental of Earl of Peterborough's estates c1671 and Taymouth (Breadalbane) sketch maps c1834; Jamaica estate papers mainly 18th cent, incl surveys, accounts, corresp and lists of slaves.

Stowe building accounts and drawings 17th-19th cent, incl house and gardens; inventories and catalogues 16th-19th cent, incl Stowe, Canons, Avington, London houses, Gosfield Hall 1813, Taymouth Castle c1862 and Biddlesden (Bucks) (GM Morgan) 1894; household accounts and papers 18th-19th cent, Stowe, Wotton, Canons, Avington and London houses; Stowe, etc garden accounts 18th-19th cent; papers rel to Bucks affairs 16th-20th cent, incl elections 17th-19th cent, militia 17th-19th cent, taxation (ship money, etc), mayoralty of Buckingham 1687-8 and cattle plague 1866-7; St Mawes (Cornwall) election papers 18th-early 19th cent; Hants militia papers 1763-75.

Personal and family papers 16th-20th cent (extensive), incl papers of the 1st Marquess of Buckingham as Lord Lieutenant of Ireland, political papers of the 1st and 3rd Dukes and of Henry, George and Thomas Grenville, papers of Sir Richard Temple, 3rd Bt, as Commissioner of Customs 1672-94, papers of the 1st Earl Nugent 18th cent and of the 1st Duke of Chandos as Paymaster-General 1705-13 and Clerk of the Hanaper; misc Knight, Campbell (Breadalbane) and Morgan family papers; diaries, personal accounts, photographs, etc; genealogical, artistic, literary and musical MSS; corresp of Sir William Andrewes (d1657) rel to Bucks affairs and manor of Grafton; antiquarian and other papers of Charles O'Conor (1764-1828, librarian at Stowe).

Huntington Library, San Marino, California. Purchased 1925 following the Stowe sale in 1921, with additional acquisitions 1939-51. *Guide to British Historical Manuscripts in the Huntington Library*, 1982, pp145-274.

[b] Further deeds 12th-19th cent, mainly Bucks but incl Cornwall, Dorset, Essex, Hants, Leics, Oxon, Somerset, Warwicks, etc; wills, settlements, financial and legal papers 16th-19th cent; misc manorial records 15th-17th cent, incl Burton Dassett (Warwicks) and Wotton, etc court rolls early 17th cent; estate records 15th-19th cent, most estates, incl leases, valuation of Cobham estates 1749, rentals 18th-19th cent (Brydges estates 1717-34, etc) and misc papers; Wotton enclosure accounts 1741-50; Bucks voters' lists 1840-4; household inventories and accounts 18th-19th cent, incl accounts for Duke of Chandos (London house) 1721-2, Stowe library catalogue *c*1800 and Breadalbane inventory 1863; personal and misc papers 16th-19th cent, incl quit roll 1717-19 and letter book 1721-2 of the Duke of Chandos, and Senegal trading ledger 1771.

Northamptonshire Record Office (Stowe collection). Purchased by J Manfield 1921 and presented to the Northamptonshire Record Society 1930. NRA 12333.

[c] Deeds 16th-20th cent, mainly Bucks; wills, settlements, trust papers and legal papers 17th-19th cent; Bucks manorial records, Wotton 1668 and Pollicotts 1754; estate records 17th-19th cent, mainly Bucks, incl surveys 1632-3, rentals 1826-40, wood accounts 1625-6, 1772-9 and labour accounts 19th cent; Avington game book 1816-75; household account book (not Stowe) 1676-9; misc inventories and other papers 17th-19th cent.

Buckinghamshire Record Office (D 104). Deposited from Stowe School 1975. (Some items had been purchased by HM Temple 1921.) NRA 19654.

[d] Family corresp and papers 18th-19th cent, incl letters to Thomas Grenville from his brother Lord Grenville 1791-1833 and others, with some misc Bateson-Harvey (of Langley, Bucks) family papers *c*1796-1836.

Buckinghamshire Record Office (D 56). Deposited by the Hon RW Morgan-Grenville 1963, 1974. NRA 25231.

[e] Letter books of the 3rd Duke 1848-50 (bankruptcy of the 2nd Duke), 1853-4, 1873-5; game book (Bucks) 1822-5.

Buckinghamshire Record Office (D/X 1039). Transferred 1989 from the Buckinghamshire Archaeological Society (which had acquired them from Major M Beaumont of Wotton House in 1947). NRA 19654.

[f] Financial papers 1827-45 (12 items).

Buckinghamshire Record Office (D 143). Deposited 1983 by Mrs JJ Whymark, whose grandfather had purchased them in 1921. NRA 25231.

[g] Map of part of the Wotton estate 1847.

Buckinghamshire Record Office (Ma/298). Purchased 1987. *Annual Report* (1988), p13.

[h] Family corresp and papers 18th-20th cent, incl appointments of and letters to the 3rd Duke of Buckingham.

In private possession. Deposited in Buckinghamshire Record Office 1963 (D 54), withdrawn 1975. (Photocopies in the Record Office.) NRA 25231.

[i] Misc estate records 17th-19th cent, incl Stowe day book 1677-80, Wotton carpenter's account 1717-20, Bucks rental 1779, Gosfield rental 1804-9 and Avington accounts 1837-9; household accounts 1814-25.

Reading University Library (BUC 11). Deposited from Rothamsted Experimental Station 1966. *Historical Farm Records*, 1973, pp41-2.

[j] Deeds 15th-20th cent, Middlesex, London and Herts; wills, trust papers and legal papers 17th-19th cent; Herts and Middlesex manorial court books 17th-19th cent; Middlesex and Herts leases 18th-mid-19th cent, surveys and plans 18th-19th cent, rentals and accounts 18th-mid-19th cent (incl rentals of whole (Chandos) estate 1712-1815), vouchers early 19th cent, estate corresp 17th-19th cent, enclosure papers 18th cent, and farm, wood and garden papers 18th-19th cent; building plans, drawings (Stowe) and accounts 18th-19th cent; household and family papers 18th-19th cent.

Greater London Record Office (Acc 262). Acquired by Middlesex Record Office from FH Marcham & Co 1947 (see JV Beckett, 'The Stowe Papers', *Archives*, vol XX, no 90, Oct 1993, p195).

[k] Chandos settlements and related papers 1696-1780.

Greater London Record Office (Acc 788). Given by Miss WA Myers. NRA 9555.

[l] Chandos estate papers rel mainly to Enfield (Middlesex) and Enfield Chase 1572-19th cent.

Enfield Local History Library (DG 91-506). NRA 25947.

[m] Legal papers rel to Whetstone property 1883.

Barnet Archives and Local Studies Centre. HMC *Accessions to Repositories 1974*.

[n] Hants rental 1737; accounts and agency papers for Middlesex (Minchendon House, Edmonton), Hants and elsewhere 1818-32.

Hampshire Record Office (19M48). Purchased from FH Marcham & Co 1948. NRA 8807.

[o] Steyning (Sussex) rental 1734.

West Sussex Record Office (Add MS 361). Presented by Hertfordshire Record Office 1948. NRA 7796.

[p] Papers of Sir Peter Temple, 2nd Bt, rel to ship money in Bucks, etc, and of Sir Richard Temple, 3rd Bt, as Commissioner of Customs 1672-94, etc; Essex and Civil War corresp of Sir Samuel Lake; Irish MSS of Charles O'Conor.

British Library, Department of Manuscripts (Stowe MSS). Among the collections at Stowe purchased by the 4th Earl of Ashburnham in 1849 and acquired for the British Museum in 1883. HMC *Eighth Report, App III*, 1881, pp2-23 *passim*.

[q] Corresp of George Grenville and the 2nd Earl Temple mainly 1761-8.

British Library, Manuscript Collections (Add MSS 42083-8). Acquired from John Murray 1930, having been sold from Stowe in 1851 (see JV Beckett, *op cit*, p192). Further papers (Add MSS 57804-37) were acquired from Sotheby's 7 Nov 1972. Five further volumes of George Grenville's correspondence 1742-62 are now in the Lewis Walpole Library, Farmington, Connecticut (NRA 22338).

[r] Case paper rel to the Lake estate 1693-1700; family corresp and papers 18th-19th cent, incl corresp of General Richard Grenville 1780-1822, corresp of the 3rd Duke as Lord President of the Council (1866-7), etc, and quittance roll of George Grenville as Treasurer of the Navy 1755-6.

British Library, Manuscript Collections (Add MSS 70956-83, 70992-7). Acquired 1992. Previously deposited in Buckinghamshire Record Office (D 55, D/X 357) by the Hon H Morgan-Grenville 1963-70. NRA 25231.

[s] Letters to General Richard Grenville from Lady Hester Stanhope 1810-20.

British Library, Manuscript Collections (Add MS 42057). Acquired 1930.

[t] Colonial Office corresp of the 3rd Duke of Buckingham 1867-8.

British Library, Manuscript Collections (Add MSS 41860, 43742). Acquired 1929, 1934.

Related collections: Temple-Gore-Langton of Newton (Somerset Archive and Record Service DD/GL, NRA 781; Buckinghamshire Record Office D/T, NRA 781); Knight and Nugent of Gosfield, papers 1720-73 (Essex Record Office D/DU 502/1-7, NRA 3505); Earls Stanhope (Centre for Kentish Studies U 1590, NRA 25095), including Grenville papers inherited or purchased by the 5th Earl Stanhope (U 1590/S2).

[45] GREVILLE, Earls Brooke and Earls of Warwick

Sir Fulke Greville, a younger son of Sir Edward Greville of Milcote (Warwickshire), married *c*1534 Elizabeth Willoughby, granddaughter of Robert, second Baron Willoughby de Broke, through whom he inherited part of the Beauchamp estates in Warwickshire and estates in Staffordshire, Northamptonshire and Lincolnshire. His grandson Sir Fulke Greville, Baron Brooke (d1628), obtained a grant of Warwick Castle in 1604, and the family also accumulated estates in Gloucestershire, Somerset and Middlesex. He was succeeded by his cousin Robert Greville of Thorpe Latimer (Lincolnshire) as second Baron. The fourth Baron (*c*1638-1677) married Anne, daughter and heir of John Dodington of Breamore

(Hampshire), through whom estates in Hampshire, Wiltshire, Glamorganshire and elsewhere were inherited. The seventh Baron married in 1716 Mary, daughter and co-heir of the Hon Henry Thynne, of Leweston (Dorset). The eighth Baron (1719-1773) was created Earl Brooke in 1746 and Earl of Warwick in 1759. Extensive sales in the early nineteenth century reduced the estates to those in Warwickshire and Somerset.

The fifth Earl of Warwick married in 1881 Frances, daughter of the Hon CH Maynard and heiress of the last Viscount Maynard's estates in Essex, Leicestershire and Northamptonshire. William Maynard of Easton (Essex), son of Sir Henry Maynard, secretary to Lord Treasurer Burghley, had been created Baron Maynard in 1628, and his son the second Baron had married in 1641 Dorothy, only daughter of Sir Robert Banastre of Passenham (Northamptonshire), through whom the Northamptonshire and Leicestershire estates were inherited. Lady Warwick died in 1938, being succeeded in the Maynard estates by her younger son the Hon Maynard Greville (d1960).

Estates in 1883: Warwick: Warwicks 8,262 acres, Somerset 1,840 acres, total 10,102 acres, worth £18,336 a year; Maynard: Essex 8,617 acres, Leics 4,411 acres, Northants 802 acres, Cambs 8 acres, Middlesex 6 acres, total 13,844 acres, worth £20,001 a year.

[a] Deeds 12th-20th cent (*c*1,200 medieval), mainly Warwicks but incl Dorset, Gloucs, Lincs, Middlesex, Northants, Somerset, Staffs and other English counties, with some for Glamorganshire and Jersey; registers and catalogues of deeds 15th-20th cent, incl Lichfield precentory cartulary 15th cent; wills, settlements and related trust and executorship papers mainly 16th-19th cent, incl the 2nd Baron Brooke decd, the debts of the 2nd Earl of Warwick, the Earl of Mansfield decd 1810-11 and the 5th Baron Monson decd 1841-4; misc legal and case papers from 16th cent, incl Verney *v* Brooke 17th cent; manorial records 13th-19th cent, mainly Warwicks (Warwick castle and borough, Alcester, etc) but incl Gloucs, Hants, Northants, Somerset, Staffs and Wilts; estate records 15th-20th cent, incl leases, surveys and valuations, accounts, etc, mainly Warwicks and Somerset but incl Bucks 17th-18th cent, Dorset 17th-18th cent, Glamorganshire 16th-17th cent, Hants 16th-18th cent, Gloucs 15th-18th cent, Lincs 17th-18th cent, Middlesex (Hackney, Holborn) 16th-18th cent, Staffs 16th-18th cent and Wilts 16th-18th cent; Somerset colliery accounts 17th-20th cent; Maynard estate accounts and papers late 19th-early 20th cent.

Papers rel to Warwick Castle 17th-20th cent, incl accounts and plans for repairs, restorations and proposed alterations, and inventories; household accounts 17th-20th cent, Warwick Castle and Brooke House (London); papers rel to Warwick and Warwicks affairs mainly 19th-20th cent; patents and appointments 16th-19th cent; family corresp and papers 16th-20th cent, incl papers of

Fulke Greville (d1606) rel to Warwicks militia, etc 1589-1600, naval and Exchequer papers of Fulke Greville, 1st Baron Brooke, Staffs lieutenancy papers of the 4th Baron 1660-72, papers rel to Sir William Hamilton late 18th cent and papers of CF Greville late 18th cent.

Warwickshire County Record Office (CR 1886). Purchased from Lord Brooke 1979, with an additional deposit 1980. (The papers were formerly kept in Warwick Castle.) NRA 21669 (partial list).

[b] Deeds and papers rel to the Middlesex (Holborn) estate 1716-1877 (6 bundles).

Warwickshire County Record Office (CR 2880). Deposited through the British Records Association 1991.

[c] Deeds for Warwicks, Lincs, etc 1782-7 (3 items); rental and valuation of estates in various counties 1779-83.

Warwickshire County Record Office (CR 1735/4/2-5). Deposited by Messrs Riders, solicitors, London, through the British Records Association 1977.

[d] Schedule of deeds 1845.

Warwickshire County Record Office. Deposited by Frere, Cholmeley & Co, solicitors, London, through the British Records Association 1992.

[e] Legal papers of Sir Fulke Greville 1590s.

Warwickshire County Record Office (CR 1987). Deposited by the Society of Genealogists through Cambridgeshire Record Office 1980. Formerly in the collection of J Harvey Bloom.

[f] Leases 1616-1731; estate accounts 1726-40 (10 vols), incl Thynne (Dorset and Somerset) estate; inventories, Warwick, Breamore and London, and account of personal estate of Lord Brooke decd 1735 (2 vols).

Public Record Office (C 113/21, 208). (In chancery, minority of 8th Baron (later 1st Earl) Brooke.)

[g] Poetical MSS of Fulke Greville, 1st Baron Brooke (1554-1628) (6 vols).

British Library, Manuscript Collections (Add MSS 54566-71). Fomerly at Warwick Castle. Purchased from Arthur A Houghton 1969. (See also P Beal, *Index of English Literary Manuscripts*, vol 1, part 2, 1980, p103.)

[h] Deeds 14th-19th cent, Essex, Northants, etc; legal papers 16th-20th cent, incl papers rel to Leics and Northants and to the purchase of property in Suffolk 1765-75; manorial records, Essex (Great Dunmow, etc) 14th-20th cent; estate papers 17th-20th cent, mainly Essex 18th-20th cent, incl maps and plans 17th-20th cent, papers rel to timber, and papers rel to the Northants and Leics estates; Easton Lodge inventory 1637, architectural drawings early 20th cent; misc family papers 17th-20th cent, incl transcript (*c*1900) of Tilty Abbey cartulary.

Essex Record Office (D/DMg). Deposited by the Hon Maynard Greville through Wade & Davies, solicitors, Dunmow 1939-52, G Eland 1961 and Mrs F Spurrier 1968, with additional deposits 1980. NRA 20041. (For further manorial records 16th-20th cent deposited in Essex Record Office by Wade & Davies and others see D/DWV M160-247 *passim* (NRA 21520), D/DQ 14/194-210. The archive at Easton Lodge was damaged by fire in 1918 and some items (including the Tilty Abbey cartulary) were lost.)

[i] Manorial records, Walthamstow Toney (Essex) 1677-1930.

Waltham Forest Archives and Local History Library. Deposited by HS Walford, the steward, before 1941.

[j] Travel journal of the 2nd Viscount Maynard 1773.

British Library, Oriental and India Office Collections (MSS Eur. E 292). *Report* (1966-7), p14.

Related collection: Barons Willoughby de Broke (Shakespeare Birthplace Trust Records Office, NRA 2638; British Library, Manuscript Collections Eg Ch 645-2116, Eg MSS 2978-3008), including Willoughby deeds and papers.

[46] GROSVENOR, Dukes of Westminster

The Grosvenor family was settled in Cheshire in the twelfth century, and acquired Eaton (near Chester) through marriage in the fifteenth. Mining interests in a neighbouring part of north Wales (Denbighshire and Flintshire) were acquired mainly in 1601. The Halkyn and Holywell (Flintshire) estates were purchased in 1704 and 1809 respectively.

Through the marriage of Sir Thomas Grosvenor, third Bt, to Mary, daughter of Alexander Davies of Ebury (Middlesex), the valuable metropolitan estates of Mayfair, Belgravia and Pimlico came to the Grosvenors. The two latter were developed principally from the 1820s.

Estates in Dorset, Wiltshire, Hertfordshire and elsewhere were acquired in the early nineteenth century, but were left to younger sons. The Moor Park (Hertfordshire) estate passed to Lord Robert Grosvenor (third son of the first Marquess of Westminster), created Baron Ebury in 1857, and the Motcombe (Dorset, etc) estate passed to Lord Richard Grosvenor (second surviving son of the second Marquess), created Baron Stalbridge in 1886.

The first Duke of Westminster (1825-1899, so created 1874) owned Cliveden (Buckinghamshire) between 1869 and 1893, and the second Duke acquired properties in Scotland and elsewhere in the early twentieth century.

Estates in 1883: Duke of Westminster: Cheshire 15,138 acres, Bucks 246 acres, Flintshire 3,621 acres, Denbighshire 744 acres, total 19,749 acres worth £38,994 a year; dowager Marchioness

(later inherited by Lord Stalbridge): Dorset 8,794 acres, Wilts 4,112 acres, total 12,906 acres worth £26,958 a year.

[a] Cheshire deeds 12th-19th cent (*c*500 medieval); Denbighshire and Flintshire deeds 15th-19th cent; misc deeds 16th-18th cent; Grosvenor family wills, settlements, inquisitions *post mortem*, etc mainly 16th-19th cent; legal papers from 15th cent, incl Welsh mining rights 16th-19th cent; Cheshire manorial records (Eaton, etc) 16th-19th cent.

Cheshire and Denbighshire estate records 16th-20th cent, incl leases ?17th-19th cent, surveys 1628-20th cent, maps 17th-19th cent, rentals and accounts 1554, 1675-mid 20th cent, tax papers 17th-18th cent, school accounts 1817-45, and papers mainly 19th-20th cent rel to buildings, forestry and sawmill, coal and gas supplies, cottage tenancies, etc; papers rel to the Chester estate mainly 18th-20th cent, incl separate rentals and accounts from 1848; Welsh (mainly Flintshire) estate papers *c*1620-mid-20th cent, incl maps 1738-40, Halkyn estate accounts 1748-80, rentals and accounts 1812-71, Llanerch woods account 1741-51, coal accounts 1736-1823, lead mining accounts and papers 1601-*c*1908, and Anglesey freeholders' list 1645 and rental 1691-1701; misc London (Middlesex) estate records 17th-20th cent, incl rentals 1677, 1679, lease book *c*1720-5 and accounts 1756-63; papers rel to Moor Park (incl plan of house) 1827-8, Motcombe estate 1820-33 (with plan of house nd) and sale of Cliveden estate 1893; records rel to estates in Scotland (Reay Forest (Sutherland), etc), Denbighshire (World's End), France and South Africa 20th cent; game books 1811-1942; stud records 1720-early 20th cent.

Accounts and papers rel to Eaton Hall, gardens and park 17th-20th cent, incl building accounts 1675-84, 1821-7 and 1870-84; Eaton household accounts and papers 18th-20th cent, incl wages books 1737-81, etc, cellar books, inventories, visitors' books, etc; Halkyn Castle building accounts 1825-6; London household accounts and inventories 19th-20th cent; Cliveden visitors' books 1873-93; records rel to Eaton nursing association 1888-99, Eaton Park Cricket Club 1898-1941 and Cheshire Hunt 19th-20th cent; papers rel to Chester and Cheshire politics and government, incl list of Chester ?chief rents 1448-9, misc shrievalty papers 17th-18th cent, account for a mayoral election 1732, and Chester and Cheshire parliamentary election papers 18th-19th cent; Flintshire yeomanry papers 1831-40; Grosvenor family patents, commissions, etc 1597-20th cent; family and personal papers *c*1600-20th cent, incl the 1st and 2nd Marquesses and the 1st Duke of Westminster; genealogical papers, papers rel to Cheshire history, etc *c*1580-19th cent; misc medieval items, incl Eaton account roll 1372-3 and rental of St Werburgh's Abbey, Chester 1449.

In private possession. Enquiries to Cheshire Record Office or Chester City Record Office. NRA 13470.

[b] Architectural drawings for Eaton Hall and Eccleston church *c*1805-22; account book of Sir Robert Grosvenor, 6th Bt 1748-55.

Chester City Record Office (Earwaker collection, CR/2/712-823). Acquired by the 1st Duke of Westminster after the death of JP Earwaker and presented to Chester Archaeological Society; transferred to the Record Office 1969. NRA 16683.

[c] Misc Welsh deeds (3) and legal papers 17th-19th cent; Flintshire (Halkyn, etc) and Denbighshire estate papers 19th-20th cent, incl surveys and valuations 1846-1933, rentals and accounts 1812-1951, papers rel to churches and chapels, and agents' letter books and notebooks 1882-1936; Holywell estate papers 18th-20th cent, incl leases and agreements, rentals 1798-1803, 1897-1925, and papers rel to St Winefride's Well 19th-20th cent; papers rel to minerals in Denbighshire and Flintshire (lead, coal, ironstone, etc) 17th- mid-20th cent, incl leases 1697-1926, lease registers and schedules 1710-1943, royalty accounts 1710-1947 and records of the Deep Level and Halkyn Mining Co 19th cent.

Clwyd Record Office, Hawarden branch (D/GR). Deposited by the Grosvenor Estate Trustees 1976. CJ Williams, *A Handlist of the Grosvenor (Halkyn) MSS*, 1988. NRA 30898.

[d] Flintshire lead smelting and farm accounts 1782-99.

Public Record Office (C 104/29, Brodhurst *v* Mawdesley).

[e] Deeds for London (Middlesex) estates (manor of Ebury, Knightsbridge, etc) 16th-20th cent; deeds for Wymondley (Herts) 13th-16th cent (24), Newmarket (Cambs) 1789-1805 and Moor Park (Herts and Middlesex) 17th-early 20th cent; wills, settlements, trust papers and executorship papers 17th-20th cent, Audley, Davies and Grosvenor; register of deeds for London estate 1623-1764; abstracts of title and other legal papers 16th-20th cent, mainly London but incl Cheshire and Welsh estates 18th-19th cent and Moor Park estate 19th-20th cent.

London (Middlesex) estate records 17th-20th cent, incl leases from 17th cent, lease books 1721-1960, trustees' minutes and memoranda 1789-1941, surveys and valuations 17th and 19th-20th cent, maps and plans from 1614, rentals and accounts 1677- mid-20th cent, letter books 1796-1819, 20th cent, agents' bills and corresp from late 18th cent, and papers 18th-20th cent rel to Grosvenor Square gardens, Grosvenor market, Grosvenor chapel and burial ground, Grosvenor Canal and Westminster Bridge; a few Cheshire and Welsh estate papers 19th cent; Swell (Somerset) estate and manorial papers *c*1696-1751; Wymondley accounts 1723-44 (6 vols); Weeting (Norfolk) accounts 1734, 1736 (4 vols); misc Dorset, Hants and Wilts estate rentals, accounts and papers

1822-34; Moor Park estate accounts and papers 1828-35; Cliveden estate and household accounts and vouchers 1884-93.

Inventories of Grosvenor House (London) 1873-1901, with papers rel to its demolition 1920s; Motcombe House inventory 1826; Newmarket household accounts 1788-9; stable account 1787-91; Grosvenor and Egerton family corresp 18th-early 19th cent, incl letters to Sir Robert Grosvenor *c*1739-54, the 2nd Earl Grosvenor and the 1st and 2nd Earls of Wilton; misc papers 18th-20th cent, incl account of supplies for Prince of Wales's household 1716, papers of Edward Boodle, solicitor, rel to the Marquess of Northampton's London estates early 19th cent, papers rel to the Cundy family, architects 1816-73 and photographs of London estate buildings 20th cent.

City of Westminster Archives Centre (Acc 1049). Deposited from the Grosvenor Office, Davies St, London W1 1965-79. Access restricted: enquiries to City of Westminster Archives Centre.

[f] Transcripts of deeds 1623-1730; deeds, legal papers and leases mainly 19th-20th cent; bill books for the Duke of Westminster's business (mainly London estates) 1907-42 (62 vols); duplicate building contract, Pimlico 1866; record of leaseholders and tenants of Lower Estate 1924-6, with plan; inventories 1929-31.

City of Westminster Archives Centre (Acc 281, 306, 439, 1050, 1667, etc). Deposited by Boodle, Hatfield & Co, solicitors, London 1965-93, all or mostly through the British Records Association.

[g] Misc Stalbridge (Motcombe, etc) deeds and papers 1629-1873.

Dorset Record Office (D/MOT formerly D1/MN). Transferred from Dorset Museum 1957. NRA 7828.

[h] Misc Stalbridge (Motcombe, etc) deeds and papers 18th-20th cent, incl maps 1898, *c*1919 and sale papers 1918-30; Gillingham (Dorset) manorial records 1615-1920; letters patent, barony of Stalbridge 1886.

Dorset Record Office (D/BHD). Deposited by Boodle, Hatfield & Co, solicitors, London, through the British Records Association 1966-90. *The Dorset Record Office 1988*, p12. NRA 17640 (partial list).

[i] Dorset (mainly Gillingham) deeds 17th-20th cent; Gillingham manorial records 1291-1935; misc papers 17th-20th cent, incl Gillingham and Motcombe enclosure papers 1809.

Dorset Record Office (D 407; D/FAN). Deposited by Farnfield & Nicholls, solicitors, Gillingham 1972-92. NRA 7828.

[j] Reading (Berks) Abbey charters 12th-16th cent, with inventories and bailiffs' accounts.

British Library, Manuscript Collections (Add Ch 19571-19659). Presented by the Marquess of

Westminster 1873. HMC *Third Report, App*, 1872, p216. (For other MSS reported on, *ibid*, pp210-16, see HMC *Guide to the Location of Collections*, 1982, p65.)

Related collection: Myddelton of Chirk (National Library of Wales, Longueville & Co collection), including (nos 1168-9) Lady Grosvenor's jointure estate, rentals and accounts 1710-29.

[47] HAY, Marquesses of Tweeddale

Sir Gilbert Hay of Locherworth (Midlothian) acquired lands in Peeblesshire (Lyne, Wester Hopprew, etc) by marriage with Mary, daughter of Sir Simon Fraser of Oliver Castle (Peeblesshire) early in the fourteenth century. Together with the hereditary sheriffdom of Peeblesshire these were held until 1686 when the office and estates were sold to the first Duke of Queensberry.

In the late fourteenth century Sir Thomas Hay married Joanna, co-heir of Hugh Gifford of Yester (East Lothian), thereby gaining part of the substantial Gifford estates which had been built up since the twelfth century. Yester became the family seat in the fifteenth century, when much of the Midlothian estate was sold. Belton (East Lothian) and Snaid (Dumfriesshire) came into the family through the marriage of the first Lord Hay (so created 1488) with the heiress of Sir William Cunningham; but Snaid was apparently alienated by the eighteenth century, as were properties in Clackmannanshire, Lanarkshire (Thankerton, etc) and Perthshire (Achmore, Rodono, etc), also possessed since the Middle Ages, whilst Belton passed to a junior branch of the Hay family. Dunfermline (Fife) and Fyvie (Aberdeenshire) were granted as security for debts by the second Earl of Dunfermline in 1646 and retained by the first Marquess of Tweeddale (so created 1694) on the fourth Earl's outlawry in 1690, though Fyvie was sold subsequently.

The sixth Marquess (d1787) bought Newhall (East Lothian) from the creditors of his cousin John Hay, father of the fifth Marquess, and inherited Linplum (East Lothian) on the death in 1760 of his brother Lord Charles Hay. Newhall, however, was bequeathed to a cousin, Edward Hay-Mackenzie, while Linplum passed by entail to Robert Hay of Drummelzier (Peeblesshire). The sixth and later Marquesses extended the family's estates by purchase in Berwickshire and Roxburghshire (Kirk Yetholm, etc). A residence in Kent (Walden Cottage, Chislehurst) was added in the nineteenth century, possibly by the ninth Marquess.

Estates in 1883: East Lothian 20,486 acres, Berwickshire 18,116 acres, Roxburghshire 4,505 acres, Fife 400 acres, Kent 10 acres, total 43,517 acres worth £26,530 a year, exclusive of mines worth £815.

[a] Writs 12th-18th cent, mainly E Lothian and Midlothian 12th-18th cent, Peeblesshire 12th-17th cent, Dumfriesshire 14th-17th cent

and Fife 16th-18th cent; Dunfermline cartularies 1555-1618 (4); inventories of writs 16th-18th cent; legal and financial papers, family settlements and marriage contracts 15th-18th cent, incl bonds of manrent 16th cent; Peebles head court papers *c*1500 and Achmore (Perthshire) barony court rolls 1535-7, 1566, with minutes 1543; Dumfermline regality court roll 1652.

Tacks 15th-17th cent, mainly E Lothian; rentals, accounts and vouchers late 16th-19th cent, mainly E Lothian and Dunfermline, but incl Lyne rental 1652 and Peeblesshire estate accounts 1671-87; Snaid rentals 1591-3, *c*1616 and accounts 1625-6; Fyvie rentals and accounts 1692-1728; Ettrick (Selkirkshire) rentals 1651-3 and accounts 1671-3; rental of Bothans (E Lothian) collegiate church *c*1560 and of the estates of Lord Jedburgh 1630; estate corresp 1627-95; papers rel to teinds, E Lothian 1592-1672 and Fife 1650-1752; Yester household accounts 1644, 1652-3, 1664-5 and misc papers 17th cent, incl some rel to building at Yester, Dunfermline Abbey, etc; patents and commissions 1629-1741; papers rel to military affairs in Scotland 17th-early 18th cent, incl roll of fencible men in Peeblesshire 1644, Fort William building accounts 1692 and inventories of Dumbarton and Edinburgh castles 1696; Haddingtonshire freeholders list *c*1820 and minutes 1821-3; misc family and other papers 17th-19th cent.

Scottish Record Office (GD 28). Presented and bequeathed by the 11th Marquess of Tweeddale 1931-69. The Dunfermline cartularies, presented 1941, have the reference RH 11/27/1-14. C Harvey, ed, *Calendar of Writs preserved at Yester House, 1166-1625* (Scottish Record Society, 1916-30). NRA 29864.

[b] Fife factor's memorandum book 1747-76.

Scottish Record Office (CS 96/288).

[c] Fife and Midlothian writs 15th-19th cent; Yester estate papers 1732-55 and teind papers 1592-1672; Dunfermline estate papers 1615-1878.

Scottish Record Office (GD 247). Deposited by Brodie, Cuthbertson & Watson, solicitors, Edinburgh 1962. Keeper's *Report* (1962), p14.

[d] E Lothian writs 1735-20th cent; inventories of writs 1543-1843, 1599-1808; legal and financial papers 18th-19th cent; accounts, corresp and papers rel to the Tweeddale estates 1703-20th cent.

In private possession. Enquiries to the National Register of Archives (Scotland) (NRA(S) 212). NRA 10747.

[e] Misc writs (E Lothian, Midlothian, Peeblesshire, etc) 16th-18th cent; inventories of writs 1659, late 17th cent; executry papers of William, Earl of Errol (d1636), and Mary, Dowager Countess of Home *c*1650-60; legal and financial papers 16th-18th cent; tacks, rentals, accounts, vouchers, corresp and papers rel to the Tweeddale estates in Peeblesshire 17th cent and

Berwickshire, Fife and E Lothian, etc 16th-20th cent, incl lordship of Dunfermline rent arrears accounts 1654-85, Fyvie accounts 1701-2, accounts of the division of Carfrae Common (E Lothian) 1769 and E Lothian timber accounts and papers 18th cent; papers rel to teinds 16th-19th cent, mainly Fyvie 16th-18th cent, Dunfermline 17th-18th cent and Stobo (Peeblesshire) 17th cent; papers rel to the estates of the Hay families of Bara (E Lothian) and of Smithfield (Peeblesshire) 17th-18th cent, incl Smithfield rental 1658; rental of the Earl of Dundee's Inverkeithing (Fife) estate *c*1662.

Yester House household accounts and papers 17th-19th cent, incl household books 1689-1767, cash books 1787-97 and garden accounts 18th cent; accounts of households at Highgate (Middlesex) 1672-4 and Bath (Somerset) 1763; household inventories 17th-18th cent, incl Pinkie House (Midlothian) 1689-1712; corresp, accounts and papers rel to building and furnishing at Yester House and Tweeddale House (Edinburgh) 17th-19th cent, incl some of William and John Adam; Yester House plans 1848; papers rel to E Lothian affairs 17th-19th cent, incl letter book of the 7th Marquess as lord lieutenant 1794-8 and election corresp 1813-18, 1841; election corresp rel to Peeblesshire 18th cent and Jedburgh (Roxburghshire) 1721-2; papers rel to the customs and excise in Scotland late 17th-18th cent and to Scottish peerage elections 1734-1833.

Patents and commissions 17th-19th cent; family accounts, vouchers and papers 16th-20th cent; papers of the 1st Earl of Tweeddale (d1653) and the 1st, 2nd, 4th, 8th and 10th Marquesses; military papers of Lord Charles Hay (d1760); letters of the 9th Marquess from the Crimea 1854-6 and of Sir William Howard Russell (1820-1907), war correspondent; literary, genealogical and misc papers 17th-19th cent, incl accounts rel to watchmen, labourers, etc, on royal ships at Woolwich 1618, personal inventory of Francis, Earl of Buccleuch 1652, accounts of William Sharp, cash keeper to Charles II 1671-2, and logs of HMS *Guernsey* 1722 and the East Indiamen *Bute* 1770-2 and *Alfred* 1781-4.

National Library of Scotland (MSS 7001-7120, Ch 7566-93; MSS 14401-14827, Ch 10685-12590). Presented and bequeathed by the 11th Marquess of Tweeddale 1944-69. HMC *Papers of British Politicians 1782-1900*, 1989, pp48-9. NRA 13563.

[f] Letter book of the 7th Marquess 1788-1801.

National Library of Scotland (Acc 6608). Purchased 1976. HMC *Accessions to Repositories 1976*.

[g] Corresp and papers of the 8th Marquess as Governor of Madras 1842-8.

British Library, Oriental and India Office Collections (MSS Eur. F 96). Deposited by the 11th Marquess of Tweeddale 1959. HMC *Papers of British Politicians 1782-1900*, 1989, p48. NRA 27520.

[h] Corresp of the 1st Marquess 1672-92.

In private possession. Photocopies in the House of Lords Record Office. NRA 16570.

[i] Corresp and personal accounts of the Earl of Gifford 1852-63.

British Library, Manuscript Collections (Add MSS 42768-71). Presented 1932 by the Dorset Natural History and Archaeological Society, which had acquired them from the 11th Duke of Bedford.

Related collections: Hay of Belton (Scottish Record Office GD 73, NRA 30415); Earls of Dufferin (Public Record Office of Northern Ireland D 1071, NRA 5700), including papers of the Earl of Gifford (1822-62) (D 1071/G).

[48] HEATHCOTE-DRUMMOND-WILLOUGHBY, Earls of Ancaster

Sir Gilbert Heathcote, first Bt (1652-1733), was Governor of the Bank of England 1708 and Lord Mayor of London 1710. He acquired estates in Rutland and Lincolnshire from *c*1716, and his son built a house at Normanton (Rutland) (demolished 1925). Sir Gilbert John Heathcote, fifth Bt (1795-1867), created Baron Aveland 1856, married in 1827 Clementina Drummond, sister and eventual heir of her brother the twenty-second Baron Willoughby de Eresby (d1870) (see below). Their son succeeded his father as second Baron Aveland and (in 1888) his mother as twenty-fourth Baron Willoughby de Eresby, and was created Earl of Ancaster in 1892.

Sir William de Willoughby (d1306), of Willoughby (Lincolnshire), married Alice Beke, co-heiress of Eresby (Lincolnshire). Their son was summoned to parliament as Lord Willoughby de Eresby in 1313. Other properties were inherited in the fourteenth and early fifteenth centuries in Holland (Lincolnshire) (from the Huntingfield family), Norfolk (from the Rosceline family) and Suffolk (from the Ufford Earls of Suffolk). Joan Willoughby, daughter and heiress of the sixth Baron, married Sir Richard Welles, but he and his son were beheaded in 1469-70. William Willoughby succeeded a cousin as tenth Baron Willoughby de Eresby in 1506, and married in 1516 Mary de Salinas, who as her dower received the reversion of Grimsthorpe (Lincolnshire) and other properties of John, Lord Beaumont. Their daughter Katherine married in 1535 Charles Brandon, Duke of Suffolk (she held his estates in dower between his death in 1545 and 1551), and secondly, in 1553, Richard Bertie. Her son Peregrine Bertie succeeded her as twelfth Baron Willoughby de Eresby in 1580, and the thirteenth Baron was created Earl of Lindsey in 1626.

The fourth Earl of Lindsey married in 1678 Mary, daughter and heir of Sir Richard Wynn of Gwydir, through whom the family acquired estates in Carnarvonshire, and was created Duke of Ancaster in 1715. On the death of the fourth Duke in 1779 the Willoughby estates passed to his elder sister Priscilla, wife of Sir Peter Burrell, second Bt, of Beckenham (Kent), who in 1796 was created Baron

Gwydir. Their son succeeded his father as second Baron Gwydir in 1820 and his mother as twenty-first Baron Willoughby de Eresby in 1828. Through his marriage in 1807 to Clementina (d1865), daughter and heiress of the first Lord Perth, the family succeeded to extensive estates in Scotland centred on Drummond Castle (Perthshire).

On the death of the fifth Duke of Ancaster in 1809 some Lincolnshire property descended to the Greathead, later Heber-Percy, family of Guy's Cliffe (Warwickshire).

On the death of the twenty-second Baron in 1870 the Willoughby, Wynn and Drummond estates all passed to the dowager Lady Aveland (see above) as Baroness Willoughby de Eresby.

Estates in 1883: Aveland: Lincs 17,637 acres, Rutland 13,633 acres, Derbys 3 acres, Hunts 2 acres, total 31,275 acres worth £46,894 a year; Willoughby de Eresby: Lincs 24,696 acres, Carnarvonshire 30,391 acres, Denbighshire 296 acres, Perthshire 76,837 acres, total 132,220 acres worth £74,006 a year.

[a] Deeds 12th-20th cent, mostly Lincs (Willoughby and Heathcote estates) 12th-20th cent but incl Rutland 13th-19th cent (mostly from 16th cent), Norfolk 12th-16th cent, Berks and Oxon (Brandon estates) 14th-16th cent, London and Middlesex (Barbican, etc) 14th-18th cent, Derbys 16th-18th cent, Wales 17th-20th cent, Kent 16th-early 19th cent and Jamaica 1699-1772; monastic charters, Barlings Abbey, Greenfield Priory and Vaudey Abbey 12th-16th cent; Huntingfield cartulary 14th cent; wills, settlements and related executorship and trust papers 13th-20th cent, Willoughby, Brandon, Bertie, Burrell, Drummond, Heathcote, etc; legal and case papers 13th-20th cent, incl copies and abstracts of deeds from 13th cent, and papers rel to succession to Willoughby and Brandon estates 16th cent, succession to Brownlow estates early 18th cent, office of Lord Great Chamberlain 1701, 1902 and peerage cases 1870, 1901; manorial records, Lincs 13th-20th cent (Edenham, Langtoft with Baston, Spilsby with Eresby, Willoughby, etc), Rutland 14th-18th cent and other counties (Devon, Norfolk, etc) 16th-17th cent.

Lincs (Grimsthorpe and Lindsey Coast) estate records 14th-20th cent, incl leases and agreements from 18th cent, surveys from 17th cent, maps from 18th cent, rentals and accounts from 14th cent, letters to London agent 19th cent, other corresp 16th-20th cent, timber accounts 19th-20th cent and farm accounts and papers mainly 20th cent; Lincs and Rutland (Heathcote) estate records 16th-19th cent, incl leases, surveys from late 18th cent, maps from 1726, valuations, rentals and accounts from *c*1720 (numerous), papers rel to fee farm rents, estate papers from early 18th cent and farm records 19th-20th cent; Lincs and Rutland combined estate records 19th-20th cent (extensive), incl valuations, accounts and vouchers, papers rel to brickyards, and Luffenham Iron Co accounts and papers 1919-38; misc Gwydir legal and estate records 18th-19th cent, incl rentals 1711-55; misc Perthshire estate papers 1865-87; other misc estate papers 16th-20th cent, incl Norfolk (Willoughby) 16th cent, Derbys (Heathcote) 1643-84, Lincs (Wynne of Folkingham) 1712-42, Yorks (Bertie) 18th cent, Norfolk (Hon Charles Willoughby) late 19th-early 20th cent and Jamaica (Heathcote) c1695-1726.

Building plans, accounts and papers mainly 18th-20th cent, incl alterations to Grimsthorpe Park by Lancelot Brown 1772, drawings for Gwydir House (London) by John Hope 1770, plans of Normanton park and gardens c1740, and Normanton alterations 19th cent; household accounts, inventories, etc, Grimsthorpe 16th-20th cent, Swinstead (Lincs) early 18th cent, Wales (Gwydir, etc) 1671-1737 and c1867, Normanton c1722-1916, Drummond Castle 1895-1932, Swinstead Hall 1933-49 and London houses; inventory of plate, Duke of Suffolk's London house 1535; stable lists and accounts 16th-19th cent.

Papers rel to Lincs and Rutland affairs 16th-19th cent, incl lieutenancy and politics; City of London shrievalty papers late 17th-early 18th cent (Heathcote); patents, commissions, etc 16th-20th cent; Willoughby, Bertie and Heathcote family papers 16th-20th cent, incl military and diplomatic papers of the 12th Baron Willoughby de Eresby late 16th cent, Civil War papers of the 1st and 2nd Earls of Lindsey, papers rel to the office of Lord Great Chamberlain, and political and commercial papers of Sir Gilbert Heathcote, 1st Bt; game books 19th-20th cent; genealogical, literary and misc papers 13th-20th cent, incl treatises ascribed to William of Leicester ?13th cent, copy of Tattershall College (Lincs) statutes c1501, muster certificate of Babergh hundred (Suffolk) c1522, notebook of Digby family of Luffenham (Rutland) 17th cent, and misc papers of Charles Heathcote-Drummond-Willoughby and EB Binns (Grimsthorpe agent) early 20th cent.

Lincolnshire Archives (ANC-9ANC). Deposited by the 3rd Earl of Ancaster and his Grimsthorpe agents and London solicitors (Messrs Warrens) 1951-69. Some of the earlier records are closed to research while conservation is in progress. HMC *Thirteenth Report, App VI*, 1893, pp203-6; *Ancaster*, 1907. NRA 5789.

[b] Lincs deeds and legal papers 16th-early 20th cent; Bertie settlements and related trust deeds 1625-1810; executorship papers, 4th Duke of Ancaster 1779-1801, incl some Lincs estate papers; other estate papers 18th-19th cent, mainly Lincs (Spilsby estate late 19th cent, etc) but incl misc Welsh estate papers 1786-late 19th cent; Grimsthorpe and Gwydir inventories 1865; Grimsthorpe, Gwydir and Drummond Castle household accounts 1823-67; account of the 3rd Duke of Ancaster as Master of the Horse 1777-8.

Lincolnshire Archives (Lind Dep 64, 97). Deposited by Messrs Warrens, solicitors, London, in

the Lindsey County Muniment Room c1940, through the British Records Association (BRA 301, 305). NRA 5757. (For later deposits from Warrens see 4ANC and 7ANC, above (NRA 5789).)

[c] Grimsthorpe household account 1581; further Bertie family papers 1555-1671; Irish account of Sir William Pelham 1579-80.

Lincolnshire Archives (10ANC). Purchased by the Lincolnshire Archives Committee and the 3rd Earl of Ancaster 1970 (Sotheby's, 23 June, lots 313-71 *passim*). The papers had passed from the Bertie family to the Greathead, later Heber Percy, family of Guy's Cliffe (Warwickshire). NRA 5789.

[d] Grimsthorpe agent's account book 1783-1810.

Lincolnshire Archives (MISC DEP 163). Deposited by AE Elvidge. *Archivists' Report 16* (1964-5), p24.

[e] Grimsthorpe estate account 1801-9.

Lincolnshire Archives (CRAGG 2/32/1). From the collection of Captain WA Cragg. NRA 4675.

[f] Carnarvonshire, Denbighshire and Merionethshire deeds and legal papers 1610-1886; wills and settlements 1654–1818, Wynn, Bertie and Burrell; Welsh estate papers 17th-19th cent, incl survey ?1766 and misc rentals and accounts from 1667; Gwydir inventories 1848, 1865-6; misc personal and genealogical papers 17th-18th cent.

National Library of Wales (Gwydir (BRA) Papers; MS 9719 E, 9720 D, 9725-6 E, 9727 D). Deposited by Messrs Warrens through the British Records Association 1940. *Annual Report 1939-40*, p25, 1940-1, p17. NRA 36325.

[g] Gwydir estates rental 1687.

National Library of Wales (MS 6414 D).

[h] Gwydir Castle visitors' book 1889-94.

National Library of Wales (MS 21802 E). *Annual Report 1981-2*, p62.

[i] Wynn of Gwydir family papers 1515-1690, incl rental and account 1568-74, survey 1605, Denbighshire shrievalty account 1606 and other letters and papers rel to public, local and family affairs.

National Library of Wales (MSS 463-70, 9051-69). Given by Sir John Williams, Bt, and Sir Herbert Lewis 1909-19. The papers are thought to have left custody at Gwydir Castle in the 1790s. They then passed through the Panton and other families. *Annual Report 1909-10*, p28, 1910-13, p34; *Calendar of Wynn (of Gwydir) Papers 1515-1690 in the National Library of Wales and elsewhere*, 1926 (including papers in Cardiff City Library). NRA 11470.

[j] Gwydir deeds and legal papers 17th-early 20th cent (mainly 19th-20th cent); Bertie trust deeds and related papers 1711-80; mortgages of Welsh estate 19th cent; Maen Homan (Nant

Conway) court book 1832-7; Carnarvonshire estate records 18th-20th cent, incl leases from 1796, maps and plans 1859-1938, rentals 1758-1866, accounts 1813-1972, corresp 1824-1935, tithe accounts 1840-91, and mining and quarrying accounts and papers 19th-20th cent; Llanrwst (Denbighshire) charity and school papers 19th-20th cent.

Gwynedd Archives, Caernarfon Area Record Office (XD 38). NRA 30191.

[k] Wynn of Gwydir deeds and wills 1629-1707; Carnarvonshire and Denbighshire rent rolls and accounts 1688-1716.

Public Record Office (C 110/139, Meredith v Wynne).

[l] Welsh (Gwydir estate) deeds 18th-19th cent, legal papers 19th-20th cent (incl sale papers 1884-97), leases and assignments late 19th-mid-20th cent, survey and maps 1784-6, particulars and valuations 19th-20th cent, rent rolls and rentals 1647-20th cent, accounts 1749-1923, letter books 1870s-1939, mining and quarrying accounts and papers 1773-mid-20th cent, and misc estate papers 19th-20th cent; Gwydir Castle building book 1884-95 and inventories 1841, 1889; Trefriw (Carnarvonshire) School Board minutes 1873-80; Eglwysfach (Denbighshire) small tithes account 1769; charity papers 18th cent.

In private possession. Enquiries to the Historical Manuscripts Commission. The records are partly those formerly in Lincolnshire Archives (3ANC 12, 4ANC) and partly those collected from the former estate office for the Gwydir properties. Not open for research while cataloguing is in progress.

[m] Perthshire, etc, charters and writs 12th-19th cent, incl lordship of Drummond and earldom of Perth; Drummond settlements and related papers; legal papers mainly 17th-19th cent, incl inventories of writs; Drummond estate papers ?18th-19th cent, incl rentals and accounts; rental of Abercairny (Perthshire) 1768-9; misc inventories of Drummond Castle, with visitors' book 1842-9; family papers late 15th-early 19th cent.

Scottish Record Office (GD 160). Keeper's *Reports*, 1954-1991 *passim*.

[n] Perth cartulary and copy of charters 1791-1929; Perth trust accounts 1798-1811, with account book 1734-7; Perthshire estate records 18th-20th cent, incl tacks 1859-1928, maps and plans, rentals 1755-66, 1812-1963 (incomplete), factory accounts 1833-1960 (incomplete), Drummond Castle day books and cash books from 1820, letter books 1870-1950 and corresp and papers 19th-20th cent; Muthill (Perthshire) parish register 1822-33; Knox survey 1810.

In private possession. Enquiries to the National Register of Archives (Scotland) (NRA(S) 827). NRA 20245. The collection is closed while conservation is in progress.

[o] Cash books of James Adams as factor 1809-16.

Scottish Record Office (CS 96/624-5).

Related collections: Heber-Percy of Guy's Cliffe (Warwickshire County Record Office CR 1707, NRA 26321; CR 611, NRA 21750); Panton of Plas Gwyn (National Library of Wales, NRA 28740), including Wynn of Gwydir legal papers 16th-17th cent; Carnarvonshire Quarter Sessions (Gwynedd Archives, Caernarfon Area Record Office XQP, NRA 28983), including papers of Maurice Wynn of Gwydir 1562-73; Williams Wynn of Wynnstay (National Library of Wales Wynnstay MSS, NRA 30545), including further Wynn of Gwydir papers 17th cent.

[49] HERBERT, Earls of Carnarvon

Henry Herbert (1741-1811), grandson of the 8th Earl of Pembroke (see no 50), inherited Highclere and Burghclere (Hampshire) from an uncle, Robert Sawyer Herbert, and was created Earl of Carnarvon in 1793. This estate was subsequently enlarged by purchases at Ecchinswell and elsewhere. Property situated mainly around Dulverton, west Somerset, including Pixton, Brushford and Bampton (just across the border in Devon), was acquired on the second Earl's marriage in 1796 to Elizabeth, daughter of Colonel John Dyke Acland and heiress to part of the estates of the Acland family, baronets, of Columb John (Devon). Christian Malford (Wiltshire) had been purchased in 1749.

Teversall and Kneeton (Nottinghamshire) were acquired through the third Earl's marriage in 1830 to Henrietta (d1876), daughter of Lord Henry Thomas Molyneux-Howard, who had inherited them from his uncle Sir Francis Molyneux, seventh Bt. They were sold about 1929. Another marriage, that of the fourth Earl to Evelyn, sister and, on his death in 1871, heir of the seventh Earl of Chesterfield, brought into the family considerable Stanhope family estates, including Bretby (Derbyshire) and Shelford (Nottinghamshire).

The fourth Earl married secondly, in 1878, Elizabeth, daughter of Henry Howard of Greystoke. In 1901 she bought Pixton and 5,000 acres in Somerset from the fifth Earl for her eldest son by the fourth Earl, Aubrey Herbert (1880-1923), who in 1910 married Mary, daughter of John Vesey, fourth Viscount de Vesci. In the 1880s the fourth Earl had bought property in Sydney and Perth (Australia), New Zealand, Canada and Italy. This passed to his widow and was apparently disposed of before the First World War.

Estates in 1883: Earl of Carnarvon: Notts 13,247 acres, Somerset 12,800 acres, Hants 9,340 acres, Derbys 120 acres, Devon 68 acres, Wilts 8 acres, total 35,583 acres worth £37,211 a year; Dowager Countess of Chesterfield: Derbys 5,209 acres, Staffs 8 acres, total 5,217 acres worth £10,760 a year.

[a] Deeds, Somerset and Wilts 13th-19th cent, Hants and Devon (Bampton) 16th-19th cent,

and Middlesex (London) 1720-1850; schedules of deeds and abstracts of title 18th-19th cent; wills, settlements, executorship and trust papers 17th-20th cent, incl wills of the Dyke family 1636-1770 and trustees' accounts of Evelyn, Viscountess de Vesci *c*1920-39; legal papers 16th-19th cent; manorial records, Hants 16th-20th cent and Kneeton 16th-17th cent; Brushford (Somerset) manor presentments 1686-1868; court rolls of Kings Brompton (Somerset) manor and hundred 1567-75 and Crediton (Devon) hundred 1510-11; St Bartholomew's Fair (Middlesex) piepowder court rolls 1622-1723.

Misc Hants and Somerset leases 18th-20th cent; Hants estate records 17th-20th cent, incl particulars of purchases 1812-33, maps, surveys and valuations 18th-19th cent, rentals 17th-20th cent, accounts, and estate corresp and papers 18th-20th cent; records of Highclere stud farm 20th cent and woodlands mid-19th-20th cent, incl survey 1877; Somerset estate records 16th-19th cent, incl terriers, surveys, rentals and accounts from 17th cent and Upton tithe papers 16th-19th cent; Christian Malford estate accounts and papers 18th-19th cent; papers rel to property in London (Tenterden St, Middlesex) *c*1838-76 and Australia and New Zealand *c*1880-1906; Derbys, Notts and Bucks (Stanhope) estate rental 1826; Bretby survey 1793 and valuation and accounts 1813-44, etc: Shelford accounts *c*1918-37; Teversall estate papers late 18th-20th cent, incl accounts *c*1771-1821; building records for Highclere Castle 1838-52, incl drawings and papers of Sir Charles Barry, and church 1869-72; Highclere household inventories and papers late 18th-20th cent, incl household accounts 1785-96, late 19th-20th cent and visitors' books from 1851; London house building papers 1776-mid-19th cent; misc household papers 19th-20th cent, incl Irish household accounts (4th Earl) 1885-6.

Sheriffs' acquittances for Notts (Molyneux family) 1648-9, 1731-2, 1746-7 and Somerset (Thomas Dyke) 1696-7; Wilts militia corresp 1799; election expenses, Wilts 1772-4 and Cricklade (Wilts) 1806; papers rel to Repton school (Derbys), Brushford school and Dulverton market 18th-19th cent; minutes of Highclere and Burghclere Horticultural Society 1923-8; appointments and commissions 17th-19th cent; family and personal accounts and papers 18th-20th cent, incl accounts of charitable gifts 1870-1922 and game books *c*1889-1965; papers of the 4th Earl, incl some rel to his visit to the Druses 1853-4; literary, genealogical and misc papers 18th-20th cent.

In private possession. Enquiries to the Rt Hon the Earl of Carnarvon, Highclere Castle, Hampshire. NRA 7289.

[b] Misc Hants deeds and abstracts of title 1758-early 20th cent; legal papers 17th-early 20th cent; Hants manorial records 1656-19th cent; Hants estate papers 18th-19th cent, incl misc leases 1732-mid-19th cent, particulars and valuations 1835-44, surveys *c*1800 and rentals and

accounts 1810-59; Highclere farm book 1780-93, timber accounts 1835-53 and labour accounts 1840-6; Hants tithe papers 1839-57; Highclere Castle building papers 1842, household accounts and vouchers 1839-55, and kennel and garden accounts 1810-34.

Hampshire Record Office (15M52). Deposited by B & JC Pinniger, solicitors, Newbury 1952. NRA 34478.

[c] Family, business, political and other corresp and papers late 18th cent-19th cent, incl some rel to Hants militia and county affairs and to the Hon Edward Herbert's murder 1870; household papers for Highclere, Tetton (Somerset) and Pixton 19th cent; misc papers, incl album of letters of the Duke of Newcastle 1706 and MS register of the Society of Antiquaries.

Hampshire Record Office (75M91). Purchased at Sotheby's, 18 July 1991, lot 384, apparently from EAM Herbert of Tetton, nephew of Aubrey Herbert. HMC *Accessions to Repositories 1991.*

[d] Trustees' accounts, Henrietta, Countess of Carnarvon 1825-54; estate papers, Teversall and Kneeton 1802-1921, Pixton 20th cent, Highclere 1855-90, Bretby 1878-84, Christian Malford 1858-73 and London (Middlesex) *c*1863-84; accounts, Australian property 1890-1910 and Portofino (Italy) 1902-13; Pixton household accounts 1911; Cricklade election papers early 19th cent; family and misc papers 18th-20th cent, incl accounts and diaries of the 2nd Earl (1772-1833) and Elizabeth, Countess of Carnarvon 1878-1913, literary and travel papers of the 3rd Earl (1800-49), and corresp and papers of Aubrey Herbert, MP, and the 4th Viscount de Vesci.

Somerset Archive and Record Service (DD/DRU, DD/HER). Deposited 1981-9 by Mrs ABD Grant, daughter of Aubrey Herbert. NRA 28627.

[e] Papers of the 4th Earl, mainly as Secretary of State for the Colonies and Lord Lieutenant of Ireland.

Public Record Office (PRO 30/6). Presented by Elizabeth, Countess of Carnarvon 1926 and by the 6th Earl of Carnarvon 1959. HMC *Papers of British Cabinet Ministers 1782-1900*, 1982, pp29-30. NRA 20656.

[f] Letter books and accounts 1837-49 of the 3rd Earl; papers of the 4th Earl; family and genealogical papers *c*1790-1929, incl literary papers of Sir AH Hardinge (1855-1933) and corresp of Sir William Heathcote, 5th Bt (1801-88).

British Library, Manuscript Collections (Add MSS 60757-61100, Add Ch 75874-8). Purchased at Sotheby's, 24 July 1978, lot 260, apparently from EAM Herbert. HMC *Papers of British Cabinet Ministers 1782-1900*, 1982, pp29-30. The groups of papers of the 4th Earl and his family sold at Sotheby's on 4 April 1977 (lot 183) and 18 June 1979 (lot 262) have not been traced.

[g] Corresp of Sir Francis Molyneux, 4th Bt (d1742), Sir William Molyneux, 6th Bt (d1781),

and Sir Francis Molyneux, 7th Bt (d1812); genealogical and misc papers 17th-19th cent.

Nottingham University Library, Manuscripts Department (Mol). Presented by the 6th Earl of Carnarvon 1977. NRA 27729.

[h] Letters to Sir Francis Molyneux, 4th Bt 1706-21; misc family papers 18th cent-1901, incl pedigree 1874.

Nottingham University Library, Manuscripts Department (Molt). Purchased at Sotheby's, 25 Feb 1992, lot 212. NRA 27729.

[i] Political and diplomatic corresp and papers of the 4th Earl of Chesterfield.

University of California Library, Berkeley, California. Purchased from the 6th Earl of Carnarvon *c*1962. NRA 6791.

Related collections: Earls of Chesterfield, Bucks estate records 1740-1810 (Buckinghamshire Record Office D/X 1099, NRA 685); Acland of Columb John (Devon Record Office 1148/M, NRA 14687).

[50] HERBERT, Earls of Pembroke and Montgomery

Richard Herbert of Ewyas, Gentleman Usher to Henry VII and natural son of the second Earl of Pembroke of the 1468 creation, married Margaret, daughter and heiress of Sir Matthew Cradock of Swansea (Glamorganshire). His son William Herbert (*c*1506-1570), a distinguished soldier and statesman, was created Earl of Pembroke in 1551. He was granted most of the Wilton Abbey estates and Baynard's Castle (London). On the death of the seventh Earl in 1683 the Wilton (Wiltshire) and other English estates (including land in Somerset and elsewhere later sold) passed to his brother as eighth Earl, but the South Wales estates passed to his daughter Charlotte, who married first the second Baron Jeffreys and secondly, in 1703, the first Viscount Windsor.

The seventh Viscount Fitzwilliam (d1816) left the bulk of his estates in Ireland and England (mainly property in Dublin and County Dublin) to his cousin Sidney Herbert (d1861), first Baron Herbert of Lea, second son of the eleventh Earl of Pembroke. The second Baron Herbert of Lea succeeded his uncle as thirteenth Earl of Pembroke in 1862.

Estates in 1883: Wilts 42,244 acres, Co Dublin 2,301 acres, Co Wicklow 230 acres, total 44,775 acres worth £77,663 a year.

[a] English and Welsh deeds 12th-19th cent, mainly Wilts (Wilton Abbey, etc) from 12th cent but incl London, Glamorganshire, Monmouthshire, etc 16th-19th cent; Irish deeds 13th-18th cent (*c*90 pre-1600), mainly Dublin and Co Dublin; wills, settlements and related papers 16th-20th cent, mainly Herbert family, incl executorship papers 1730-61, 1862-71 and 1939-63 (Sir Sidney Herbert, Bt); legal and case

papers 17th-19th cent, incl registers of deeds; manorial records 16th-20th cent, mainly Wilts.

Wilts estate records 16th-20th cent, incl surveys and valuations from 16th cent, maps and plans 18th-20th cent, rentals 1755-20th cent, accounts from 16th cent, corresp 1553-20th cent (mainly from 1733), reports and memoranda 18th-20th cent, and papers rel to enclosure 1785-1866, tithes mainly 19th cent, woodlands and timber 1748-20th cent, farms in hand 1879-1912, buildings 20th cent and sales 19th-20th cent; misc papers rel to other English and Welsh estates 16th-18th cent, incl surveys and accounts of 1st Earl's properties in Dorset, Somerset, Glamorganshire, etc mid 16th cent; Irish estate records late 17th-20th cent, incl surveys 1762, 1837 and 1850, maps and plans 1692-1850, rent accounts 1751-1806 and estate accounts mid-19th-early 20th cent; accounts and papers rel to former Fitzwilliam estate in Salop *c*1862-73.

Papers rel to Wilton House 17th-20th cent, incl plans and drawings from *c*1650, inventories and sale catalogues, rebuilding and restoration accounts and papers early 19th cent, corresp, printed material and photographs; Wilton household accounts 18th-20th cent, brewing and cellar accounts 18th-19th cent, stables accounts 1755-1825, garden accounts 1791-1830 and papers and plans rel to the park 17th-20th cent; accounts and papers rel to houses in London (Privy Gardens, Whitehall) and Richmond Park *c*1755-1801, incl inventory of Fitzwilliam moveables at Pembroke House *c*1800.

Patents, commissions, etc, Herbert and Fitzwilliam 17th-20th cent; Herbert personal and family papers 17th-20th cent, incl military and official papers of the 11th Earl late 18th-early 19th cent, official and political corresp and papers of the Hon Sidney Herbert 1833-61 and Royal Household papers of the 14th Earl 1895-1905; Fitzwilliam official and family corresp 1639-1815; diaries of Sir Matthew Dekker (father-in-law of the 6th Viscount Fitzwilliam) 1726-48; misc MS and printed material 17th-20th cent, incl Civil War pamphlets rel to the 4th Earl and genealogical and heraldic papers; game books 1843-1939; papers of the Earls of Pembroke as Visitors of Jesus College, Oxford 1653-1742 and 20th cent; misc Wilton Abbey records late 13th-early 16th cent, incl inventory of charters 1287, rental and custumal 1316, survey *c*1538, Wilton borough rent accounts 1361-73 and Alvediston farmers' accounts 1484-1509.

Wiltshire Record Office (WRO 1422, 2057, etc). Deposited from Wilton House by the 17th Earl of Pembroke 1977-93. NRA 16612 (Sidney Herbert papers), 22080 (list in progress). Some documents less than 100 years old are not available for research.

[b] Survey of Wilts and Dorset estates 1756; Wilts plans 1783-1803.

Wiltshire Record Office (WRO 1553). Deposited by Wiltshire Archaeological Society 1979. NRA 1335.

[c] Map of Grovely Wood near Wilton by DL Heniage 1589.

Wiltshire Record Office (WRO 212B). Deposited by Wiltshire Archaeological Society 1952.

[d] Wilton estate agent's diaries 1810-40.

Wiltshire Record Office (WRO 867). Deposited through Salisbury and South Wiltshire Museum 1967. NRA 16171.

[e] Misc estate papers from 18th cent; plans of Wilton House and park from 18th cent, with inventory 1960; drawings for other houses 18th-early 19th cent, incl house in Whitehall; family and personal papers 17th-20th cent, incl papers rel to honours and appointments, and diplomatic corresp of Sir Michael Herbert 1879-1903; misc papers, incl a genealogical MS (Herbert family) c1632 and Fitzwilliam pedigree late 17th-early 18th cent.

In private possession. Enquiries to Wiltshire Record Office. NRA 22080.

[f] Inventory of Wilton House 1561.

Victoria and Albert Museum, National Art Library. HMC *Accessions to Repositories 1982.*

[g] Irish deeds and legal papers 18th-20th cent; Irish agreements 1857-1948, estate plans and drawings 1864-1969 (412 items) and estate corresp 1836-1947; misc Dublin, etc estate papers 19th-20th cent, incl Dublin railways, schools, drainage, etc and maintenance of Merrion Square.

National Archives of Ireland, Dublin (Acc 1011). Deposited from the Pembroke Estates Management Office, Dublin 1972. NRA 29975.

[h] Papers of Sir Robert Pye as executor of the 4th Earl and rel to his financial affairs c1630-53.

Sheffield Archives (Elmhirst papers, EM 1351-62). Deposited by AO Elmhirst 1959. NRA 4707.

[i] Family corresp of Lord and Lady Herbert of Lea 1856-61.

British Library, Manuscript Collections (Add MS 59671). Presented 1976.

[j] Travel journal of the 13th Earl 1870.

Alexander Turnbull Library, Wellington (National Register of Archives and Manuscripts in New Zealand, B 105).

Related collections: Marquesses of Bute (National Library of Wales, NRA 581); Herbert, Earls of Powis (no 51); Dukes of Beaufort (National Library of Wales, NRA 12100, 12101), including records that descended through the daughter of the 2nd Earl of Pembroke (1468 creation).

[51] HERBERT, Earls of Powis

Edward Herbert (1583-1648), of Chirbury (Shropshire) and Montgomery Castle (Montgomeryshire), was a great-grandson of Sir Richard Herbert of Montgomery, a Gentleman Usher to Henry VIII, and a great-great-grandson of Sir Richard Herbert, brother of the first Earl of Pembroke (so created 1468) (see no 50). Edward Herbert married in 1589 Mary, daughter and heir of Sir William Herbert of St Julians (Monmouthshire), who brought estates in Monmouthshire, Carnarvonshire, Anglesey and County Kerry. He was created Baron Herbert of Chirbury in 1629.

Florentia, sister and co-heir of the fourth Baron (d1691), married her kinsman Richard Herbert, a younger son of Matthew Herbert of Dolegeiog (Monmouthshire) by Anne, daughter of Charles Foxe of Bromfield (Shropshire). Their son Francis Herbert (d1719) married Dorothy, daughter and co-heir of John Oldbury (d1702), a London merchant. Henry Arthur Herbert (c1703-1772), of Oakly Park (near Bromfield), son of Francis and Dorothy, succeeded in 1748 to the estates of his distant kinsman the third Marquess of Powis (see below). He was created Baron Herbert of Chirbury in 1743 and Earl of Powis in 1748.

The Herberts of Powis Castle, like the Herberts of Chirbury, owned estates in both Montgomeryshire and Shropshire. Sir Edward Herbert, second son of the first Earl of Pembroke of the 1551 creation (see no 50), purchased Red Castle, later Powis Castle, near Welshpool (Montgomeryshire) in 1587. His son was created Baron Powis in 1629 and his great-grandson Earl (1674) and Marquess (1687) of Powis. The family also owned property in Shropshire (Oswestry, etc, formerly a property of the Earl of Craven), Middlesex (Hendon, originally granted to the first Earl of Pembroke) and Northamptonshire (Heyford, etc, inherited from the Parr family). The first Earl of Powis of the 1748 creation sold the Middlesex and Northamptonshire properties in the 1750s, and other outlying properties were disposed of in the 1820s, leaving the Powis estates concentrated in Montgomeryshire and Shropshire.

On the death of the second Earl without issue in 1801 his estates were inherited by his nephew, the son of his sister Henrietta, who in 1784 had married the second Baron Clive. The first Baron Clive, a descendant of the Clive family of Styche (Shropshire), had made extensive purchases in Shropshire and elsewhere, including Montford, near Shrewsbury, in 1761, Walcot, near Bishop's Castle, in 1763, and Oakly, from the Earl of Powis, in 1771. The second Baron Clive was created Earl of Powis in 1804, and the Clive estates were soon afterwards divided: the Montford, Walcot and other estates in Shropshire remained with the Earls of Powis, but the Oakly estate passed to a younger son, Robert Henry Clive, who in 1819 married Harriet, Baroness Windsor, sister and co-heir of the sixth Earl of Plymouth.

Estates in 1883: Montgomeryshire 33,545 acres, Radnorshire 19 acres, Denbighshire 9 acres, Salop 26,986 acres, total 60,559 acres worth £57,024 a year.

[a] Deeds 13th-20th cent, mainly Montgomeryshire and Salop (Herbert estates) but some for

Anglesey, Ireland (from 16th cent) and elsewhere; Herbert and Clive trust and executorship
papers 16th-19th cent, incl settlements, wills and
inventories, and papers rel to settlements of
1751, 1804-7, etc; legal and case papers
16th-20th cent, incl Irish estate 17th cent, the
forfeiture of the Powis estates 1689, and the
affairs of Lady Mary Herbert (her Spanish mining interests, etc) 18th cent; manorial records
14th-19th cent, mainly Montgomeryshire and
Salop, incl hundred of Chirbury from 14th cent,
borough of Montgomery from 15th cent, barony
of Powis from 16th cent and manors and bor-
oughs of Llanfyllin (Montgomeryshire), Oswestry
and Pool 17th-19th cent; Irish manorial records
1676-80.

Montgomery and Salop estate records (Herbert
of Powis and Herbert of Chirbury, Montgomery
and Oakly) 15th-20th cent, incl leases, surveys
and maps, rentals and accounts, vouchers, corresp, and papers rel to timber, enclosure and
tithes; papers rel to minerals in Montgomeryshire
and Salop 17th-18th cent, incl lead mining,
Mathraval (Montgomeryshire) Forge iron works
(1742-53) and Clee Hill (Salop) workings;
papers rel to other Welsh estates 16th-19th cent,
incl Anglesey, Carnarvonshire, Cardiganshire
(lead and silver mining papers, etc), Merionethshire, Monmouthshire (St Julians) and
Radnorshire; papers rel to the Middlesex and
Northants estates 17th-18th cent, and to Ribbesford (Worcs) 1690s-1760; papers rel to the
Castle Island (Co Kerry) estate 16th-early 19th
cent, incl leases, surveys, rentals and accounts;
records of the Clive estates in Salop and elsewhere mid-18th-20th cent, incl rentals for the
Clive (later Powis) estates in Salop from 1780;
legal and estate papers for the Lloyd of Trefnant
(Montgomeryshire) estates 1760s-1820s;
Ormsby-Gore estate papers 1820s; rentals for the
Oldbury estates (Middlesex, etc) 1704-9 and the
Mytton estates (Salop) 1784.

Papers rel to Powis Castle mainly 18th-19th cent,
incl inventories, library catalogues, household
accounts and papers rel to the gardens, park and
farm; papers rel to other Herbert and Clive
houses 17th-19th cent, incl Castle Island
mid-17th cent (plan and accounts), Oakly Park
1748-9 (plans), Lymore (Montgomeryshire),
Walcot, Powis House (London), Clive House in
Berkeley Square, Claremont (Surrey) (rebuilding 1771-80) and Madras (cellar books
1798-1803); papers rel to Montgomeryshire and
Salop county affairs 16th-19th cent, incl lieutenancy, commissions of the peace, elections
(Montgomery, Montgomeryshire, Ludlow
(Salop) and Bishop's Castle (Salop) 18th-19th
cent), roads and bridges, Montgomery Castle
1644-50, Montgomery poor law union early 19th
cent, Machynlleth (Montgomeryshire) toll
accounts 1632, Salop shrievalty accounts 1597-8
(Foxe) and 1654-5 (Herbert), and Clun Hospital
(Salop) papers late 18th cent.

Herbert and Clive family papers 16th-20th cent,
incl political and literary corresp and papers of

the 1st Baron Herbert of Chirbury, papers of
Francis Herbert of Oakly and of the Duke of
Powis late 17th cent, Indian and other papers of
the 1st and 2nd Barons Clive, and papers of the
2nd Earl of Powis rel to Chartist disturbances
1831-42 and the proposed union of the sees of
Bangor and St Asaph 1835-49; other family
papers 16th-19th cent, incl accounts of Sir
Charles Foxe 1569-1630, business and personal
papers of John Oldbury mainly late 17th cent
and papers of General John Carnac 1760-7;
genealogical and misc papers 16th-19th cent, incl
notebook of the Revd William Hicson of Mon-
don (Essex) 1583-99; Bromfield Priory account
early 15th cent; Caus (Salop) ministers' accounts
1460-93.

National Library of Wales. Deposited by the
Powysland Club 1930, the 4th, 5th and 6th Earls
of Powis 1932-82 and the Trustees of the Powis
estates 1982-90. *Annual Reports*, 1932-90 *passim*.
NRA 20203, 20151, 23682 (partial lists).
Related Montgomeryshire manorial records
1579-18th cent were deposited by JB Willans of
Dolforgan in 1976 (*Annual Report*, 1976, p80;
NRA 30537).

[b] Herbert of St Julians rental 1583 and survey
with rental 1633.

Society of Antiquaries of London (Wakeman and
Morgan collection, MS 790).

[c] Household accounts of the Marquess of
Powis 1686-1700.

British Library, Manuscript Collections (Add MS
38864). Purchased at Sotheby's, 18 May 1914,
lot 1,258. HMC *Fifteenth Report, App II*, 1897,
pp20-1 (Hodgkin MSS). (For further Herbert
papers see also Add MSS 7081-2, (m) below.)

[d] Deeds ?16th-20th cent, mainly Salop, Montgomeryshire and Radnorshire (Clive properties:
Styche, Walcot, Montford, Oakly, etc); trust and
legal papers 16th-20th cent, incl executorship
papers of the 1st Baron Clive and attorneys'
minutes 1774; Salop manorial records 14th-19th
cent, incl borough, hundred and honour of Clun
14th-16th cent; Salop estate records (mainly
Clive, later Powis, properties) 18th-20th cent,
incl leases, surveys and maps, rentals and
accounts, corresp, field books 19th-20th cent and
papers rel to enclosure, tithes, timber, drainage,
churches and railways; Oakly Park rentals and
accounts ?18th-early 19th cent; Oswestry estate
records 16th-19th cent; particulars for estates in
Monmouthshire 1769, 1771 and Radnorshire
1769; papers rel to Markham property in Kent
18th-19th cent; accounts and papers rel to
houses and household management 18th-19th
cent, incl Styche, Walcot, Berkeley Square,
Hayes Mews and Ludlow Castle (plans and
papers 18th cent); papers rel to Styche gardens
19th cent and Walcot home farm; papers rel to
Salop affairs 17th-20th cent, incl militia, Bishop's
Castle and Ludlow elections, Clun school, town
hall and hospital, and Lydbury North school,
etc; misc family papers 18th-19th cent, incl
accounts of the 1st Baron Clive and game books.

Shropshire Records and Research Unit, Shropshire Record Office (552, 1043, 2561). Deposited by the 6th Earl of Powis 1953-71 and others. NRA 11563 (summary notes), 17099 (partial list).

[e] Clun ministers' accounts 1517-18.

Shropshire Records and Research Unit, Shropshire Record Office (1386). Found in the former Walcot estate office, Lydbury North, and deposited by Lt-Col WP Kenyon 1964.

[f] Legal papers, mainly 19th cent and rel to Montgomeryshire and Salop estates, incl abstracts of title and summaries of wills and settlements; Walcot estate papers late 17th-late 18th cent; Salop and Montgomeryshire estate papers mainly 19th cent, incl papers rel to manorial rights, enclosure, tithes, churches, schools and railways; Clun Hospital papers 19th cent.

Shropshire Records and Research Unit, Shopshire Record Office (1015, 3651). Deposited by Salt & Sons, solicitors, Shrewsbury 1959, 1977-8. NRA 11563 (summary notes).

[g] Abstracts of title, legal papers and case papers early 19th cent, mainly rel to Oswestry.

Shropshire Records and Research Unit, Shropshire Record Office (800). Deposited by Longueville & Co, solicitors, Oswestry 1957-8. NRA 11563 (summary note).

[h] Corresp of the 3rd Earl of Powis rel to the South Salopian Yeomanry Cavalry mainly 1848-72.

Shropshire Records and Research Unit, Shropshire Record Office (2183). Transferred from the Shropshire Yeomanry Museum 1969. NRA 33287.

[i] Papers of the 4th Earl of Powis as lord lieutenant of Salop 1896-1951.

Shropshire Records and Research Unit, Shropshire Record Office (1665, 1735). Presented by the Duchess della Grazia 1966.

[j] Salop (Clive) estate papers 18th cent, incl rentals and accounts; household papers, Walcot, Oakly and Claremont 1770-c1777; Shrewsbury election papers 1734-75; agency papers of John Ashby 18th cent, incl letters from the 1st and 2nd Barons Clive.

Public Record Office (C 109/71-8). NRA 34890.

[k] Herbert family papers 16th-18th cent, incl diplomatic and other papers of the 1st Baron Herbert of Chirbury 1615-39, parliamentary diaries 1640-1 and notes of the proceedings against the Earl of Strafford 1641.

Public Record Office (PRO 30/53). Deposited by the 5th Earl of Powis 1956. HMC *Tenth Report, App IV*, 1885, pp378-98. NRA 8665. (Other items reported on by the Commission in 1885 (pp398-9) were deposited in the National Library of Wales in 1959. A further item (p398) was among miscellaneous MS volumes sold from the library of Powis Castle at Sotheby's, 20 Mar 1923.)

[l] Herbert family corresp and papers 17th-mid-18th cent, incl papers of the 1st Baron Herbert of Chirbury and his brother Sir Henry Herbert (1593-1673), Master of the Revels.

National Library of Wales (MSS 5295-5313). Purchased from Messrs Quaritch 1916, having left Ribbesford (Worcs) on the death of the 4th Baron Herbert of Chirbury in 1738.

[m] Letter book of Lord Herbert of Chirbury as ambassador to France 1619-20, with his Tractatus De Veritate.

British Library, Manuscript Collections (Add MSS 7081-2).

[n] Corresp and papers 1748-1851, mainly of the 1st and 2nd Barons Clive; plan of Walcot Hall nd.

British Library, Oriental and India Office Collections (MSS Eur. G 37). Deposited by the 5th Earl of Powis 1956. NRA 29349.

[o] Corresp and papers of Henrietta Clive, Countess of Powis 1792-1823.

British Library, Manuscript Collections (Add MS 64105). Presented by Mr and Mrs B Ginsberg 1987.

Related collections: Herbert, Earls of Pembroke and Montgomery (no 50); Earls of Plymouth (Shropshire Records and Research Unit, Shropshire Record Office SRO 22).

[52] HILL, Marquesses of Downshire

Sir Moyses Hill (d1630) acquired estates in Counties Antrim and Down in the late sixteenth and early seventeenth centuries. They were increased by purchase and inheritance, and the marriage of his grandson William Hill (d1693) to Eleanor Boyle brought the Blessington (County Wicklow) estate into the family. Trevor Hill was created Viscount Hillsborough in 1717, and his son Earl of Hillsborough in 1751 and Marquess of Downshire in 1789. In 1786 Arthur Hill (d1801), later second Marquess of Downshire, married Mary Sandys, heir not only through her uncle the second Baron Sandys to the Worcestershire and East Anglian estates of the Sandys family, but also through her mother to the estates of the Blundell, Alexander, Lee, Vanlore and Trumbull families.

William Trumbull (d1635) acquired the Easthampstead (Berkshire) estate in 1627-8. His grandson Sir William Trumbull married Judith Alexander, daughter of the fourth Earl of Stirling and eventual co-heir to property in Berkshire, Buckinghamshire, Somerset, Surrey and elsewhere, including estates inherited from the Lee and Vanlore families. William Trumbull, son of Sir William, married Mary Blundell, daughter and co-heir of Viscount Blundell (d1756), through whom the Dundrum (County Down) and Edenderry (King's County) estates descended. It was Mary, daughter and heir of William Trumbull and Mary Blundell, who married in 1760 Colonel Martin

Sandys, brother of the second Baron Sandys (d1797), and their daughter Mary who married Viscount Fairford, later second Marquess of Downshire.

The Sandys barony was recreated for Mary, Marchioness of Downshire in 1802, and on her death in 1836 she was succeeded in the barony and in the Sandys estates by her second son Lord Arthur Hill.

Estates in 1883: Co Down 78,051 acres, Co Wicklow 15,766 acres, King's Co 13,679 acres, Co Antrim 5,787 acres, Co Kildare 1,338 acres, Berks 5,287 acres, Suffolk 281 acres, total 120,189 acres worth £96,691 a year.

[a] Deeds for Irish estates late 16th-20th cent; wills, settlements and related papers, Hill family 17th-20th cent and Boyle and Blundell families 18th cent; Irish estate papers mainly 18th-20th cent, incl leases, surveys, maps, rentals, accounts, vouchers and tithe papers; Irish estate corresp (Hill estates) 18th-20th cent (extensive), incl letters to members of the Hill family and their agents; corresp rel to the Blundell estates in Ireland and to the Easthampstead estate 18th-19th cent; Irish farm accounts 1837-1919; papers rel to Hillsborough Castle (Co Down) 18th-20th cent, incl inventories and plans; household accounts 1794-1895, mainly Hillsborough, etc but incl Easthampstead 1888-92; papers rel to Irish affairs mainly 18th-19th cent, incl Hillsborough corporation books 1740-1841, Hillsborough turnpike minutes 1762-87 and papers rel to Co Down politics; Hill family papers 17th-19th cent, incl appointments, commissions, and personal and political corresp of the 1st, 2nd and 3rd Marquesses of Downshire.

Public Record Office of Northern Ireland (D 607, 671). Deposited by the representatives of the 7th Marquess of Downshire 1958 and earlier. Purchased 1992. NRA 21035.

[b] Co Down and Co Antrim estate records 1744-1969 (9 vols), incl Kilwarlin (Co Down) and Carrickfergus (Co Antrim) rentals 1744-6 and cash books 1802-3, 1904-30.

Public Record Office of Northern Ireland (D 2784/23). Purchased from a dealer 1990-1. *Annual Report 1990-1*, p9.

[c] Deeds c1200-19th cent, mainly Berks but also Bucks and Kent (Lee), Cambs, Suffolk, Worcs, etc (Sandys), Somerset (Vanlore), other English counties and Ireland; wills, settlements and related papers, with other legal and financial papers, Trumbull, Alexander, Vanlore, Lee, Blundell and Sandys families 16th-18th cent and Hill family 18th-19th cent; misc legal papers 14th-19th cent; misc manorial records, Berks, Bucks, Cambs, etc 14th-19th cent; misc estate papers (leases, surveys, rentals, etc) 14th-19th cent, incl Berks mainly 16th-19th cent, Bucks 17th-18th cent, Cambs, Worcs, etc 16th-18th cent and Ireland 17th-18th cent; design for lodge at Easthampstead c1630; household inventories and accounts 17th-18th cent, Easthampstead, Ombersley (Worcs), etc.

Official and local papers mainly 17th-18th cent, incl shrievalty of Berks 1739-40 and Hants 1607, Berks commission of the peace 18th cent, Worcs subsidy assessments early 17th cent and Isle of Ely drainage papers 17th cent; Berks forest papers 15th-19th cent; appointments and commissions 17th-19th cent; misc family corresp and papers 16th-19th cent, Trumbull, Alexander, Lee, Blundell, Sandys and Hill, incl legal MSS of Sir William Trumbull, Trumbull family corresp rel to its Yorks estates mainly 17th cent, accounts and papers of the 5th Earl of Stirling c1722-39, and military papers of Lord Robert Bertie (husband of a Blundell co-heiress) 1741-81; misc papers, incl papers of the Landen family, bellmakers 14th-16th cent.

Berkshire Record Office (D/ED, Acc 622, 662). Deposited by the representatives of the 7th Marquess of Downshire 1954-76. HMC *Downshire I-VI*, 1924-95. NRA 7580.

[d] Court book for Tilehurst (Berks) and other manors 1646-7.

Berkshire Record Office (D/EB/M3). Deposited by the British Records Association 1946. NRA 3501.

[e] Berks and Wilts deeds 16th-18th cent (1 bundle).

Berkshire Record Office (D/EB/T 120-1). Deposited by the Public Record Office of Northern Ireland through the British Records Association 1951. NRA 3501.

[f] Easthampstead estate accounts 1729-57 and household accounts 1719-24, with dairy book 1870-2; estate book (Bucks, etc) and notebooks of the 5th Earl of Stirling 1717-38; rent account (Tilehurst, etc) 1749-55 and letter book 1737-9 of Robert Lee; Ombersley farm accounts 1729-60 (1 vol); Downshire provision account 1850-4; account rel to the Hon Mrs Blundell 1786-95; corresp of the 6th Marquess 1910-11.

Berkshire Record Office (D/EZ 91). Purchased 1993. Sold at Sotheby's, 21 July 1992, lot 257 (part).

[g] Sir William Trumbull's memorials of his embassy to Constantinople 1687-8.

British Library, Manuscript Collections (Add MS 34799). Purchased 1895.

[h] Papers of Sir William Trumbull 1685-91.

British Library, Manuscript Collections (Add MSS 52279-80). Purchased at Sotheby's 30 July 1963, lots 594, 596. For other Trumbull papers sold in 1963, and now widely dispersed, see HMC *Annual Review 1989-90*, pp25-8.

[i] Diplomatic and political corresp and papers of William Trumbull (d1635) 16th-early 17th cent, Sir William Trumbull c1660-1715 and GR Weckherlin (1584-1653, grandfather of Sir William Trumbull); family corresp and papers c1620-1720, Trumbull, Weckherlin, Cotterell, Dormer, Bridges, Stubbes and Dumaresque families, with Easthampstead library catalogue,

medical and culinary receipt books and verse collections 17th-early 18th cent.

British Library, Manuscript Collections (Dep 8826). Purchased 1989. HMC *Annual Review 1989-90*, pp23-8; *Downshire I-VI*, 1924-95. NRA 7864, 7580 (part).

[j] Legal commonplace book of Sir William Trumbull, with inserted letters and papers.

British Library, Manuscript Collections (Dep 8990). Purchased at Sotheby's, 18 July 1991, lot 394. (Another commonplace book, *c*1657, was presented in 1990 by L Heyworth, Esq. Add MS 70590.)

[k] Account book of Sir William Trumbull as Secretary of State 1695-7.

British Library, Manuscript Collections (Dep 9190). Purchased 1993. Sold at Sotheby's, 21 July 1992, lot 257 (part).

[l] Further Trumbull papers 16th-17th cent, incl two legal commonplace books of Sir William Trumbull, Spanish diplomatic tracts 1588-1631 and a treatise on maritime law.

Cambridge University Library (Add MSS 8863-8). Sold at Sotheby's, 18 July 1991, lots 393, 395.

[m] Account books (2 vols) and papers of Richard Archdale, London merchant (great-grandfather of Judith Trumbull) 1623-39.

Guildhall Library, London (MSS 23953-5). Sold at Sotheby's, 14 Dec 1989, lot 220.

[n] Account books, Trumbull family 1632-1733 (3 vols) and Martin Sandys 1742-68 (1 vol).

In private possession. Sold at Sotheby's, 21 July 1992, lot 257 (part).

[o] Naval accounts of the Earl of Orford (great-great-great-uncle of Mary Sandys) 1689-99.

Untraced. Sold at Sotheby's, 14 Dec 1989, lot 229.

[p] Papers of Cardinal Granvelle, Spanish statesman *c*1532-61 (10 vols).

Untraced. Sold at Sotheby's, 26 Apr 1990, lots 379-81. NRA 7133.

Related collection: Barons Sandys (Hereford and Worcester Record Office 705:56, NRA 1492).

[53] HOPE, Earls of Hopetoun, later Marquesses of Linlithgow

Sir James Hope (d1661) of Hopetoun (West Lothian), a younger son of Sir Thomas Hope of Craighall (Fife), first Bt, married Anne, daughter and heiress of Robert Foulis of Leadhills (Lanarkshire). Their descendants acquired estates in West Lothian, Midlothian, East Lothian (Ormiston, Luffness, etc), Fife (Rankeillour, Rosyth, etc), and Dumfriesshire. Charles Hope (1681-1742) was created Earl of Hopetoun in 1703. Craighall (Fife) was purchased from Sir Thomas Bruce Hope of Craighall, sixth Bt, in 1729.

The Scottish estates of the Johnstone family, Marquesses of Annandale (see no 54), were inherited by the third Earl of Hopetoun (1741-1816). On his death they passed to his daughter Anne, whilst the Hopetoun estates passed to his half-brother, Major-General John Hope (1765-1823), who succeeded as fourth Earl. Property in East Lothian (Luffness) and Fife (Rankeillour, Craighall) passed to other branches of the Hope family. The seventh Earl was created Marquess of Linlithgow in 1902.

Estates in 1883: Lanarkshire 19,180 acres, W Lothian 11,870 acres, E Lothian 7,967 acres, Dumfriesshire 2,549 acres, Fife 941 acres, total 42,507 acres worth £39,984 a year, exclusive of minerals worth £3,974.

[a] Writs, Dumfriesshire and Lanarkshire 16th-18th cent, Fife 15th-18th cent and E, Mid and W Lothian 14th-19th cent; inventories of writs 16th-19th cent, incl Leadhills cartulary 17th cent and inventory of leases and grants of mines and minerals 1556-1770; misc wills and settlements 17th-19th cent, mainly Hope family; accounts of the guardians of the 1st Earl of Hopetoun 1684-1704; executry accounts of the 2nd Earl of Hopetoun 1783; legal and case papers 16th-20th cent, incl Johnstone family late 17th-18th cent; Hopetoun barony court book 1700-59; head court of the sheriffdom of Bathgate (W Lothian) minutes 1706; Kirkliston (W Lothian) regality court book 1670-1747.

Tacks 16th-19th cent, mainly Lanarkshire and E and W Lothian, with some for Dumfriesshire, Fife and Midlothian; estate records 16th-20th cent, mainly Lanarkshire, E and W Lothian, Dumfriesshire and Fife, incl surveys, maps, particulars, valuations, rentals 17th-20th cent, accounts and vouchers 17th-19th cent, corresp 17th-20th cent, and papers rel to teinds (16th-18th cent), drainage, improvements, canals and railways; Airthrey (Stirlingshire) valuation 1654 and rentals 1656, 1672; Castle Campbell (Clackmannanshire) barony rental 1655; Leadhills lead and silver mining papers 1610-20th cent, incl leases of mines, bar lead and other accounts, plans and sections, contracts of sale, papers rel to exports to Holland, etc, and Hildestoun silver mines accounts 1607-17; W Lothian colliery papers 18th-19th cent, incl Bathgate coal mining accounts, vouchers, leases and papers, and papers rel to Humbie and Priestinch collieries *c*1832-55; papers rel to Kirkliston (W Lothian) linen weaving 18th-19th cent; papers rel to game 18th-20th cent, incl Hopetoun game books 1881-1951 and shooting leases 1816-75; Dumfriesshire and W Lothian (Annandale) estate rentals, accounts and papers 17th-18th cent; W Lothian (Fairholme family) estate papers 17th cent; misc Lanarkshire estate papers, Foulis family early 17th cent.

Hopetoun House building accounts and papers 1698-19th cent, incl papers of James, John, Robert and William Adam, works journal 1782-4 and account of parks and improvements

1700-94; Hopetoun inventories 18th-20th cent, incl library early 19th cent and livestock and implements 1818-23; Hopetoun household accounts, vouchers and papers c1700-20th cent, incl diet books 18th-19th cent, cellar books 1791-1925 and visitors' books 1830-1934; papers rel to farm and gardens 18th-20th cent, incl dairy books 1830-64 and farm diaries 1799-1811; misc household papers 17th-20th cent, Hope and Johnstone, incl Leadhills building papers 1736-40 and inventories 1683, 1770, Rankeillour building accounts 1815, Luffness household inventory 1825 and Lubenham Hall and Papillon Hall (Leics) accounts, etc 1850-72; personal inventories 17th-20th cent, incl the 3rd Earl of Hopetoun 1781, Thomas Fairholme 1672, John Fairholme 1694 and the Marquesses of Annandale mid-17th-mid-18th cent.

Linlithgowshire (W Lothian) election papers and misc lieutenancy papers 18th-19th cent, incl some rel to the Linlithgowshire Yeomanry Cavalry 1804-26, volunteer infantry, and militia 1808-37; misc local papers 19th-20th cent, incl Abercorn (W Lothian) parish poor fund minutes and papers 1840-7 and minutes of the Rogue Money Society of Abercorn 1811-55.

Patents and commissions 18th-20th cent; family corresp, papers, accounts and vouchers 17th-20th cent, incl papers of the 1st Earl rel to horse breeding and racing 1695-1736, mining and other papers of Sir James Hope (d1661), military papers of the 4th Earl of Hopetoun, Australian papers of the 1st Marquess of Linlithgow, and Indian and other papers of the 2nd Marquess of Linlithgow; papers of General Sir Alexander Hope of Luffness (1769-1837), incl letter book as trustee of the 5th Earl of Hopetoun 1823-5, and General Charles Hope (1768-1828); Peninsular War letters of General Sir James Archibald Hope 1812-14; letters of James Joseph Hope-Vere, MP, to JP Wood 1823-38; misc corresp of Sir Thomas Hope, 1st Bt, of Craighall 1645-6; misc family papers, Johnstone 17th-18th cent and Fairholme of Craigiehall 17th cent; misc literary, genealogical and other papers 16th-20th cent, incl account book of Sir George Bruce of Carnock, treasurer of the king's silver mines at Hildestoun (Lanarkshire) 1610-12; charters of David II 1356 and Robert II 1375.

In private possession. Enquiries to the National Register of Archives (Scotland) (NRA(S) 888). NRA 17684.

[b] Writs, Lanarkshire 18th-19th cent and E, Mid and W Lothian 16th-20th cent; inventories of writs 16th-19th cent; misc settlements 17th-19th cent, mainly Hope family but incl Sir Alexander Livingstone 1683; legal and case papers 17th-20th cent, incl some rel to Dalmeny church (W Lothian) and Leadhills parish.

Tacks, E and W Lothian 18th-20th cent; misc E and W Lothian rentals, valuations and plans 17th-19th cent, incl W Lothian estate rental 1787; Costertoun (Midlothian) rental 1724; Wamphray (Dumfriesshire) rental 1800; rental of Sir James Dalzell's Blackness (W Lothian) estate 1817; estate papers 18th-20th cent, incl some rel to Wamphray; mining leases and papers, Leadhills 17th-20th cent; papers rel to Union Canal 1815-51 and to Edinburgh & Glasgow Railway 1855-1905; Wamphray inventory 18th cent; inventory of Niddry Lodge, Kensington 1854; misc papers 16th-20th cent, incl some rel to W Lothian freeholders 1789-1877.

In private possession. Enquiries to the National Register of Archives (Scotland) (NRA(S) 2717). NRA 29885.

[c] Legal corresp and papers and misc W Lothian election papers c1835-95.

In private possession. Enquiries to the National Register of Archives (Scotland) (NRA(S) 395). NRA 12273.

[d] Ormiston factory accounts and ledgers c1800-15, mainly rel to lead sent from Leadhills to London.

Scottish Record Office (GD 253/207, 212-14). Deposited by D & JH Campbell, solicitors, Edinburgh 1969. NRA 13863.

[e] Lead mining diary and letter books of Sir James Hope 1646-61.

St Andrews University Library. Formerly in the possession of P Marshall of Glasgow and deposited 1967. NRA 10987.

[f] Leadhills mining register 1671-80.

Bodleian Library, Oxford (MS Eng.misc.e.186). Purchased 1929.

[g] Accounts of the 2nd Earl of Hopetoun with his agent William Robertson 1759-77.

National Library of Scotland (MSS 988, 9238). Purchased 1935, 1967.

[h] Corresp and papers of the 2nd Marquess of Linlithgow as Viceroy of India 1936-43.

British Library, Oriental and India Office Collections (MSS Eur.F 125). Deposited by the 3rd Marquess of Linlithgow 1964. NRA 20532.

Related collections: Hope-Johnstone of Raehills (no 54); Hope of Luffness (Scottish Record Office GD 364, NRA 10172); Hope of Craighall (Scottish Record Office GD 377, NRA 10171).

[54] HOPE-JOHNSTONE of Raehills

The Johnstones, a prominent Border family, had land in Dumfriesshire by the thirteenth century, and rose to the peerage in the seventeenth century. James Johnstone, second Earl of Hartfell, was created Earl of Annandale in 1661, and his son William Marquess of Annandale in 1701. The latter married first Sophia, heiress of John Fairholme of Craigiehall (West Lothian) and second Charlotte, heiress of John Vanden Bempde of Hackness (Yorkshire, North Riding).

On the death of the third Marquess without issue in 1792 the Scottish estates passed to his great-nephew the third Earl of Hopetoun (see no 53), and then to Lord Hopetoun's eldest daughter Anne (d1818), wife of Admiral Sir William Johnstone Hope (1766-1831). Her descendant established his claim to the earldom of Annandale in 1986. The Yorkshire estate, however, was inherited by Sir Richard Vanden Bempde Johnstone (1732-1807), first Bt, of Hackness, son of John Johnstone (a younger son of Sir William Johnstone of Westerhall, Dumfriesshire) by Charlotte, Marchioness of Annandale. His descendant was created Baron Derwent in 1881.

The Craigiehall (West Lothian) estate passed to Henrietta Johnstone, daughter of the first Marquess of Annandale, who married the first Earl of Hopetoun, and thence to their second son the Hon Charles Hope-Vere (1710-91).

Estates in 1883: Dumfriesshire 64,079 acres, Lanarkshire 1,287 acres, total 65,366 acres worth £28,236 a year.

[a] Writs, mainly Dumfriesshire 14th-19th cent and Craigiehall 17th-18th cent; inventories of writs 16th-20th cent; misc wills and settlements 16th-19th cent; misc executry papers 18th-20th cent; minutes of the curators of the 1st Marquess of Annandale 1672-3, 1682 and of the 3rd Marquess 1758-74; legal and case papers 16th-20th cent, incl many rel to the Annandale peerage; stewartry of Annandale minutes 1716; Newbie (Dumfriesshire) barony court minutes 1656 and Moffat (Dumfriesshire) regality court books 1700-48.

Estate records 16th-20th cent, mainly Dumfriesshire, incl tacks 16th-20th cent, surveys, valuations and particulars 17th-20th cent, maps and plans 18th-20th cent, rentals 16th-20th cent, feu ledgers 1890-1957, factory and estate accounts and vouchers 16th-20th cent, Leadhills (Lanarkshire) barony accounts late 18th-19th cent, factory and estate corresp 17th-20th cent, and papers rel to losses under the Commonwealth 1655-62, Dumfriesshire woodlands 18th-20th cent, shooting 1870-1965, commons and enclosures 1763-1833, roads and bridges 1777-1839, drainage 1847-60, the surveying of the Hope-Johnstone estates 1758-1879 and teinds 16th-20th cent; Craigiehall estate papers late 17th-early 18th cent, incl rentals and accounts; misc accounts and papers of Alexander Trotter, factor of the Earls of Home 1659-68.

Accounts, papers and plans rel to building at Raehills 1781-20th cent; misc accounts rel to building at Moffat (Dumfriesshire) late 17th-early 18th cent; particulars of Raehills Great Park 1786 and papers rel to Raehills garden 20th cent; accounts and papers rel to building at Craigiehall and Edinburgh late 17th-early 18th cent, incl letters of the architect Sir William Bruce 1694-1701; Lochwood (Dumfriesshire) building account 1722; accounts, inventories and other household records 17th-20th cent, incl Raehills, Moffat, Newbie, Lochwood and Edinburgh; misc

personal inventories 17th-19th cent; Lochmaben (Dumfriesshire) election papers 1704; Dumfriesshire election corresp 1804-7; papers rel to Moffat parish and grammar schools 1639-20th cent; papers rel to Moffat well 1748-1822, Moffat fair 1841-68 and Johnstone and Applegarth churches 18th-20th cent.

Patents and commissions 17th-18th cent; family accounts and papers 17th-20th cent, incl papers of the 1st Marquess of Annandale and the 2nd and 3rd Earls of Hopetoun; letters of James 'Secretary' Johnstone (1665-1737); business corresp of James and John Hope, WS c1767-1851; papers of Admiral Sir William Johnstone Hope (1766-1831) and of John James Hope-Johnstone, MP 1844-6; misc papers rel to the agents of the 3rd Earl of Annandale at Riga c1650-70; accounts and papers rel to the Earl of Annandale's Troop of Horse 1650-91; corresp and papers of the 18th Earl of Crawford (d1698); misc papers of the Fairholme family of Craigiehall late 17th cent; literary, genealogical and misc papers 17th-20th cent, incl subscription letters rel to the Melville Monument 1814-15.

Papers of the Johnstone family of Westerhall (Dumfriesshire) 1696-1913, incl misc deeds and estate papers 17th-early 19th cent, rental of Westerhall barony 1807, legal papers rel to the Grenada estates of Sir Frederick Johnstone 1835-7 and papers of Sir James Johnstone (1697-1772), 3rd Bt, of Westerhall; misc deeds and papers of cadet branches of the Johnstone family, Marquesses of Annandale 16th-18th cent.

In private possession. Enquiries to the National Register of Archives (Scotland) (NRA(S) 2171). HMC *Fifteenth Report, App IX*, 1897. NRA 12630.

[b] Dumfriesshire writs late 14th cent-1780; inventory of writs 1744; legal papers rel to the Annandale peerage case 1819-91; Moffat rentals 1759-91 and teind papers 1589-1852; misc Dumfriesshire estate papers 19th-20th cent; minute book of the patrons of Moffat parish and grammar schools 1831-46 with related papers 1639-1873.

In private possession. Enquiries to the National Register of Archives (Scotland). Deposited in the Scottish Record Office by Hope, Todd & Kirk, WS, Edinburgh 1962 and withdrawn 1980. NRA 32485.

[c] Inventory of Annandale estate titles 1484-1817.

Scottish Record Office. Deposited by Tait & Crichton, WS, Edinburgh 1961. Keeper's *Report* (1961), p4.

[d] Curators' accounts of the 3rd Marquess of Annandale 1745-1800.

Scottish Record Office (CS 96/12).

[e] Legal and estate papers of the 1st Marquess 1681-1719.

Harvard University, Baker Library, Boston, Massachusetts. RW Lovett and EC Bishop, *Manuscripts in the Baker Library: A Guide to Sources for Business, Economic and Social History*, 1978, p279.

Related collections: Hope, Earls of Hopetoun (no 53); Barons Derwent (North Yorkshire County Record Office ZF, NRA 972); Johnstone of Westerhall (Scottish Record Office GD 1/510, GD 2/330, CS 96/1961, CS 96/2321; Edinburgh University Library La. II 73); papers of Sir William Pulteney, 5th Bt (1729-1805) (Huntington Library, San Marino, California), including Johnstone of Westerhall family correspondence.

[55] HOWARD, Earls of Carlisle

The Dacre family owned land in Cumberland from the thirteenth century and acquired Naworth and Gilsland (Cumberland) by marriage in the fourteenth century. Further lands were added by purchase, royal grant and inheritance, including (from *c*1488) estates in Cumberland, Westmorland, Northumberland and County Durham (Morpeth, etc) and the North and East Ridings of Yorkshire (Hinderskelf and Grimthorpe) belonging to the barony of Greystoke.

Following the death of the fifth Lord Dacre (of the North) in 1569, his eldest daughter Anne, later Countess of Arundel, inherited the barony of Greystoke (see no 37), but the Naworth, Hinderskelf (later Castle Howard), Morpeth and Grimthorpe estates passed to a younger daughter, Elizabeth, who married Lord William Howard (1560-1640), a younger son of the fourth Duke of Norfolk. Charles Howard (1629-85), his great-grandson, was created Earl of Carlisle in 1661. His daughter Mary married Sir John Fenwick, on whose execution in 1697 some of the Fenwick property in Northumberland was granted to the Earl of Carlisle. Additions were also made to the County Durham estates in the 1690s, by purchase from the Fetherstonhaugh family.

Purchases and exchanges of land, including some with the Dukes of Devonshire, increased the Cumberland, Yorkshire and Northumberland estates in the course of the eighteenth and nineteenth centuries. These estates were administered from offices at Naworth (Cumberland and Northumberland), Castle Howard (Yorkshire) and Morpeth (Northumberland and Durham). Much of the Morpeth estate, however, was sold *c*1888-90 and in 1915. On the death of Rosalind, Countess of Carlisle, in 1921, the estates were divided mainly between her only surviving son, who inherited Castle Howard and most of the Yorkshire estates, and her grandson, the eleventh Earl, who received Naworth Castle, parts of the Cumberland estates and the remaining property in Northumberland. Other relatives inherited small portions of the Cumberland and Yorkshire estates.

Estates in 1883: Cumberland 47,730 acres, Northumberland 17,780 acres, Yorks NR 13,030 acres, total 78,540 acres worth £49,601 a year.

[a] Deeds 12th-19th cent, mainly Cumberland, Yorks ER and NR, Co Durham and Northumberland; wills, settlements and executorship papers 16th-20th cent; legal and financial papers 16th-20th cent; manorial records, Cumberland (Gilsland, etc) 15th-20th cent, Yorks ER and NR 16th-20th cent, Co Durham 16th-17th cent and Northumberland (Morpeth and Naworth estates) 17th-18th cent.

General estate accounts 19th cent and corresp 17th-19th cent (Naworth, Castle Howard and Morpeth estates); Naworth estate papers 14th-20th cent, incl leases 17th-19th cent, surveys 16th-19th cent, valuations (Greystoke and Dacre lands) 1396-1486 (3), rentals and accounts 16th-19th cent, corresp 17th-19th cent, tithe papers 17th-19th cent, valuations, accounts and corresp rel to woods 18th-19th cent, fisheries papers 17th-19th cent, colliery and mining papers 18th-19th cent, and home farm accounts, vouchers and papers 18th-20th cent; Yorks ER and NR estate papers 15th-20th cent, incl leases and agreements 18th-20th cent, surveys 1435-20th cent, valuations 1537-20th cent, rentals 17th-20th cent, accounts 15th-20th cent, vouchers 18th-20th cent, Castle Howard estate corresp 18th-20th cent, and papers rel to enclosure 17th-19th cent, drainage (Rye and Derwent) 18th-20th cent, rectories and tithes 16th-20th cent, Methodist chapels 19th cent, woods 17th-20th cent, gamekeeping 18th-20th cent, lime kilns and brickworks 19th cent, quarries 20th cent, home farm 18th-20th cent, market gardens 20th cent and Castle Howard Inn 1770-1836; Co Durham estate papers 17th-20th cent, incl leases and agreements 17th-19th cent, rentals and accounts 17th-18th cent, lead mining papers 1678-1786 and coal mining papers 18th-20th cent; Northumberland (Morpeth estate) papers 17th-20th cent, incl leases 18th cent, valuations 18th-19th cent, rentals and accounts 17th-20th cent, corresp 18th-20th cent and coal mining papers 18th-20th cent; Cambs accounts 1712-43; Hunts survey and rental 1690-1708.

Old Hinderskelf Castle and Castle Howard building accounts and papers 1681-19th cent, incl corresp of the 3rd Earl with Nicholas Hawksmoor and Sir John Vanbrugh *c*1700-36, and papers rel to decoration 18th-19th cent and chapel alterations 1871-6; papers rel to house contents (Castle Howard, Naworth Castle and London) 1693-20th cent, incl inventories of silver, china and furniture, catalogues of books, prints and paintings, and corresp rel to purchases of works of art; household accounts, etc rel to Naworth Castle 1694-5 and to Castle Howard 1687-20th cent, incl papers rel to fires at Castle Howard 1932, 1940; papers rel to Castle Howard gardens and waterworks 18th-19th cent.

Cumberland lieutenancy papers *c*1700-30 and election papers 18th-19th cent; papers rel to Yorks elections and local government 18th-20th cent; papers rel to Cumberland, Yorks and Northumberland agricultural societies 19th-20th

cent; corresp and papers rel to Castle Howard
Roman Catholic chapel 18th-20th cent, Yorks
Methodist chapels 19th cent and Yorks parishes
17th-20th cent; papers rel to Yorks roads
19th-20th cent; Yorks poor relief and charity
papers 18th-20th cent, incl Castle Howard
Friendly Society papers 1796-1834; schools
papers 19th-20th cent.

Family papers 1595-20th cent, incl patents and
commissions; corresp and papers of the 4th Earl;
political, Irish and other papers of the 5th and
7th Earls; political and other corresp and papers
of Rosalind, Countess of Carlisle; misc legal and
estate papers of the Fenwick family 1615-1741,
incl Northumberland leases, rentals and accounts
17th-18th cent, papers rel to Northumberland
affairs 1682-3, and papers of Sir John Fenwick
17th cent; letters and accounts of George
Augustus Selwyn, MP 18th cent.

In private possession. Enquiries to the Librarian,
Castle Howard, Yorkshire. Access restricted.
HMC *Fifteenth Report, App VI*, 1897; *Papers of
British cabinet ministers 1782-1900*, 1982, pp32-3;
Papers of British politicians 1782-1900, 1989, p55.
Partial list NRA 24681. Some HMC-reported
MSS, with others from Castle Howard, were sold
at Hodgson's, 20 July 1944, lots 230-48: see
HMC *Guide to the Location of Collections*, 1982,
pp11-12.

[b] Yorks NR bailiffs' accounts 17th cent, with
memoranda and accounts of James Danby, agent
to the 1st Earl of Carlisle 1662-76, and household accounts 1696-8.

British Library, Manuscript Collections (Add MS
32163). Presented by Mrs William Collins 1884.

[c] Agency account 1788; letters to the Revd
John Forth, Castle Howard agent 1788-1815.

York City Archives Department (YL/Munby/Acc
54: 32, 98-119). Deposited by the Munby family
in York Central Library. NRA 14178.

[d] Welburn (Yorks NR) court book 1742-1851.

North Yorkshire County Record Office. Deposited
by Welburn parish council 1976.

[e] Grimthorpe manorial records 1748-1835.

Hull University, Brynmor Jones Library (DD
CV/71). Deposited by Messrs Crust, Todd &
Mills, solicitors, Beverley 1981. NRA 6482.

[f] Corresp of James Loch (1780-1855), agent,
rel to the Castle Howard estate and to Queen
Victoria's visit 1850.

Scottish Record Office (GD 268). Deposited by the
Hon Spencer Loch 1990. Keeper's *Report*
(1990-1), p39.

[g] Cumberland deeds late 12th-20th cent;
Northumberland (Naworth estate) deeds
17th-19th cent; family settlements and legal
papers 17th-20th cent; Cumberland manorial
records 16th-20th cent, incl barony of Gilsland
court books, etc 1576-1939, surveys 17th-18th
cent and accounts 16th-19th cent.

Receivers' accounts for Cumberland,
Westmorland, Yorks, Co Durham, Northumberland, Salop, etc 1530-1; Cumberland estate
records 16th-20th cent, incl leases 16th-20th
cent, surveys 16th-18th cent, maps and plans
17th-20th cent, particulars 17th-19th cent, valuations 18th-20th cent, rentals and accounts
16th-20th cent, corresp, stewards' accounts and
vouchers 18th-20th cent, and papers rel to enclosure 18th-19th cent, tithes and church patronage
17th-19th cent, woods 18th-19th cent, gamekeeping 18th-19th cent, fisheries 17th-19th cent,
corn mills 18th-19th cent and lead mining
17th-18th cent; colliery papers 18th-20th cent,
incl day books, accounts and plans; corresp and
papers rel to limestone and granite quarries
18th-20th cent; papers rel to Brampton
(Cumberland) Scotch Tweed Mill Company Ltd
19th cent; farm papers 18th-20th cent; papers rel
to water supply and to draining and hedging, etc
19th-20th cent; road and railway papers
18th-20th cent; Northumberland rentals
18th-19th cent; Yorks (Castle Howard estate)
rentals and accounts early 19th cent, 1917-39.

Papers rel to building work at Naworth Castle
19th-20th cent, incl corresp with Philip Webb
and Anthony Salvin; plans rel to 1 Palace Green,
Kensington, mainly by Philip Webb 19th cent;
papers rel to Naworth Castle contents 17th-20th
cent, incl inventories 1832-68 and lists of books
and papers 17th-20th cent; Naworth Castle
household books and accounts 1613-19th cent;
Cumberland taxation papers 17th cent; papers
rel to local politics 19th-20th cent, incl East
Cumberland election 1880; corresp rel to Carlisle Waterworks Bill 1897-1925; papers rel to
Brampton Rural District Council 19th-20th cent;
papers rel to building a new church at Brampton
19th-20th cent; Cumberland poor relief papers
18th-20th cent; corresp of the 9th Earl and
Rosalind, Countess of Carlisle 1878-1912.

*Durham University Library, Archives and Special
Collections* (HN). Deposited by the 11th Earl of
Carlisle from Naworth Castle and Boothby estate
office 1954-60 and by Messrs Cartmells, solici-
tors, Brampton 1967-82. NRA 11493 (partial
list). Some books and manuscripts from Naworth
Castle were dispersed by sale at Sotheby's, 11
April 1927, lots 744-70 and 27 Oct 1947, lots
261-533. The residue of Lord William Howard's
collection of printed books was purchased at
Sotheby's (14 Dec 1992, lot 171) by Durham
University Library.

[h] Cumberland, Co Durham and Northumberland deeds, legal papers and estate papers,
accounts and corresp late 19th-20th cent, incl
papers rel to Netherton (Northumberland) colliery c1950-60 and executorship papers, Rosalind,
Countess of Carlisle 1921-49.

*Durham University Library, Archives and Special
Collections* (HN). Transferred from S Walton, a
former agent 1982. Documents less than 30
years old closed to research.

[i] Cumberland estate letter books c1898-1943;
Castle Howard estate letter book 1908-31; letter

books rel to Leif Jones (secretary to Lady Carlisle) 1907-30.

Durham University Library, Archives and Special Collections (HN). Transferred by Lord Henley, grandson of S Walton 1982. Documents less than 30 years old closed to research.

[j] Misc Dacre and Howard of Naworth deeds and papers 13th-18th cent (*c*30 medieval), incl licence to crenellate Naworth 1335, and legal and case papers rel to Dacre claims 16th-18th cent; Cumberland manorial records 16th-18th cent; Cumberland agreements and tenancy papers 18th cent, survey book 1570, particulars 17th cent and rental 16th cent; grant of Brampton fair 17th cent.

Cumbria Record Office, Carlisle (Aglionby MSS, vols V-VIII). Deposited by Major Mounsey-Heysham. NRA 6315.

[k] Gilsland bailiffs' papers, with instructions from Lord William Howard, 1613.

Cumbria Record Office, Carlisle. Deposited by D Mawson 1988. County Archivist's *Report* (Jan-March 1988), p9.

[l] Ainstable and Irthington (Cumberland) manorial records and surveys 16th-17th cent.

Public Record Office (SC 2/165/2,16; LR 11/80/912; LR 2/212/1-12; LR 2/213/53-8).

[m] Askerton (Cumberland) surveys 16th cent.

Public Record Office (E 164/42/61-7; E 315/399/49-137).

[n] Northumberland (Morpeth estate) deeds 14th-19th cent; Co Durham deeds 16th-18th cent; Northumberland legal papers 17th-19th cent; manorial records, Morpeth 17th-19th cent; Northumberand estate records 16th-20th cent, incl leases and agreements 17th-20th cent, surveys and maps 17th-20th cent, valuations 18th-19th cent, rentals and accounts 17th-20th cent, vouchers 18th-20th cent, corresp 18th-20th cent, and papers rel to Morpeth estate buildings 19th-20th cent, enclosure 18th cent, tithes 16th-17th cent, 19th cent, woods 18th cent, Morpeth mills 17th-18th cent and brickworks 18th cent, and collieries 18th-20th cent; Co Durham surveys 17th cent and leases 18th cent; survey of all Northumberland properties 1718; papers rel to Co Durham and Cumberland lead mines 18th cent; Northumberland Quarter Sessions papers 17th cent and election papers 18th-19th cent; papers rel to election of Morpeth free burgesses 18th cent and to Morpeth fairs and markets 18th-20th cent; Morpeth Town Hall papers 19th-20th cent; papers rel to rural district councils 20th cent; Morpeth grammar school 18th cent and Northumberland schools 20th cent; Fenwick family corresp and papers 18th-19th cent, incl papers rel to Morpeth elections 18th cent.

Durham University Library, Archives and Special Collections (HN). Sent from Castle Howard to Boothby muniment room 1933 and deposited by

the 11th Earl of Carlisle 1954, 1960, with additional material from Messrs Cartmells, solicitors, Brampton 1967-82. Documents less than 30 years old closed to research. NRA 11493 (partial list).

[o] Northumberland (Morpeth estate) survey 1569-70.

Public Record Office (E 164/37).

[p] Cumberland, Northumberland and Yorks rentals and receivers' accounts 1760-7.

Public Record Office (C 114/169-70, Musgrave *v* Carlisle).

[q] Letter book of the 2nd Lord Dacre of Gilsland as Warden of the Marches towards Scotland 1523-4.

British Library, Manuscript Collections (Add MS 24965). Acquired 1862.

[r] Papers and corresp of the 1st Earl of Carlisle 17th cent, incl accounts 1679-80 and papers rel to his governorship of Jamaica.

British Library, Manuscript Collections (Sloane MSS 2717, 2723-4).

[s] Account roll of clerk of the kitchen and steward to the 4th Lord Dacre of the North rel to households at Kirkoswald and Naworth (Cumberland) and Morpeth and Horsley (Northumberland) 1541-2.

Bodleian Library, Oxford (MS Eng.hist.c.267). Purchased 1941 (Davis & Orioli catalogue 103, no 182).

[t] Letters to Rosalind, Countess of Carlisle, from Gilbert Murray 19th-20th cent.

Bodleian Library, Oxford (MSS Gilbert Murray). Given by Stephen Murray and Rosalind Toynbee, and by Gilbert Murray's literary executors 1958. NRA 16865.

Related collections: Fitzalan-Howard, Dukes of Norfolk (no 37); Barrett-Lennard of Belhus (Essex Record Office D/DL, NRA 8987), including Dacre family and Cumberland estate papers 15th-18th cent; Howard of Corby (in private possession, NRA 7034), including Cumberland deeds and estate papers 13th-20th cent; Howard of Greystoke (Cumbria Record Office, Carlisle D/HG, D/HGB, NRA 23768, 23774), including Cumberland estate papers 15th-20th cent.

[56] INGILBY of Ripley

The Ingilby family owned Ripley in the West Riding of Yorkshire by the mid-fourteenth century. In 1398 John Ingilby was associated with the foundation of the Carthusian monastery of Mount Grace in the North Riding. During the reign of Elizabeth I family lands in the North Riding were disposed of and further West Riding properties, including Dacre and North Deighton, were subsequently bought.

Lincolnshire estates (Harrington and Kettlethorpe) were gained through the marriage of Sir

John Ingilby (d1815) to Elizabeth, daughter and heir of Sir Wharton Amcotts, first Bt, of Kettlethorpe (d1807). Kettlethorpe passed at the death in 1854 of Sir William Amcotts-Ingilby into the possession of his sister Augusta and her husband Robert Cracroft of Hackthorn, Lincolnshire. The former Amcotts estate of Washingborough (Lincolnshire), which had passed to the Buckworth family, was acquired by the Ingilbys in the early nineteenth century and sold in 1840.

Estates in 1883: Yorks WR 10,609 acres, Lincs 1,271 acres, total 11,880 acres worth £13,538 a year.

[a] Deeds, mainly Yorks 12th-20th cent and Lincs 12th-18th cent (*c*250 medieval); abstracts of title 17th-19th cent; wills and settlements 16th-20th cent, incl some of the Amcotts family; inquisition *post mortem* for Sir William Ingilby 1618; legal and trust papers 14th-20th cent, incl executorship papers of the 2nd Earl of Cumberland *c*1577-1611; bonds, recognisances and other financial papers 16th-19th cent; manorial records for North Deighton (Yorks WR) 1397-1793 and for Dacre with Hartwith and Ripley 16th-18th cent; Bewerley manor verdicts 1702 and Armley manor estreats 1740-3; Brinkhill and Driby (Lincs) manorial records 1387-1632.

Yorks estate records 15th-20th cent, incl leases and tenancy papers 16th-20th cent, surveys, valuations and particulars 16th-19th cent, misc maps and plans 17th-20th cent, rentals 1481-19th cent, accounts 17th-20th cent, and corresp and papers rel to tree planting and wood sales late 18th-mid-19th cent and enclosures 16th-19th cent; papers rel to Yorks livings and tithes 16th-19th cent, incl Ripley rectory valuation 1534-5, Studley (Yorks WR) prebend tithe books 1583-1637 and Studley leases and rentals from 17th cent; Bewerley lead mining and Dacre (Yorks WR) and North Deighton quarrying papers 18th-19th cent; Lincs estate papers 18th-20th cent, incl misc leases 1729-1856, surveys and valuations 1811-53, rentals and accounts *c*1807-1914, and misc corresp and papers 19th-early 20th cent; London (?Middlesex) estate rental 1807-13; accounts of the Sheffield estate of the 2nd Earl of Shrewsbury 1454-5, 1458; Ripley Castle inventories 1794, 1845, 1850, 1918 and misc household accounts 1822-66; household account book (? of Sir Marmaduke Constable of Everingham) 1570-1.

Papers rel to Knaresborough Forest (Yorks WR) 16th-18th cent; Yorks official papers 16th-19th cent, incl escheator's quietus 1533-4, West Riding feodary's accounts 1572-7 and sheriff's quietus (Sir John Ingilby) 1781-2; papers of Sir William Ingilby as justice of the peace 1660-82 and as treasurer of lame soldiers in the West Riding 1674; North Deighton constable's accounts 1647-8; Ripley market and fair toll books 1708-78; Ripley girls' school expenses 1817-19, vestry minute book 1859-75 and

clothing club account book 1879-1906; Lincoln poll books 1727; N Lincs poll book and register 1834.

Patents and commissions 1600-19th cent; misc family papers 16th-20th cent, incl warrants, receipts and payments of Sir William Ingilby as treasurer of Berwick 1557-60, continental tour diary (Sir John Ingilby) 1727-9 and diaries of Sir William Ingilby, 3rd Bt 1857-1914; Ripley Castle weather records 1848-1907; literary and other papers 12th-20th cent, incl 14th cent extracts from Fountains Abbey charters, an Ingilby pedigree 1598, two parliamentary diaries Feb-Mar 1699 and misc papers of the Amcotts family 17th-19th cent.

West Yorkshire Archives Service, Leeds. Deposited by Sir Joslan Ingilby 1963 and by Sir Thomas Ingilby 1982-90 (Acc 2662, 2922, 3061). HMC *Sixth Report, App,* 1877, pp352-95. NRA 11614. Most of the manuscripts reported on in 1877 were dispersed by sale at Sotheby's, 21 Oct 1920, or by private sales. HMC *Guide to the Location of Collections,* 1982, pp32-3; *Annual Review 1990-1,* p26.

[b] Fountains Abbey (Yorks WR) deeds 12th-16th cent (25), stock accounts 1480-93, rent accounts 1527-36 and survey 1540; Yorks shrievalty quietus 1564.

West Yorkshire Archive Service, Yorkshire Archaeological Society (MD 335/66, 67). Presented by Lt-Colonel PL Bradfer-Lawrence and Mrs EB Grey 1972. *Guide to the Archive Collections of the Yorkshire Archaeological Society 1931-83,* 1985, p55. NRA 546.

[c] Dacre rent books 1824-1930.

Kirby, Son & Atkinson, solicitors, Harrogate. NRA 7145.

[d] Misc deeds for Ripley, Killinghall, etc *c*1413-1593; rental of Sir William Ingilby's lands 1589.

North Yorkshire County Record Office (ZAA). Purchased 1984 (Sotheby's, 6 Nov, lot 965).

[e] Ripley Castle inventory 1773.

Public Record Office (C 105/17).

Related collection: Cracroft-Amcotts of Hackthorn (Lincolnshire Archives AMC, NRA 2596).

[57] INNES-KER, Dukes of Roxburghe

By the late Middle Ages the Ker family owned considerable estates, mainly in Roxburghshire, including Altonburn and Cessford (acquired 1467). In 1602 Robert Ker, created Earl of Roxburghe in 1616, was granted forfeited estates of Francis Stewart, Earl of Bothwell, including former Kelso Abbey property in Roxburghshire (Kelso, Sprouston, etc), Berwickshire (Little Newton, etc), Selkirk and elsewhere. He also acquired an East Lothian estate (Broxmouth, Pinkerton, etc), and in 1627 bought the barony of Broughton

(Midlothian), with property in Edinburgh and West Lothian, from Sir William Bellenden.

William Drummond (afterwards Ker), youngest son of the second Earl of Perth by Jean Ker, the first Earl of Roxburghe's daughter, succeeded as second Earl in 1650. His grandson John Ker was created Duke of Roxburghe in 1707. On the death of the third Duke in 1804 William Bellenden, seventh Baron Bellenden and heir male of the second Earl, inherited the Roxburghe estates and title. (After the death of the first Baron Bellenden in 1671 his estates and title had passed to a younger son of the second Earl.) The title was dormant from the death of the fourth Duke in 1805 until 1812, when his cousin Sir James Innes (1736-1823), sixth Bt, of Innes (Morayshire) established his claim as fifth Duke.

Morayshire property was owned by the Innes family as early as the thirteenth century. In 1578 the estates of the Crombie and Rothmackenzie (Banffshire) branch of the family were added to those of Innes of Innes. Sir James Innes, third Bt, married a daughter of the first Earl of Roxburghe in 1666. The sixth baronet sold his family estates to the second Earl Fife in 1767. His marriage to Mary, daughter of Sir John Wray, twelfth Bt, by Frances Norcliffe, brought him the Norcliffe estate of Langton (Yorkshire, East Riding), which descended to his wife's nephew on her death in 1807. He also had property at Huish (Devon), apparently disposed of after his succession as Duke of Roxburghe.

Estates in 1883: Roxburghshire 50,459 acres, Berwickshire 6,096 acres, E Lothian 3,863 acres, total 60,418 acres worth £50,917 a year.

[a] Berwickshire, E Lothian and Roxburghshire writs 12th-19th cent, Ker family, incl Kelso Abbey charters and bulls 12th cent-1593; Mid and W Lothian, Stirlingshire, Orkney, etc writs 15th-17th cent, Bellenden family; Innes writs 12th-18th cent, mainly Banffshire and Morayshire, with some for Aberdeenshire, Ross and Cromarty, etc; Langton (Yorks, ER) deeds 1608, 1808-10; inventories of writs and registers of title 15th-19th cent; wills, settlements, trust, legal and financial papers 15th-20th cent, Ker, Bellenden and Innes, incl Roxburghe succession case papers 1805-12; barony court records, Broxmouth 1659-1735 and Kelso 1741-1926.

Berwickshire, E Lothian and Roxburghshire estate papers 16th-20th cent, incl tacks and tenancy papers 17th-19th cent, surveys, valuations and plans 17th-19th cent, rentals, accounts, vouchers, corresp, and papers rel to Tweed fishings 17th-18th cent and quarrying late 18th-mid-19th cent; papers rel to teinds and stipends 17th-19th cent, mainly Roxburghshire but incl Selkirk, Dunbar, and Falkirk (Stirlingshire) 17th-18th cent; misc papers for Ker estates in Northumberland (Ford, etc) 17th-18th cent and for Bellenden family estates in Mid and W Lothian and elsewhere 15th-17th cent, incl Kerse (Stirlingshire) 1568-1609; Banffshire and Morayshire (Innes) estate papers c16th-18th cent, incl

tacks and tenancy papers, rentals, vouchers, accounts, papers rel to teinds and to Spey fishings, and letters of the 1st Marquess of Argyll to his factor Sir Robert Innes 1654-7; misc English estate papers (Innes) 18th-early 19th cent, incl Huish cash and rent book 1775-91 and Langton survey and valuation 1807; Inverchroskie (Perthshire) estate records 1841-52; misc Orkney estate papers (bishop of Orkney) 1550-87, incl Birsay rental c1564; rental, Dorchester, Pyrton and Thame hundreds (Oxon) 1625.

Household records, Broxmouth and Floors (Roxburghshire) 17th-20th cent, incl misc Floors building accounts 17th-19th cent, Broxmouth plans and elevations 18th cent, inventories 17th-19th cent, accounts 1619-20th cent, and Floors library catalogue 1804, sales accounts 1813 and related papers 18th-19th cent; misc inventories and accounts 17th-19th cent for Edinburgh, London, Bath and other households, incl Henley Park (?Oxon) inventory 1727; papers rel to Roxburghshire affairs 17th-20th cent, incl heritors' papers 18th-20th cent, papers rel to freeholders and elections 18th cent, and Roxburghshire and Selkirkshire lieutenancy papers 1715; Berwick election accounts (William Ker) 1710; papers rel to Kelso burgh 16th-20th cent, incl customs and fair accounts 1627 and treasurer's accounts and vouchers 1795-1818; Moir Mortification Fund records 1849-97; memorandum book of the 5th Duke as JP for Devon 1795.

Patents and commissions 16th-19th cent; Innes and Ker family papers 16th-20th cent, incl papers rel to the Middle March and feuds with the Kerrs of Ferniehirst 16th-17th cent, corresp of the 1st Earl c1591-1650 and of Margaret, Countess of Roxburghe (d1753), accounts of Captain Innes's company 1760, corresp and papers of Sir Henry Innes, 5th Bt, and of the 5th Duke, legal accounts 19th cent, Peninsula War diaries of Lady Susanna Dalbiac 1811-12, and corresp of the 6th and 7th Duchesses with Queen Victoria 1879-1901; misc Bellenden family papers 15th-17th cent, incl business letters of the bishop of Orkney to Sir John Bellenden, Justice Clerk 1569; genealogical and misc papers 15th-20th cent, incl papers rel to Sciennes convent (Midlothian) 1555-83 and fortifications at Langholm and Wauchope (Dumfriesshire) c1556.

In private possession. Enquiries to the National Register of Archives (Scotland) (NRA(S) 1100). HMC *Fourteenth Report, App III*, 1894, pp1-55. NRA 10542. A Kelso Abbey charter 1159 was deposited in the National Library of Scotland 1941.

[b] Innes legal and family papers c1582-1700, with inventories of plenishing 1644-8.

Scottish Record Office (RH 15/82/10, 16; RH 15/90/1; RH 13/11). NRA 10542.

[c] Writs and inventories of writs 17th-19th cent, mainly Roxburghshire and E Lothian; marriage

contract of Sir James Innes 1666; legal and financial papers late 19th-20th cent; rental of the Duke of Roxburghe's estates *c*1729; genealogical and misc papers 19th cent.

In private possession. Enquiries to the National Register of Archives (Scotland) (NRA(S) 1100). NRA 10542.

Related collections: Bellenden family papers 1533-1622 (National Library of Scotland Advocates' MS 22.3.14); Earls Fife (Aberdeen University Library, Department of Special Collections and Archives MS 3175, NRA 35370), including Innes of Innes papers 13th-18th cent.

[58] KERR, Marquesses of Lothian

Mark Kerr (d1584), last abbot of Newbattle (Midlothian), acquired the monastic lands of Newbattle and Prestongrange (E Lothian). These passed to his son Mark (d1609), created Earl of Lothian in 1606. Prestongrange was sold in 1622 but Newbattle was inherited by Anne, daughter of the second Earl of Lothian (d1624), who in 1630 married William Kerr (d1675), son by his first wife of Robert (d1654), first Earl of Ancram. William Kerr, who was raised to the earldom of Lothian in 1633, bought the barony of Jedburgh (Roxburghshire) from the first Earl of Haddington in 1637. His son William (d1703), created Marquess of Lothian in 1701, inherited Ancrum and Woodhead (Roxburghshire) on the death of his uncle the second Earl of Ancram (d1690), son of the first Earl by his second wife. The second Marquess succeeded his cousin Robert Kerr, second Lord Jedburgh (d1692) in his Roxburghshire estates (Oxnam, Crailing, etc). Papers of the Barons Somerville may have been transferred to Newbattle from the family's nearby seat at Drum (Midlothian) on its sale by the fourteenth Baron Somerville (1765-1819).

Blickling Hall (Norfolk) was purchased by Sir Henry Hobart (d1625) from Sir Edward Clere. The Norfolk estate was augmented by the marriage in 1717 of John Hobart (created Earl of Buckinghamshire 1746) to the daughter and co-heir of Robert Britiffe of Baconsthorpe, which brought him Briningham, Hunworth and Stody (purchased by the Britiffes from Sir Edmund Bacon, second Bt, in the seventeenth century). On the death of the second Earl of Buckinghamshire in 1793 the earldom passed to his half-brother but the Norfolk estates descended to his daughter and co-heir Caroline, wife of the second Baron Suffield. At her death in 1850 they devolved upon the eighth Marquess of Lothian, grandson of her sister Henrietta (d1805). Land in Gedney, Holbeach and Whaplode (Lincolnshire), acquired by the Hobart family about 1721, descended to the second Earl's fourth daughter Emily, wife of the second Marquess of Londonderry, and thence, when she died in 1829, to the seventh Marquess of Lothian, to whom she also bequeathed the Stewart estate of Bellaghy (County Londonderry). These Lincolnshire and Irish properties, however, were sold by 1859.

Gunnersbury (Middlesex) and Bere Ferrers (Devon) were properties of Sir John Maynard (1602-90), whose daughter and co-heir Elizabeth married Sir Henry Hobart, fourth Bt. They apparently passed to Hobart's son, the future first Earl of Buckinghamshire, on the death in 1721 of Maynard's widow, Mary, Countess of Suffolk. Both estates were later sold, Gunnersbury in 1739. Marble Hill (Middlesex) belonged to the first Earl's sister Henrietta, Countess of Suffolk (d1767).

(For records of the Melbourne and other estates of the Lamb family, inherited in the twentieth century by the Kerr family, see no 25).

Estates in 1883: Roxburghshire 19,740 acres, Midlothian 4,548 acres, Norfolk 8,073 acres, total 32,361 acres worth £45,203 a year, exclusive of £6,296 for mines.

[a] Midlothian and Roxburghshire charters and writs 12th-19th cent, incl Newbattle Abbey charters and papal bulls 1140-16th cent; misc writs 15th-19th cent, incl Lanarks 15th-17th cent and Fife 17th-19th cent; inventories of writs 16th-19th cent; wills, settlements, executry, trust and legal papers 16th-20th cent, incl Macdonald of Clanranald trust papers 1824-36 and legal papers rel to the dowager Marchioness of Londonderry 1828-38; bonds, discharges and other financial papers 16th-19th cent; Midlothian and Roxburghshire estate records 16th-20th cent, incl tacks 16th-19th cent, maps and plans 18th-20th cent, valuations 1824,1888, rentals 17th-19th cent, factory and chamberlainship accounts and vouchers 17th-20th cent, factory corresp 1822-70, estate papers and papers rel to teinds 16th-19th cent; Newbattle (Midlothian) coal mining papers 16th-19th cent, incl tack 1594 and accounts 1726-1870; estate accounts for Innerleithen (Peeblesshire) 1566-7 and Pitfirrane (Fife) 1674-83; Mybster (Caithness) rent ledger 1838-47; Blickling estate plans *c*1858 and corresp 1858-67; Gedney, Holbeach and Whaplode rentals, accounts and papers 1807-56; Bellaghy accounts and papers 1811-42; Ingestre and Hopton (Staffs) estate accounts 1834.

Misc house building accounts 17th-19th cent, incl Newbattle 1696-1732, Ferniehirst (Roxburghshire) 1633, 1707-12 and Ancrum and Lothian House (Edinburgh) early 18th cent; household inventories 17th-20th cent, incl Ferniehirst 1646, Newbattle and Ancrum 1719, Lothian House 1788 and Newbattle library inventory and valuation 1926; household accounts, Newbattle and Monteviot (Roxburghshire) 1624-1887, incl Newbattle cellar books 1833-60; Monteviot weather records 1881-99; Blickling Hall visitors' book 1932-9; papers rel to Marshgate House (Surrey) mid-18th cent.

Papers rel to local affairs 15th-19th cent, mainly Roxburghshire, incl Roxburghshire lieutenancy letter book 1804; records of the Edinburgh Regiment of Militia 1789-1855 and the Midlothian

Fencible Light Dragoons 1794-1800; papers rel
to the 3rd Militia Battalion, Royal Scots 1880-7;
Huntingdon election accounts and papers 1820;
appointments, commissions and family and political papers 16th-20th cent, incl corresp of the
1st Earl of Ancram (d1654), political papers of
the 3rd Earl of Lothian (d1675), letters of the 1st
Earl of Haddington 1620-33 and Charles II
1649-51, accounts of the 3rd Marquess as High
Commissioner of the General Assembly 1733-8,
journals and papers of the 6th, 7th and 9th Marquesses, and corresp and papers of the 11th
Marquess (1882-1940); notebook of Sir Thomas
Kerr of Redden c1620-59; letters received by
Henrietta, Countess of Suffolk; accounts of Sir
Patrick Murray Threipland, 5th Bt 1838-78;
accounts of the 7th Regiment of Dragoons 1697;
misc records of the 3rd Regiment of Foot Guards
1710-19; literary, antiquarian, genealogical and
other papers 16th-20th cent, incl accounts of
David Pringle, surgeon apothecary, 1676-81 and
genealogical corresp of Arthur Herbert Kerr
(1862-1930).

Deeds and papers of the Somerville family, Barons Somerville 1447-1755, mainly rel to Lanarks
(Carnwath, etc) and Midlothian (Drum, etc),
incl marriage settlements 1631, 1651 and 1674;
deeds and misc papers of the Somerville family
of Aston Somerville (Worcs) c1290-1651, mainly
rel to Warwicks and Worcs, incl Gloucs coroner's
roll 1397-8, Kington and Bishampton (Worcs)
manor court roll 1493, marriage settlement 1568
and inquisitions *post mortem* 1537, 1578.

Scottish Record Office (GD 40). Deposited on loan
1932-72 by the 11th and 12th Marquesses of
Lothian and purchased from the 12th Marquess
1991. HMC *First Report, App*, 1870, pp116-17;
Papers of British Cabinet Ministers 1782-1900,
1982, p35. NRA 10737.

[b] Curatory accounts and Midlothian and Roxburghshire rentals and accounts 1901-30.

Scottish Record Office (CS 96/2725-2902).

[c] Estate accounts 1782-93.

Scottish Record Office (GD 237/230/3). Deposited
by Tods, Murray & Jamieson, solicitors,
Edinburgh 1969. NRA 32483.

[d] Letters of the 9th Marquess to his agent rel
to the Roxburghshire election 1868.

Scottish Record Office (GD 1/631). Purchased
from Margaret PJC Payne 1972.

[e] Midlothian and Roxburghshire factory
accounts 1883-9; Newbattle coal mining
accounts 1703-11, 1746-52; London household
accounts 1707-8; Newbattle household accounts
1708-10, 1842-3 (with Monteviot) and cellar
books 1830-78; catalogues of the libraries at
London and Newbattle 1666-1876, with related
papers 1643-1899; misc family papers 17th-19th
cent, incl Italian tour journal 1624-5 and other
papers of the 1st Earl of Lothian (d1675), notebooks of the 6th Marquess, sporting diary of the
7th Marquess 1816-24, misc literary papers of

the 8th Marquess, and diaries and letter books of
the 9th Marquess; MS narrative by the 2nd Earl
of Buckinghamshire of his Lord Lieutenancy of
Ireland 1777-80; returns of the 11th Regiment of
Dragoons 1752-6; historical, literary and misc
papers 15th-20th cent, incl a book of hours 15th
cent, log and letter books of Admiral Sir John
Pennington 1628, 1631-2 and sermons 17th cent
(3 vols).

National Library of Scotland (MSS 5730-5841).
Presented 1950 by the Newbattle trustees under
the will of the 11th Marquess of Lothian.

[f] Roxburghshire tacks c1773-85.

National Library of Scotland (Dep 301/110).
Deposited by Tods, Murray & Jamieson, solicitors, Edinburgh 1979. NRA 29083.

[g] Estate, building and other accounts of the 3rd
Marquess 1733-43; misc family papers
c1643-1821.

National Library of Scotland (MS 2980 (iv), Ch
2120-35). Presented by Mrs Murray Thomson
1941.

[h] Letters of the 5th Marquess to his factor
Francis Brodie 1808-10.

*Edinburgh University Library, Special Collections
Department* (MS Dk.8.4 (Brodie)).

[i] Misc Newbattle chamberlainship papers
1814-24.

Midlothian District Libraries (LT/1). NRA 26051.

[j] Misc vouchers of the 5th Marquess
1779-1800.

*Birmingham University Library, Special Collections
Department* (MS BUL 6/iv/12). Purchased 1959.
HMC *Accessions to Repositories 1959*, p2.

[k] Diary of the 6th Marquess 1817-20.

Edinburgh Central Library. Presented 1924.

[l] Deeds 12th-19th cent, incl Norfolk and
Suffolk 12th-19th cent, Lincs 14th-17th cent,
and Kent, London and Middlesex 16th-18th
cent; abstracts 16th-19th cent; wills, settlements
and trust papers 15th-19th cent, mainly Hobart
and Kerr; legal case papers 16th-19th cent, incl
some rel to the dispute over the will of Sir John
Maynard (1602-90) and Lady Belmore's divorce
c1780-94; records of Hobart and Harbord (Bri-
(Barons Suffield) Norfolk manors (Blickling, Briningham, Hevingham, Hunworth, Stody, etc)
13th-20th cent, incl court rolls for Gallows and
Brothercross hundred 1545 and Grimshoe and
Weyland hundred 1554-7, 1599-1603; Mendles-
ham (Suffolk) manorial accounts 1437-8;
Moulton (Lincs) manorial papers c1558-1624.

Leases 15th-19th cent, mainly Norfolk, incl
Clere of Blickling lease register c1577-99; Blickling estate records 15th-20th cent, incl maps and
plans 18th-20th cent, terriers, particulars, valuations, surveys, rentals and accounts 15th-20th
cent, vouchers 17th-20th cent, corresp 18th-20th
cent, Blickling agent's papers 1847-20th cent,

wood and timber accounts 1858-96, farm, labour and game records 19th-20th cent, tithe papers 17th-19th cent, Walsingham sheep reeve's accounts 16th cent, and papers rel to the restoration of Blickling church 1876 and Stody parsonage 1881; misc Lincs estate papers 17th cent (incl some rel to fen drainage), 1830-6; Gunnersbury and Marble Hill estate papers 1723-53, incl Twickenham rental 1723; Bere Ferrers estate corresp and papers 1721-69; papers rel to the ancestral Norfolk estate of the Harbord family 16th-19th cent, incl valuation 1821, rent books 16th cent, 1742-65, Plumstead farm accounts 1823-5 and legal and estate papers late 18th-early 19th cent; Roxburghshire rental 1826; Midlothian estate report 1830.

Blickling building papers 17th-20th cent, incl accounts 1619-21, plans 18th-20th cent and architectural letters and papers of William Ivory (1746-1801), Joseph Bonomi 1794-7, William Burn 1864-71 and Sir Digby Wyatt 1870-2; Blickling household records 17th-20th cent, incl inventory 1793, accounts from 1630, cellar accounts 1842-1901, stable accounts 1797-1800 and papers rel to the library early 19th cent; misc Hobart London household accounts 17th cent, with building papers of Samuel Wyatt (1737-1807); misc papers rel to Marble Hill House mid-18th cent and account of goods sold from Stanwell House (Middlesex) 1624-5.

Duchy of Lancaster (Norfolk, Suffolk and Cambs) receiver's accounts 1384-1408 and records 17th cent, incl accounts of deodands and suicides 1641-57; papers rel to Norfolk affairs 14th-20th cent, incl assessment for an aid 1346-7, subsidy assessments 1662-3, lieutenancy journals and papers c1676-1821, election papers 1733-5, accounts of prisoners and maimed marines 1728-37, records of Elizabeth Hele's charity 1791-1804 and Blickling school 1884-1904, and churchwardens' accounts for Baconsthorpe 1663-1713 and Fakenham 1777-80; Botesdale (Suffolk) school records 1631-43, 1713-32; papers rel to Corpus Christi College, Cambridge 16th-18th cent and Wellingborough (Northants) navigation 1758; Northants shrievalty accounts (Sir Thomas Drury) 1740; Middlesex pipe roll *temp* William III; St Ives (Cornwall) election papers 1721-66.

Hobart family bills, accounts and papers 16th-19th cent, incl appointments 17th-18th cent, personal inventories 1673 (Sir Henry Hobart) and c1734 (Brigadier John Hobart), accounts of Mary, Countess of Suffolk 1690-1721 and Elizabeth Bristow 1723-7, and papers of Henrietta, Countess of Suffolk; corresp and papers of the 2nd Earl of Buckinghamshire; misc Harbord family papers 18th-19th cent, incl accounts of Lady Suffield's charitable donations 1802-23 and corresp of the 3rd Baron Suffield 1812-21; misc Kerr family accounts and papers 19th-20th cent, incl some papers of the 7th Marquess of Lothian; family corresp of the 2nd Marquess of Londonderry and his wife 1790-1828; corresp and misc papers of Sir Thomas Drury, 1st Bt c1745-59; misc papers

15th-20th cent, incl Carrow Priory (Norfolk) cellarer's accounts 1455-6, 1484-5, 1529-30 and memorandum book of William Ffolkes 1752-67.

Norfolk Record Office (Blickling Hall MSS MC 3, MC 184). Bequeathed by the 11th Marquess of Lothian 1940 and transferred from Blickling Hall 1941-92. HMC *Seventeenth Report*, 1907, pp45-51, and *Lothian*, 1905. NRA 4641. The record office has microfilm copies of other miscellaneous Blickling Hall papers, including a manor court book 1789-1935, estate rentals and accounts 1793-1802 and household inventories 1850, sold at Sotheby's, 13 Dec 1993, lot 286.

[m] Misc Norfolk deeds and legal papers 16th-17th cent; Norfolk manor court rolls (Wymondham and Horsham St Faith) 1636-72 and estate accounts 1665, 1707-8; Norwich election expenses 1786-7; continental travel journals and antiquarian papers of Henry Hobart (d1799); misc papers 18th cent.

Norfolk Record Office (COL/13/1-42). Part of the Colman Library collection presented by Timothy Colman 1955. The papers were collected by the Marquess of Lothian's librarian James Bulwer (1794-1879) and acquired by JJ and JR Colman 1879. NRA 32977.

[n] Misc Blickling estate papers 19th cent, incl farm account 1893.

Norfolk Record Office (R 158D, R 159D). Presented by Dr JI Sapwell 1977. NRA 27820.

[o] Architectural plans by William Ivory 1765-85, Joseph Bonomi 1793 and Humphry and John Adey Repton early 19th cent; estate plan by James Corbridge 1729; misc volumes, incl the 'Cecilian Commonwealth' by Lord Burghley (1520-98), ship money case papers c1636, legal treatise by Sir Matthew Hale (1609-76) and diaries of the 8th Marquess of Lothian c1849-57.

In private possession. Enquiries to the Administrator, The National Trust, Blickling Hall, Norfolk. The Blickling psalter and homilies were sold with 166 other MS volumes from Blickling in 1932. HMC *First Report, App*, 1870, p14 and *Guide to the Location of Collections*, 1982, p40.

[p] Corresp and papers of the 2nd Earl of Buckinghamshire and of Henrietta, Countess of Suffolk.

British Library, Manuscript Collections (Add MSS 22358-9, 22625-9). Presented by the executors of John Wilson Croker 1858. Croker received them from Emily, Marchioness of Londonderry, to whom they had been bequeathed by her father the 2nd Earl of Buckinghamshire.

Related collections: Earls of Buckinghamshire (Buckinghamshire Record Office D/MH, NRA 1; Bodleian Library, Oxford Tanner MSS); Barons Suffield (Norfolk Record Office, NRA 4650); Marquesses of Londonderry (Durham County Record Office D/LO, NRA 11528; Public Record Office of Northern Ireland D 654, D 655, etc, NRA 25609).

Select index

The primary purpose of this index is to act as a means of reference to families mentioned in the text and to their principal estates and seats. Individuals are included only in a landowning context, and place-names are indexed only when significant records for those places are described in the text. Institutions and corporations are also indexed where the text notes significant surviving records.

A reference to an entry number followed by a letter (eg 10a, 20k) indicates the specific group of papers in which the reference occurs. Where a number only is cited (eg 10, 20), there is a reference in the introductory or closing paragraph or paragraphs and generally also in one or more of the groups of papers described in the entry.

Argyll, Synod of, 13a
Argyll, Dukes of, *see* Campbell
    Earl of Argyll's Regiment of Foot, 13a
Argyllshire, estates in, 13, 14, 15, 24, 29, 43a
Arley (Warwicks), 38
Arlington Street (London), 41a
Armaddy (Argyllshire), 14
    Castle, 14a
Arran (Buteshire), 30, 40a
    lifeboat, 30e
Arthington (Yorks WR), charity school at, 38a
Arthingworth (Northants), 27
Arundel (Sussex), 37
    Castle, 37
    college, 22a, 37a
Arundell family
    Barons Arundell of Wardour, 2
    of Lanherne (Cornwall), 2
Ashburnham House (London), 3a, 3d, 30
Ashburnham House (Westminster), 30
Ashburnham Place (Sussex), 3a
Ashburnham family, Barons and Earls of
    Ashburnham, 3, 12, 16p
Ashburton, Barons, *see* Baring
Ashby, John, agent to the Barons Clive, 51j
Ashill (Norfolk), 23b, 23c
Ashley family, of Wimborne St Giles (Dorset), 4
Ashley-Cooper family, Earls of Shaftesbury, 4
Ashridge estate (Beds, Bucks and Herts), 27, 33
    Park, 27c, 33a
Ashton Gifford (Wilts), 20a
Ashton Hall (Lancs), 30
Ashwick (Somerset), 39a
Ashwood Park (Herefs), 16n
Aske (Yorks NR), 32
Askerton (Cumberland), 55m
Astley (Warwicks), 33a
Aston Somerville (Worcs), 58a
Aston family, Barons Aston of Forfar, 21
Atholl, Dukes of, *see* Stewart-Murray
Aubigny (France), 42
Auchlyne House (Perthshire), 14a
Auchterhouse (Forfarshire), 29a
Aust (Gloucs), 16l
Austerfield (Yorks WR), 26e
Austria, deeds relating to, 20k
Aveland, Barons, *see* Heathcote
Avington (Wilts), 44
    House, 44a
Ayrshire, estates in, 6b, 9, 18, 30a, 31, 43a
Ayston (Rutland), 11

Bachymbyd (Denbighshire), 5
Baconsthorpe (Norfolk), 58
Badenoch (Inverness-shire), 42
Baggrave (Leics), 25
Bagot family, Barons Bagot, 5
Bagot's Bromley (Staffs), 5
Baillie family, of Jerviswood (Lanarkshire) and
    Mellerstain (Berwickshire), 6
Baillie-Hamilton family, Earls of Haddington, 6
    Charles, MP, 31a
Balcaskie (Fife), 29
Balcomie (Fife), 18
Balfe family, of Runnamoat (Co Roscommon),
    21

Ballinbreich (Fife), 32
Bampton (Devon), 49
Bampton (Oxon), 20
Banastre family, of Passenham (Northants), 45
Banff Castle (Banffshire), 29a
Banffshire, estates in, 31a, 42, 57
Bar (Ayrshire), 18h
Bara (E Lothian), 47e
Barbados, 18a
Barbreck (Argyllshire), 13
Baring family, Barons Ashburton, 24
Barking (Essex), 41
Barking (Suffolk), 3
    Hall, 3i
Barlings Abbey (Lincs), 48a
Barlow, Elizabeth, heiress of Hardwick (Derbys),
    later Countess of Shrewsbury, 17
Barnstaple (Devon), elections at, 39a
Barrett-Lennard family, baronets, of Belhus
    (Essex), 55
Barrow-upon-Humber (Lincs), 21a
Barrow-upon-Trent (Derbys), 25d
Barrowby (Lincs), 17a
Barrs (Argyllshire), granite quarry at, 14a
Bateson-Harvey family, of Langley (Bucks), 44d
Bath (Somerset), 14a, 43a, 47e, 57a
    Priory, 39
Bath, 3rd Earl of, *see* Granville, William
Bathgate (W Lothian), 53a
Bawtry Hall (Yorks WR), 26c
Baynard's Castle (London), 50
Beachampton (Bucks), 41
Beauchamp family, Earls of Warwick, 19a, 45
Beauchamp family, Barons Beauchamp of Hatch,
    12c
Beauchief Abbey (Derbys), 38a
Beaufort, Dukes of, *see* Somerset family
Beaulieu Abbey (Hants), 18g
Beaumont, John, Baron Beaumont, 48
Beauvale (Notts), 25f
Beckford, William, of Fonthill (Wilts), 30
Bedfont, East (Middlesex), 7
Bedford (Beds), barony of, 19
Bedford, Dukes of, *see* Russell
Bedfordshire, estates in, 3, 11a, 12, 16a, 16g, 19,
    27, 28, 30a, 33, 37a, 40e
Belfast (Co Antrim), 4
Belgravia (Middlesex), 46
Bellaghy (Co Londonderry), 58
Bellenden family, Barons Bellenden, 57
Bellfield (Fife), 29a
Belton (E Lothian), 47
Belton (Lincs), 27
    House, 27a, 27b
Bennett, Frances, of Beachampton (Bucks),
    heiress of estates in Bucks, Notts and Yorks, 41
Bentinck family, Dukes of Portland, *see*
    Cavendish-Bentinck
Bere Ferrers (Devon), 58
Berkeley (Gloucs), 7
    Castle, 7a, 7f
    St Andrew's chantry in, 7a
Berkeley Square (Middlesex), 7a, 7c
Berkeley family
    Earls of Berkeley and Barons Fitzhardinge, 7,
    25d, 37
    Barons Berkeley of Stratton, 7, 27a

Printed in the United Kingdom for HMSO
Dd301351 12/95 C7 G559 10170